POLITICS IN
CENTRAL AMERICA

POLITICS IN LATIN AMERICA,
A HOOVER INSTITUTION SERIES

General Editor, **Robert Wesson**

Copublished with Hoover Institution Press,
Stanford University, Stanford, California

POLITICS IN CENTRAL AMERICA

Guatemala, El Salvador, Honduras, and Nicaragua

Thomas P. Anderson

PRAEGER SPECIAL STUDIES • PRAEGER SCIENTIFIC

Library of Congress Cataloging in Publication Data

Anderson, Thomas P., 1934-
    Politics in Central America.

    (Politics in Latin America)
    Bibliography: p.
    Includes index.
    1. Central America—Politics and government—
1951-   . 2. Violence—Central America. 3. Central
America—Economic conditions. 4. Central America—
Social conditions. I. Title. II. Series.
JL1416.A52   972.8′052   81-15787
ISBN 0-03-060618-7   AACR2

*The Hoover Institution on War, Revolution and Peace,
founded at Stanford University in 1919 by the late President
Herbert Hoover is an interdisciplinary research center for
advanced study on domestic and international affairs in the
twentieth century. The views expressed in its publications
are entirely those of the authors and do not necessarily
reflect the views of the staff, officers, or Board of Overseers
of the Hoover Institution.*

Published in 1982 by Praeger Publishers
CBS Educational and Professional Publishing
a Division of CBS Inc.
521 Fifth Avenue, New York, New York 10175 U.S.A.

23456789 052 98765432

Printed in the United States of America

In Memory of
Herbert Warden Everley

Editor's Preface

This is the first-born of what should become eventually a large family of monographs on Latin American politics. It is hoped that in due course they will include studies of all Latin American countries plus various questions of foreign relations, regional problems, and so forth. They are intended to be primarily factual, with minimal theoretical analysis or interpretation, in order to be useful for all those, students, academics, journalists, or the proverbial intelligent reader, desiring background knowledge on Latin American political developments.

It is appropriate that our series opens with a study by Thomas P. Anderson of the four "volcanic" countries of Central America. It is here that political tensions are at their height and American attention is concentrated. Important beyond their size and wealth, these countries may well be precursors of greater explosions or indicators of broader trends. Their problems—including divided societies, inequality, and misgovernment—are like those of Latin America in general, only more severe; and understanding them will carry far toward measuring the troubles of the rest of the region. They seem now to stand near a watershed, and major change probably lies ahead. Professor Anderson's work is a valuable map showing how they have come to the present crucial turnings.

Robert Wesson

Author's Preface

A study such as this, which covers four separate, though related countries must, of necessity, have in it a bewildering number of names of individuals and organizations. As far as individuals are concerned, the reader would do well to keep in mind the Spanish practice of including the mother's family name after the father's family name when giving the complete name of a person. Thus: Fidel Chávez Mena or Hector Dada Hirezi; the names Mena and Hirezi are mothers' family names and only occasionally used. Sometimes a person will be generally known by the mother's family name; hence, Maximiliano Hernández Martínez, the tryant of El Salvador, is always known as General Martínez. The use of the mother's family name can be most helpful, as in distinguishing Anastasio Somoza García from his son Anastasio Somoza Debayle. In this work, whenever the mother's family name is commonly tacked on, it has been given at least once or twice.

Central Americans have an even greater passion for abbreviating the names of organizations to initials or acronyms than do North Americans. In order to help the reader get through the alphabet soup of abbreviations, an appendix has been prepared which follows the last page of the text and gives important initials and their meaning in both Spanish and English, country by country. The reader would also be well advised to remember that the titles of organizations can be misleading. The Revolutionary Party in Guatemala is revolutionary in name only, while the National Democratic Union in El Salvador is in fact a communist group.

The plan of the book is to give two chapters detailing the last decade of political and social history in each country. The first of these carries the political process up to the most recent crisis and the second follows that process into mid-1981. The third chapter on each country attempts to analyze the political, social, and economic forces at work, not in any rigidly mechanistic manner, but rather through suggesting what has been the process of interaction and what might be the results of such a process in the future. A final section in each of these chapters suggests some, though by no means all, of the possible United States options in its dealing with that country. The final chapter of the book returns to the basic themes stated in the first chapter of the work.

There are extensive footnotes throughout, but the most important basis of the study has been the data received in the literally hundreds of interviews with political figures, in and out of government, which the author has conducted over the last several years. For those interested in additional readings on Central America, a bibliographic essay has been provided, dealing chiefly with works which are readily available and which are printed in English.

Thomas P. Anderson

Acknowledgments

The author would like to thank the many persons who consented to be interviewed for this study. I can only hope that I have correctly expressed their points of view. Deserving of special thanks are Blanche Blum and Angela Collison, my typists, who had to put up with my often original notions of spelling. John McAward and his organization, the Unitarian Universalist Service Committee, also were very helpful in providing me several opportunities to visit Central America and participating in their investigations of human rights problems. It has been a pleasure to work with Robert Wesson of the Hoover Institution on the editing of this volume. I appreciate his many valuable suggestions. This has been a very complex study and, while I have taken pains not to make any errors of fact, I would not be surprised if a few may have crept in. They are, of course, solely my responsibility.

Contents

LIST OF TABLES, FIGURES, AND MAP

POLITICS IN
CENTRAL AMERICA

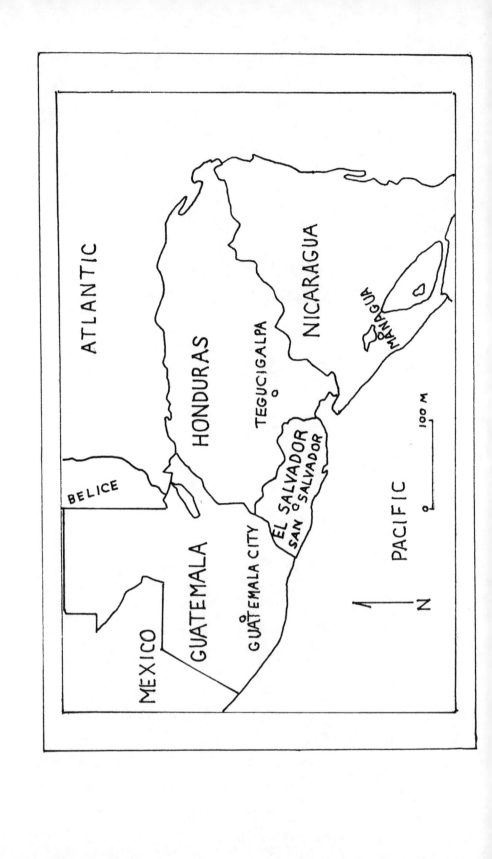

1

A Social
and Political Overview

To undertake an explanation of the politics of any one country is difficult enough. To attempt to explain the politics of four of them within the confines of a single work may seem presumptuous; yet there are certain reasons which make possible a comparative study of the four Central American countries of Guatemala, El Salvador, Nicaragua, and Honduras. This is not to say that their political traditions are identical. Any such statement would raise the hackles of a politically aware Central American, but there are similarities as well as divergences in the political life of these nations. On the other hand, Costa Rica—the fifth Central American state to be carved from the ruins of the Central American Federation—while having certain factors in common with the rest, has developed a unique political tradition in which violence has been largely eliminated and relative democracy is the rule. It has therefore been excluded from this study, though the reader who wants a contrast to the almost unrelieved pattern of violence in the other Central American republics might do well to undertake a study of Costa Rican institutions.

Active peaks dot the area, such as Guatemala's Volcán del Fuego, which broods over the capital like a pagan god; the jet black Izalco of El Salvador, a tombstone marking one of the bloodiest massacres of Central American history; and the lovely Momotumbo, which can be seen from the windows of the formerly Somoza-owned Hotel Intercontinental, across Lake Managua. But the volcanoes also serve as an ominous symbol here, as they did for Malcolm Lowry when he wrote his violent and tragic masterpiece, *Under the Volcano*. This study will focus on the eruptive violence of the region, not simply as a phenomenon, but rather as a symptom of grave social and economic injustices which have so far made a peaceful and democratic life there impossible. Its primary thesis will be that this political violence and, at times, the near chaos, are the result of the increasingly desperate struggle of certain entrenched groups to retain land, prestige, and power at any price.

This work is designed to be short on theory and long on political facts, and designed also to focus on the present situation rather than the past. Nevertheless, some background on the region is necessary, along with a discussion of some of the region's most important political, social, and economic institutions.

The region invaded by the Spanish *conquistadores* was by no means entirely made up of volcanoes, although the backbone of the New World runs through the region, hugging the Pacific coast of it fairly closely in Guatemala, where it is at its highest, and then broadening out through El Salvador, a land of lush mountain valleys among a tangled welter of low peaks, and becoming confused and choppy, like a breaking sea, in Honduras. Nicaragua resembles El Salvador in its broad plains and relatively low mountains. Lakes dot the mountain valleys, most impressively—Ilopango in El Salvador; Lake Managua, now an open sewer and a chemical bath, in Nicaragua; and, largest of all by far, Lake Nicaragua, the ever-tempting waterway for a possible isthmian canal.

In addition to the mountain valleys, where the largest part of the populace dwells, and in which three of the four countries have their capitals—Managua, nearly at sea level, being the exception—there is a littoral plain that begins on the Pacific coast of Guatemala, broadens out through El Salvador, and runs through the other two countries and into Costa Rica. This, too, is a populous area, given to cotton growing and cattle raising as well as sugar and fruit growing, while the foothills of the mountains yield some of the finest coffee in the world. But in addition to the prosperous Pacific littoral, there is a different lowland region running along the Atlantic, or north, coast, beginning with Guatemala's Petén and going on through the Mosquito coast of Honduras and Nicaragua. In this gloomy region, population today is sparse, though the Maya once throve in the Petén. It is a region of swamps, jungles, meandering rivers that, until the airplane, were the only means of egress, but it is also regarded as a region of promise and potential untapped wealth (see Table 1.1).

When Alvarado and the other *conquistadores* stormed down from Mexico, they found civilization already flourishing, chiefly among Maya and related Toltec tribes, but also among the Aztec-linked Pipil of El Salvador. The newcomers subjugated, exploited, and, largely through their diseases, nearly killed off these people. But eventually a conglomerate race appeared, the mestizo, part Indian and part European. El Salvador, Nicaragua, and Honduras are predominantly mestizo nations, with a few Indians, while Guatemala remains some 40 percent Maya in speech and culture. This requires some qualification because, as *indio* and mestizo literally move in shade from one to

TABLE 1.1. Central America at a Glance

Item	El Salvador	Guatemala	Honduras	Nicaragua
Area	8,000	42,000	42,000	57,000
Population	4.9	7.0	3.2	2.3
Density	590	190	78	40
Literacy	50%	38%	47%	50%
Life expectancy	58	52	53	54
Per capita income	630	1,000	600	700
Gross domestic product	3,060.7	6,966.7	1,947.7	1,545.9
Percent of GDP from manufacture	18.0	16.3	16.4	24.1

Notes: Area in square miles; population in millions; density per square mile; per capita income in dollars; figures are for 1979. The economic data are from *Latin America Regional Report*, 2 October 1980; figures in millions of dollars.

the other, the real distinction has come to be between indio, or *indígene*, and *ladino*, the latter being any person, of whatever ethnic origin, who takes on European ways. Thus, saying that Guatemala is 40 percent Maya means that 40 percent of its population is outside the dominant Spanish-European culture of the *ladinos*.

Along the Atlantic coastal region, there is a large admixture of African blood, the result of a migration of English-speaking blacks from the West Indies. This goes back to the time when Britain had control of most of the Atlantic coast area, a remnant of which is Belize, also claimed by Guatemala. This black population is largest in Honduras and Nicaragua and nonexistent in El Salvador, which has no Atlantic coast.

POLITICAL INSTITUTIONS

Led by a *criollo* aristocracy (of European ancestry), Central America joined in the independence movement against Spain. At first claimed by Mexico, the region has asserted its independent existence by 1822 and established a Central American Confederation, comprising the five traditional states of Central America. But this unity did not last. Poor communications and the incessant struggle of liberals and conservatives had broken the confederation into its constituent parts by the 1840s, and separate governments were established.

Each of these governments was republican in form, with a presidential system generally modeled on that of the United States. But while it was possible to import the forms of such a government, it proved impossible to impart much of the spirit. While the government of the United States grew organically out of colonial institutions, the newly established Central American governments represented a total break from the traditions of the colonial past. In colonial times, there had been virtually no local governments reflecting the will of the governed, but instead, a multitude of often overlapping authorities created by the crown-administered edicts written in Spain and imposed upon the new world. Further, instead of following the common-law system presumed in the United States as the basis of government, the Central Americans were saddled with a Roman law system which held that authority came from above and which gave very little scope to judicial review.

The constitutions of Central America, both in the nineteenth century and in the twentieth, have reflected the confusions arising from the grafting of an alien governmental structure onto a Hispanic legal system. A good constitution, as Napoleon reminded us, should be "short and obscure," like that of the United States, which, with all its amendments, can be printed on half a dozen pages. The current (1965) constitution of Guatemala runs, in the fifteenth edition, to 129 pages and contains 270 articles.[1] As there is little judicial discretion, even the most minute details of what we could term "positive law" find their way into the constitution itself, making the document inflexible and constricting. Most Central American constitutions are likewise difficult to amend.

This means that almost every major governmental upheaval, through coup or civil war, results in a new constitution being established. The constitutions become no more than party platforms and statements of aspirations for the current groups in power. They represent an ideology rather than a simple set of rules for governing.

Whatever the constitution might say, the fact is that the president generally concentrates most of the authority of the republic in his own hands. This may be, as some authorities declare,[2] because of the traditional Hispanic need for *caudillos*—strong, often military leaders exhibiting the traditional macho virtues and passing out rewards to their followers and punishments to their enemies. But, in any case, the very nature of the constitutional system has made this concentration of power practically inevitable. When constitutions are so constricting that nothing can be accomplished within their framework, the temptation of the executive branch will be to rule by decree, outside constitutional restraints. Presidents play a large part in the life of Central America. Sometimes they use their mandate to effect reform and then they step down, as did José Arevalo in Guatemala. Sometimes they are more or less benevolent dictators, such as Tiburcio Carías Andino in Honduras. Often they are despots, such as Maximiliano Hernández Martínez in El Salvador or the various Somozas of Nicaragua. Occasionally they are demonic figures of legendary cruelty, such as Manuel Estrada Cabrera of Guatemala. There are even instances of ineffectual presidents, dominated behind the scenes by some minister of defense or a past president. But even in these cases the power remains in the institution of the presidency, no matter who might wield that power.

With the fall, in July 1979, of Anastasio Somoza Debayle, there remained no long-term personalist presidents on the scene, who flaunted or manipulated constitutions in order to keep themselves in power for decades. Instead, the system which has evolved in Guatemala, and in El Salvador until the coup of October 1979, has been one of rotation in office involving a rather highly selective group of individuals in the military establishment. In El Salvador this was achieved through a single ruling party that dominated the presidential elections, while in Guatemala a more complex system has developed in which a group of feuding, but interrelated, parties contend for the presidency. Indeed, as of the start of 1980, there was technically only one president among the four nations under discussion, that of Guatemala, elected in 1978. The three other states were under juntas, or governing committees, and in the case of Nicaragua, it would have been difficult to pick out any one person as the strongman of the regime. But this, of course, was an exceptional situation.

The legislative assemblies of all but Nicaragua have been traditionally unicameral. Only Nicaragua, under the now-defunct constitution, saw fit to impose a Senate on top of the assembly. In any case, the powers of these assemblies, however imposing they may appear in the constitutions, are in fact generally weak. The presidents often manage to assure that their own party has the majority of the seats, and where this is not so, the assemblies are often bypassed or ignored. The corruption in the elections to these bodies is proverbial and often leads to a majority of venal time servers, ready to be bought by the highest bidder. Guatemala proudly claims to have a "semi-parliamentary" system, because the Congress can compel the resignation of a minister. But the Congress cannot, short of impeachment, bring down a president and, in fact, the military keeps a tight rein upon its powers.

The judiciary, too, although it occasionally functions much better than one has a right to expect under the circumstances, is essentially a broken reed. Short of the Supreme Court, judicial posts are not highly regarded and they are woefully underpaid. The temptation is to do as little as possible while holding office. Under most of the constitutions which have been established in the region, the borrowed principle of judicial review has been given some scope. But this is so alien to the traditions of the law that it has had limited effectiveness. In a region in which power has often come from naked force, it is a brave Supreme Court indeed that dares defy the executive. As a South American dictator once put it: "If the Supreme Court grants habeas corpus to my enemy today, who will grant habeas corpus to the Supreme Court tomorrow?"

Despite these problems of the governmental system in the countries under discussion, there are times when the laws are obeyed, the judiciary functions, and even the legislature plucks up its courage and acts with resolution and independence. At first glance, it appears that the system does not function much of the time because men are corrupt, but the reality lies in the fact that the social and economic system upon which the laws are erected is itself corrupt.

POWER GROUPS

One of the most important historical groups in Central America includes those who control the land.[3] Even in colonial times, the crown and its agents left the great *hacendados* broad latitude to deal with the Indian laborers and to control the local administration of justice. With the coming of independence, this oligarchy broadened its scope to the national level of politics, making and unmaking presidents, raising frequently the standard of revolt, through the simple process of arming its own followers. In rural Honduras to this day, many of the great landholders bear the honorary title of colonel.

The advent of such cash crops as coffee, bananas, cattle, and sugar greatly concentrated the land in the hands of a few. In El Salvador and Guatemala, whole communities of Indians were dispossessed of their lands through a combination of fraud and force. The landed oligarchies became very conscious of their own status as this concentration took place. In El Salvador the myth grew early in the twentieth century that there were 14 families—*los catorce*—who owned most of the land and controlled the political power. Although not literally true, the myth is significant in its suggesting of how the man in the street perceives the situation in the country. In Guatemala the concentration of wealth in the hands of the few was almost as tight as in El Salvador. Honduras and Nicaragua were slower to develop such concentrations, the latter only achieving it during the Somoza era.

While one can speak of certain old families who trace their prosperity well back into the nineteenth century, such as the García Granados family of Guatemala or the Escalón family of El Salvador (both of which got their start with successful military presidents), the landed oligarchy is in fact an ever-changing group that frequently coopts vigorous newcomers. Sometimes a revolution will end in wholesale expropriations resulting in a new landed gentry. Often a successful political or military figure will cement his position by the purchase of an estate, and perhaps by a marriage into the aristocracy. Successful merchantile or banking families often follow the same route into the landed class.

The concentrations of landholding which result from the growth of large estates can be startling. Estimates for Guatemala, and El Salvador before its recent land reform, suggest that about 2 percent of the population owned some 60 percent of the land. The expropriation of 376 estates in El Salvador gave the government a quarter of the arable land in the country.[4] Similarly, the expropriation of the estates of Somoza and his major supporters in Nicaragua, after the civil war, gave the government about 25 percent of the farmable land for its land-reform schemes.

The present century has seen the rise of industry in Central America. Some of this industry is foreign owned, but much of it is the work of local entrepreneurs. Much of it is the service industry, hotels and the like, or light manufacturing, of plastics, textiles, cement, beer, and other readily salable items. In some cases the industrial class represents relatively new arrivals to Central America. The Noltenius family in El Salvador, the Kongs of Guatemala, or the Handal family in Honduras are names that come to mind. The successful industrialist or businessman seldom remains separate from the landed wealthy. If he does not own land by inheritance, he quickly acquires it and his children will probably think of themselves primarily as landholders rather than as entrepreneurs. Thus, land and other forms of wealth become interlocked.

Although still influential in the political process, the oligarchy no longer ruled directly by the middle of the century. In each of the states being discussed, they had forfeited much of the direct political control to the professional military. In each case this was the result of the catastrophic great depression of the 1930s. Only the "firm hand" of a military ruler appeared able to stave off social chaos, and such communist revolts as that which tried to seize El Salvador in 1932.[5] Thus, Jorge Ubico in Guatemala, Maximiliano Hernández Martínez in El Salvador, Tiburcio Carías Andino in Honduras, and Anastasio Somoza García in Nicaragua all stepped in and presumably saved their respective countries, insuring themselves a long period in office. In Honduras there was a resurgence of traditional civilian political rule, which was ended again with the rise of Oswaldo López Arellano. Guatemala, too, had its nine years of revolution, but in the end, all succumbed to military governance.

The military, which has come to have such a dominant influence, has had a long period of evolution. In the nineteenth and the early twentieth century, the profession of arms was something that most members of the landed gentry indulged in as officers at some point in their career, either during internal strife or in one of the frequent Central American wars. The peacetime army tended to be a rather sorry affair of impressed peasants commanded by underpaid and demoralized officers. This began to change with the establishment of military academies, such as the *Politécnica* in Guatemala and the *Escuela Militar* in El Salvador. The emphasis from then on was on professionalism, with the students receiving a thorough grounding in mathematics, engineering, and science, along with more military subjects. The students of such schools tended to be recruited at a much younger age than are our own West Pointers. Generally a student would have ten years of education upon entry and be in his mid-teens. One graduated as a second lieutenant at around 19. Like novices in a seminary, the cadets, taken in at an impressionable age, learned to have no other loyalties but to their calling. The people they knew best were those in their own class, or *tanda*, and in these small groups (for the classes were never large), such a feeling of brotherhood grew that even being on opposing sides in a coup or revolution could not break the sense of kinship. This explains the frequent leniency toward the military instigators of an unsuccessful coup.

As professionalism and esprit de corps increased, new opportunities to extend the education of the military were sought. The coming of World War

II brought in Uncle Sam to fill that role. It appeared to the United States that one of the best ways to bind the Latin American nations to its cause was to train their military. The process has continued ever since, with large numbers of officers shipped off to train at Fort Bragg or at Fort Gulick in Panama. Some young officers, such as Anastasio Somoza Debayle, even received part of their military education at West Point. To the officer class, one of the most tragic aspects of the 1969 war between Honduras and El Salvador was that it was fought between officers who had gotten to know each other well in Panama and elsewhere as they learned the profession of arms. Not all the continuing education of the modern Central American officers is military. The command schools of the various countries often feature courses in economics, business management, and government. Sometimes soldiers are even sent to universities to learn these things. This makes sense in the context of military rule. The able minister of economics of the Lucas government in Guatemala is a professional soldier, Col. Julio Tulio Búcaro.

While the establishment of military academies with regular entrance requirements did not entirely eliminate favoritism and nepotism in the selection of candidates, it did tend to open careers to the talented and ambitious. The military, which still does not pay very well, began to attract the sons of the lower middle class, people who could scrape together just enough money to educate their sons to the point where they might enter the academy. Thus, the sons of functionaries and small farmers, of taxi drivers and bank clerks, found their way into the profession of arms and became officers and gentlemen.

As the political dominance of the armed forces increased, this last fact was responsible for a great deal of tension between the landed oligarchs and the soldiers, with the former tending to see the latter as parvenus and upstarts. Socially, if a soldier rose to be a minister of state, or even president of the republic—which became the highest military rank—he had to be at least tolerated by the landed wealthy, if for no other reason than the favors the soldier could do for one. A rising officer might even be allowed to marry the unprepossessing daughter of some great family. Upon retirement, however, an officer who had found himself rubbing shoulders with the elite because of his political importance, often found that the circle of his acquaintanceship magically shrank to nothing as he was discarded by those he could no longer aid.

Not all officers fit the lower-middle-class stereotype, of course. A few still come from the oligarchy. Gen. Romeo Lucas García of Guatemala is, for instance, related to the García Granados clan. It may also happen that some impressed peasant manages to work his way up through the ranks to the very top. This happened in the case of Gen. Juan Melgar Castro, the former Honduran strongman. But, by and large, the pattern described above still holds.

To insure against this, the officer class has begun to buy land on its own. In Guatemala this process is very far advanced and is officially encouraged by the military. The great transversal highway which has opened up the vast, fertile regions of central Guatemala is often referred to as "the highway of the generals" because the officers have helped themselves generously to the now-valuable lands along either side of the road. Before the overthrow of the Somozas, the leading figures in the National Guard had taken over not only a good deal of the land, but a great deal of the rest of the wealth of Nicaragua as well. And it is a rare general or colonel in Honduras or El Salvador that has not acquired his coffee *finca* or hacienda. While the meager salaries of the officer class would not permit the accumulation of much wealth, there are many "freebies" that come to the officers in the way of housing and goods and credit, and for those lucky enough to land a position in the security forces or the government, the opportunities for graft are almost unlimited. Sometimes an officer will overreach himself, such as the unfortunate Colonel Rodríguez, the onetime chief of staff of the Salvadorean army, convicted in the United States of attempting to sell guns to the Mafia; but, in general, the well-regarded soldier is virtually above the law.

While the oligarchy and the military, linked in an uneasy symbiotic relationship, control most of the political power, the urban middle class is not entirely ineffective. This middle sector of society, neither very wealthy nor near destitution, supplies the shock troops of the political parties and is generally the most active and knowledgeable element in political campaigns. Contrary to popular North American mythology, this middle sector, ranging all the way from officers in the banks to teachers in the schools and bureaucrats in the ministries, is quite extensive, especially in the capital cities, as the neat suburban houses in many neighborhoods attest. Large areas of each capital remind one strongly of similar housing in San Diego or Miami, and the inhabitants would not appear out of place in those cities.

This is, for the most part, a class with aspirations, hoping to make it to the top, or at least to the point of becoming landholders. This is why some of the sons go off to the military academy. But the real preserve of the middle sector, where its political values are nourished, is the local university. Generally disdained by the U.S.-educated oligarchy, the local universities offer the promise of upward mobility and prestige to the middle class. Previously, there was but one university per country—San Carlos in Guatemala, a colonial institution; and the more recent national universities founded in the other three countries in the nineteenth century. But of late, there has been a proliferation of new universities, chiefly sponsored by the Catholic church and, in particular, the Jesuit order. Thus, Rafael Landívar University came into existence in Guatemala City; the *Universidad Centroamericana* opened in San Salvador, and is commonly known as the UCA; and another UCA opened in Managua—all are Jesuit run. These were at first fondly imagined, by the inherently conservative middle class, to be less radical than the state-run universities, but they actually soon became more radical, thanks to the doctrines propounded at Medellín, Columbia, by the Catholic bishops in 1969.

The October coup of 1979 in El Salvador was largely hatched at the UCA and three members of its faculty have subsequently sat on the revolutionary junta. Honduras has a powerful university, the *Universidad Nacional Autónoma de Honduras* (UNAH), a refuge for the left wing of the Liberal Party. The conservatives in El Salvador, finding themselves unable to control either of the existing institutions of higher learning, recently founded José Matías Delgado University, a rather improvised institution whose chief distinction seems to consist in the 1950s dress code it imposes on its students.

Law continues to be the predominant field of study at the various universities, for, as befits Roman law countries, there is a great need for lawyers. But even in the faculty of law, the supply has outrun the demand and many *licenciados* of the law find themselves without employment in their field. Indeed, most students find that the university is not always the ticket to a better life that it pretends to be, and the increasing frustrations fuels the radical politics of the university crowd. Repressive states have learned to think of the universities as their enemies. Sometimes an authoritarian government will seize control of the national university and attempt a reform of the system. The government of El Salvador took over the National University following the abortive coup of 1972, but soon found that it had a tiger by the tail. The students expressed their displeasure in various ways, which included assassinating the rector of the university in 1978. Recently, that university has been the haven of left-wing militants.

Not only do the capital cities harbor a large middle class, but also they tend to be the largest seats of unionized labor. Labor has made unsteady progress in Central America. In the four countries, there were no unions to speak of until the 1920s and growth was slow thereafter. The failure of the 1932 revolution set back union activity in El Salvador until after World War II. Guatemala, which had a virtual ban on unions until that same date, saw a remarkable growth of union activity between 1945 and 1954, only to have this dramatically brought to an end by the counterrevolution of Castillo Armas. Unionism in Guatemala is today weaker than it was in 1950, but is gradually growing, despite assassinations and other harassment. In Honduras, the year 1954 marked a major breakthrough when the banana-company unions humbled the great foreign corporations. On the other hand, Nicaragua always maintained firm governmental control of union activity until after the 1979 civil war. In some countries, it has been almost impossible to call a legal strike, even when strikes were theoretically legal. El Salvador had exactly one legal strike between the implementation of its labor code in 1955 and the coup of 1979, although there were plenty of strikes.

In predominantly rural and agricultural countries, it is hard to draw the line between industrial unionization and farm workers' movements. Most major confederations embrace both; however, in some instances, peasant unions have been illegal. El Salvador would never grant *personería jurídica*, or legal personality, to the various peasant organizations of the 1970s. This does not mean that peasant organizations have not been effective, but their lack of legal status in El Salvador and Guatemala has led to frequent clashes with the authorities.

Unions can and do exert considerable political pressure and only the most repressive governments can totally ignore their influence. In Honduras, where unionization has been traditionally strongest, the unions have generally thrown their weight behind the Liberal Party. But the military leader, Oswaldo López Arellano, cleverly used the support of organized labor when he overthrew civilian rule in 1972 and established an authoritarian government.[6]

Unionism is something new for the *campesinos*, the tillers of the soil who form some 80 to 90 percent of the population of the region. For most of the postconquest period, they have been unrelentingly exploited by those who owned the land. The system has varied. The early conquerors demanded and received the tribute labor of the Indians in the *encomienda*, or controlled district, or rounded them up for work projects in the *repartimiento*, or distribution system. These cruder forms of exploitation soon gave way to the system of peonage, including virtual debt slavery. Peonage was only abolished in Guatemala in 1931 when Jorge Ubico became president and substituted a system of employment cards, by which the peasantry had to prove they had worked so many days a year on the large estates or be dragooned into the army. These cards accomplished the same end as did peonage and they lasted until 1944.

Not all the *campesinos* were landless *peónes* by any means. Perhaps half of the *campesinos* in the region owned some land, though only a few owned enough to be self-sufficient. Others farmed garden plots, known as *milpas*, on the estates of the wealthy and divided their time between cultivating the lands of the *hacendado* and their own plots. These peasants were known as *colonos*. All in all, the lot of the peasantry has been a precarious one. Their lot sank during the "liberal" period of the nineteenth century as village after village saw its communal lands confiscated and absorbed into the estates of the mighty. The twentieth century, with its rapid growth in population, has only accentuated the competition over the land, most dramatically in El Salvador.

Land reform, designed to give lands back to the peasantry, was a major goal of the abortive revolutionary period in Guatemala. Honduras tried it in the late 1960s and 1970s. In Nicaragua, a dramatic effort at redistribution of the land seized the estates of Somoza and his supporters in 1979—almost 25 percent of the arable land—and then began to confiscate parts of other estates in 1980. El Salvador, under the second junta, in March 1980, decreed a massive land-reform scheme in an attempt to stave off civil war. The success of such schemes depends on the determination and planning of those involved, as well as the political climate. Honduras's land-reform program has dragged under the military governments of Melgar Castro and Paz García, for political reasons. The land-reform scheme in Nicaragua, on the other hand, is perfectly in accordance with the ideology of the ruling Sandinista movement and is being pushed through with vigor and careful planning. The program of El Salvador has many of the chaotic aspects of the entire country's social and political life.

In recent years, the peasantry has received fresh support, in its struggle for social justice, from an institution long regarded as the mainstay of the landed oligarchy: the Catholic church. The church itself had once been a great landholder, but the liberal reforms of the nineteenth century ended that and the church, always ready to make friends with the mammon of wickedness, soon embraced the new class of liberal landholders and preached patience and submissiveness to the peasants. The old-style clergyman, ritualistic, concerned with the theology of the next world and the pleasures of this one, can still be found, but in dwindling numbers. Some support for the traditional social order still exists among the higher clergy, in the person of such men as Bishop Arnoldo Aparicio in El Salvador and Cardinal Mario Casariego (soon to retire) in Guatemala.

But the church had long had a more advanced theology of social justice, dating back to the encyclical of Leo XIII, *Rerum Novarum*, in the late nineteenth century. This was restated and reenforced by Pius XI in *Quadragesimo Ano* and by John XXIII in *Mater et Magistra*. When the bishops of Latin America met in Medellín, in 1969, they were inspired by these doctrines to proclaim a theology of liberation, stressing social justice for the poor. Since that time, many clergy members, both native and foreign, have sought to put these ideals into practice. This was frequently a risky business. Two foreign priests were murdered in Honduras for their participation in the land-reform movement in 1975, and no less than seven were slain in El Salvador during the presidencies of Molina and Romero. Priests, such as Father Hemógenes López, the martyr of San José Pinula, have also been slain in Guatemala. Even the higher clergymen have suddenly lost their old complacency. The denunciation of his regime by Archbishop Miguel Obando y Bravo of Managua was a serious blow against the power of Anastasio Somoza Debayle, and the critical support which Monsignor Obando has since given to the Sandinista government has helped it immeasurably in gaining the confidence of the Nicaraguan people. The most celebrated clerical opponent of tyranny was, of course, Archbishop Oscar Arnulfo Romero y Galdámez of San Salvador, whose bitter feud with the dictator Carlos Humberto Romero (no relation) became known as "the war of the two Romeros." Monsignor Romero's intransigent opposition to human rights violations under the second junta finally earned him a martyr's crown when he was shot down while saying mass on 24 March 1980. His death drove many priests and nuns to a more radical position, though some will continue to say, with Cardinal Casariego, "Medellín was optional, and I have opted out."[7]

The events at the next Latin American-bishops conference in Puebla, Mexico, in 1979, appeared at first to strengthen the position of the conservatives. Pope John Paul II, appearing personally, warned against political involvement and seemed to repudiate the theology of liberation. Nevertheless, the tendency begun at Medellín continues. No fewer than three Catholic priests held ministerial rank in the Nicaraguan cabinet in early 1981. Plainly, any solution for the problems of Central America must take the role of the church into account.

THE VIOLENT LAND

The politics of the area under discussion has long been bound up with violence. Examples readily suggest themselves to even the most casual observer. From 10,000 to 30,000 people were killed in the great peasant uprising in El Salvador in 1932. Both Guatemala and El Salvador have had a history of political murder on an unprecedented scale during the last decade. Some 20,000 people have been killed, for political reasons, in Guatemala since 1970 and over 2,000 were killed in the first year of the Lucas government. El Salvador had an equally bloody reputation during the same period. Six hundred persons lost their lives in political crimes in the last year of the Romero government, while under the second junta, an equal number were killed in 1980 alone.[8] The Nicaraguan civil war cost an estimated 40,000 lives, or almost 2 percent of the entire population. This does not include those who died by assassination in the jails of the Somoza regime. Honduras has been relatively quiet since the violence surrounding the expulsion of 80,000 Salvadoreans in 1969 and the subsequent war between the two countries, but its political life also abounds in examples of almost-casual murder.

Indeed, even without political turmoil, the society of these four countries might still be styled violence prone. In El Salvador, murder and manslaughter together rank as the second highest cause of death in normal times, lagging behind only intestinal diseases, and well ahead of respiratory ailments, the third highest killer in the country.[9] In 1960, a normal year, that country had 1,313 arrests for murder while having only 243 traffic fatalities.[10]

The reasons for the propensity to violence would require a highly complex sociopsychological study, one that is only hinted at in current writing on the subject, but it is possible to make certain suggestions concerning the deeper roots of this cultural malaise.

To begin with, like much of Hispanic America, this is a death-oriented society. Poverty and malnutrition combine to insure a very high infant-mortality rate (something of the order of 120 per 1,000 live births). Death becomes a constant and familiar companion. The church, too, is death oriented, or was before its recent transformation. The use of relics and even whole bodies of saints is common, while rural people still hold a festival for the passing of a "little angel" (a child below the age of ability to reason), with the dead child as centerpiece in *ladino* areas of rural Guatemala.[11]

Life being brief, the emphasis shifts from prolonging one's life to living and dying in a heroic manner. As Octavio Paz so beautifully wrote: "Death defines life. . . . Death illuminates our lives. If our deaths lack meaning, our lives also lacked it. . . . Tell me how you die and I will tell you who you are."[12] For most men, to die tamely, of some disgusting disease, is thus a disgrace, an unworthy death. The best death is that which gives one the chance to display one's manhood to the fullest. Here the concept of machismo is very important. It is a term against which most North Americans take offense, but it is a very real part of the regional culture of Central America and does not mean the kind of swaggering bravado that comes to our minds.

Rather, machismo is the noble defiance of death. It is the willingness to dare, to take physical risks, in the face of hopeless odds. Therefore, it has more to do with Don Quixote than with Don Juan. No one has put it as well as Julius Rivera has in his brilliant study, when he wrote:

> A Macho gambles with Destiny, ready to win or lose. He gambles with death, he gambles with God. A burning love affair is a victory over Destiny; a revolution, a victory over death; sin a victory over God. When the three come together, man has accomplished his fulfillment.[13]

Skill in arms and pride in their possession are traits in *ladino* society handed down from the time of the *conquistadores*. Every poor man has his machete; every man who can afford it, his firearms. You can be sure you have won the confidence of a Central American man when he shows you his collection of weapons, which, these days, can include even an automatic rifle. These weapons are there to be used. While it might seem cowardly to assassinate or to shoot from an ambush, to the people of the region, the very act of killing requires courage and machismo.

These tendencies can be exaggerated, but the acceptance of violence as the normal means of settling disputes, including political ones, is what sets the two cultures apart. The *golpe de estado* (or coup d'etat) and the *cuartelazo* (or barracks uprising) are not regarded as aberrations, but rather as normal parts of the political process and sometimes the only, or best, way of affecting change.

With these points in mind, we can, beginning with Guatemala, work our way southward through four Central American states and their political order.

NOTES

1. Republic of Guatemala, *Constitutión de la Republica de Guatemala*, 15th ed. (Guatemala City: Ministerio de Gobernación, 1978).

2. Julius Rivera, *Latin America: A Sociocultural Interpretation*, enlarged ed. (New York: Irvington-Halsted, 1978), pp. 4, 53. He relates the need for *caudillos* to the authoritarian family structure.

3. Thomas Melville and Marjorie Melville, *Guatemala: the Politics of Land Ownership* (New York: The Free Press, 1971).

4. *New York Times*, 3 March 1980.

5. Thomas P. Anderson, *Matanza: El Salvador's Communist Revolt of 1932* (Lincoln: University of Nebraska Press, 1971) describes this revolt.

6. James A. Morris and Steve C. Ropp, "Corporatism and Dependent Development: A Honduran Case Study," *Latin American Research Review* 12, no. 2 (1977):41.

7. *Latin America Political Report*, 15 June 1979.

8. *New York Times*, 12 March 1980, quotes estimate of Archbishop Oscar Romero, that 600 were killed in the first two months of 1980.

9. *This Week Central America and Panama*, 11 February 1980.

10. Thomas P. Anderson, "The Social and Cultural Roots of Political Violence in Central America," *Aggressive Behavior* 2 (1976):251, quoting Alastair White, *El Salvador* (New York: Praeger, 1971), p. 251.

11. Anderson, "Cultural Roots," p. 252, cites Richard N. Adams, "La Culture del Ladino del Poblado y del Campo," in *Encuesta sobre la Cultura de los Ladinos en Guatemala* (Guatemala City: Editorial del Ministerio de Educación Pública, 1956) pp. 84, 168.

12. Octavio Paz, *The Labyrinth of Solitude* (New York: Grove Press, 1961), p. 54.

13. Rivera, *Latin America*, p. 5.

PART I
GUATEMALA

2

Guatemala:
The Revolution that Failed

Guatemala, the most populous country of Central America and the second largest after Nicaragua (if one excludes Belize, which Guatemala claims), borders on both the Atlantic and the Pacific, with the majority of the population living in the Pacific highlands at altitudes between 3,000 and 8,000 feet. The capital itself is at almost 5,000 feet. The country had a population of 3.3 million in 1940, and the estimate for 1980 is 6.7 million, of whom about one-eighth live in and around Guatemala City. Although not as poor as some of its neighbors, its per capita income has remained low, with that for 1974 being $620, and that for 1980 being about $950.[1]

Modern Guatemala lives in the shadow of the abortive revolutionary movement of the late 1940s and early 1950s, which sought to transform the traditional patterns of land tenure and political control. Since the coup of 1954, which ended the period of reform, politics in Guatemala has to be seen mostly in the context of an attempt to keep the lid on the situation and prevent a return to the leftist reformism of the pre-1954 era.

Before a revolution brought down the last of them in 1944, Guatemala's history could be told largely through the lives of a series of strongmen who dominated long periods and stamped their personalities upon the state. The first of these was the Indian peasant, Rafael Carrera, a proclerical conservative, who ruled from 1838 to 1865. After his death in office, the liberal, anticlerical faction gained control; and a great leader emerged in the person of warlike Justo Rufino Barrios (president, 1871-85), who died in battle trying to fulfill his dream of reuniting the Central American Confederation, which had broken up in 1838. Barrios was a hard, dictatorial man, but he did try to modernize and improve the country. Much less can be said for the lawyer, Manuel Estrada Cabrera, who continued (1898-1920) the liberal tradition in name only. Famous for his vanity and his cruelty, he has been given a just memorial in Nobel Prize winner Miguel Angel Asturias's novel *El Señor Presidente*. Eleven years after his long-suffering subjects had overthrown Estrada, they found the perennial anarchy ended by still another strongman, Jorge Ubico (1931-44), brave as a lion and insensitive to human needs.

The land over which these dictators ruled was a primitive one, without paved roads and, until the coming of the airlines in the 1930s, without easy access to the outside world. Further, almost 50 percent of the populace were Maya-Toltec Indians who resolutely refused to give up their culture and thus stood outside the national life. In many ways, although exploited, the Maya were better off than their *ladino* neighbors (*ladinos* being persons, of whatever ethnic background, who have adopted European-Hispanic ways). The *indigenes* at least had a fairly cohesive society and a mutual-support system based upon a syncretism of the Catholic and pagan religions, upon the *cofradías*, or religious brotherhoods, and upon an unofficial but well-known system of chiefs and leaders. Colorful costumes even identified each village and status level and affirmed the loyalty of the individual to the group.

But even the Indians could not resist the steady exploitation by the great landholders, and still less resistant were those who lived in *ladino* municipalities and were poor. Some 2 percent of the populace owned over 60 percent of the land and used the labor of much of the rest of the population. Before Jorge Ubico took over, the common system was one of debt peonage—legal under Guatemalan law—supplemented by contract laborers brought down from the mountains in gangs as virtual slaves to labor seasonally on the haciendas and coffee *fincas*, thus supplementing the meager income from their own minute landholdings. The system was not entirely without benefits for the migratory workers, for, as Richard N. Adams points out, this supplementary income allowed the Indian communities of the southwest piedmont to maintain their separate villages.[2]

Ubico eliminated the debt peonage, substituting a vagrancy law in 1934 that required persons owning less than a certain amount of land to carry with them (as noted earlier) cards showing that they had been employed on the great estates for a fixed number of days each year. Further, to get a stronger grip on the country, he substituted for locally elected *alcaldes*, or mayors, a system of *intendentes*, or governors appointed by himself.[3]

Like Barrios and Estrada before him, Ubico befriended and encouraged foreign planters to establish themselves in the country, as a means of pulling the country out of the economic shambles caused by the great depression. Many Germans and other foreigners established large estates, but nothing compared to the vast holdings of the North American-based United Fruit Company (UFCO), which had begun operations early in the present century.

UFCO had extensive tracts given to the raising of bananas and had also invested in the railroad, in coffee *fincas*, and other productive enterprises. Only in Honduras was its hold greater than in Guatemala. Peasant labor organizations were ruthlessly crushed, despite consistent attempts to organize, starting in the 1920s. Urban labor, too, was stifled in its attempts at collective bargaining.

Just as the coming of the great depression had seen the establishment of a number of long-term dictatorships throughout Latin America, so the ending of World War II heralded a revival of liberal, democratic aspirations throughout the region. The Latin Americans, participating in a war to make the world safe for democracy, wanted some of it themselves. In 1944, Ubico, like Martínez in neighboring El Salvador, was forced to step down by his military officers. In his place, he installed a trusted friend in the presidency, but this satisfied no one and a military triumvirate took over, determined to hold free elections.

The overwhelmingly successful candidate in the election of December 1944 was the distinguished educator and scholar Juan José Arévalo Bermejo, who, through his long years in exile in Argentina, had become a symbol of the opposition to tyranny, and who campaigned as a reformer under the banner of the newly formed *Partido de Acción Revolucionaria* (PAR). Arévalo lacked political experience and his life abroad had left him out of touch with Guatemalan realities, but he was determined to create a new nation built on the principles of justice. He enfranchised the Indians and other illiterates, instituted a social security scheme, built and staffed rural schools, and encouraged peasants' cooperative movements to pool their resources for buying and selling. Heartened by the overthrow of Ubico, a new labor movement had sprung into existence, the *Confederación General de Trabajadores Guatemaltecos* (the General Confederation of Guatemalan Workers—CGTG). The Arévalo regime was generally favorable to urban labor, and the Labor Code of 1947 gave confederation workers protection against arbitrary dismissal, against unfair competition from company unions, and against raids among members of rival groups. Union officers were protected in the performance of their duties and strikes were authorized for all urban workers except public servants. A labor union could be recognized in a factory if 25 percent of the workforce belonged, and a system of labor inspectors and labor courts was created to deal with violations of the code and with arbitration. Under this encouragement, the CGTG, Guatemala's largest labor group, grew to 104,000 members by 1954.[4]

Arévalo's labor legislation did not extend to peasants, who were still not allowed to strike. But a peasant mass movement was formed in 1950, the *Confederación Nacional de Campesinos Guatemaltecos* (CNCG), and the succeeding president lifted restrictions upon *campesino* strikes in 1951.

This new president was an army major, Jacobo Arbenz Guzmán, who had been one of the men responsible for Ubico's ouster and had sat on the triumvirate. A cloud hung over his name because of his alleged role in the 1949 assassination of fellow triumvir and rival Col. Francisco Javier Arana, an event which remains mysterious to this day, although it seems unlikely that Arbenz actually ordered the assassination.[5] Arbenz got 266,000 votes, or 65 percent of the total, against eight other candidates including Gen. Miguel Ydígoras Fuentes, the minister of communications under Ubico. The election of the man who styled himself "*el soldado del pueblo*" has been called "of questionable honesty,"[6] but it probably did reflect the enthusiasm of the average Guatemalan for a reform policy which had benefited so many. A revolt, following the election, by Col. Carlos Castillo Armas was unsuccessful; and Castillo was pardoned, a move which Arbenz no doubt later regretted.

Arbenz launched a whirlwind of reform measures, which included a crackdown on, and an auditing of the books of, Empresa Eléctrica, in which it was discovered that the company was making an actual annual profit of 107 percent. It was forced to cut its rates and raise its wages to give a profit margin of 10 percent.[7] The Central American Railway came in for similar treatment. But the major action of the government was Decree 900, the land-reform act of 1952. Article 32 declared that uncultivated holdings of six *caballerías* or more (a *caballería* being about 111 acres) were *latifundios* and therefore subject to confiscation under the 1944 constitution. Parts of smaller uncultivated parcels might also be taken. No cultivated land would be touched and the land would be paid for at tax-assessed value, in 3 percent bonds maturing in 25 years.[8] This struck hard at such giants as UFCO, which had over half a million acres and only 43,000 in cultivation, much of the rest being reserve banana land, but it also struck at the rural oligarchy that had traditionally run the country. However, by the standards of the present day, this land-reform scheme was quite moderate.

Soon charges were flying that Arbenz was a communist, and indeed, his wife was a member of the party. He was denounced from the pulpit by the archbishop of Guatemala City, Msgr. Mariano Rossell y Arellano, and in the domestic and foreign press, particularly in the United States. There were certainly communists in the government, such as José Manuel Fortuny, a leader of the PAR, and Victor Manuel Gutiérrez. Some of these communists had indeed insinuated themselves in high places, but, as Adams points out, Arbenz himself was essentially a Guatemalan nationalist.[9] The real desire of Arbenz appears to have been to cement his own power among the peasants and workers.

The specter of a communist state in the Western Hemisphere was raised by the U.S. Congress, the State Department, and the CIA. The fact that Secretary of State John Foster Dulles was a member of the law firm of Sullivan and Cromwell which had drawn up UFCO's contract with the Ubico government in 1936, and that his brother Allen had been on the board of directors of UFCO, largely escaped notice in the United States, but not in Latin America.[10] The CIA approached Ydígoras Fuentes, the leading figure among the defeated candidates in the 1951 election, and, when he hesitated to cooperate in a coup, approached Col. Carlos Castillo Armas, then in exile. Bolder than Ydígoras, Castillo allowed himself to be drawn into the plan. Several things aided his cause. First, a shipment of Czech arms, with which Arbenz had planned to arm the peasants and workers, as a counterweight to the suspect regular army, was seized by the army at the docks in May 1954—a fact given considerable publicity in the United States, as proof Arbenz was a communist. Secondly, Arbenz began to stir up labor trouble in the neighboring Central American countries, leading to the wholehearted cooperation of Honduras and Nicaragua in the overthrow scheme. Castillo Armas, with fewer than 200 men, launched his invasion across the Honduran border. The most powerful weapon in his arsenal was a heavy machine gun, but the CIA had provided a B-26 bomber which its pilot flew out of a Nicaraguan airfield to give support to the invaders. The invasion was successful because the army refused to turn over the shipment of arms to the workers and simply stood aside and watched.[11] It is quite possible the military, by itself, would have gotten rid of Arbenz, even without a CIA-backed invasion. The peasants were thus unarmed, and, in fact, Arbenz showed something less than heroic determination to fight to the death, escaping as quickly as he could to an embassy.

There followed a severe crackdown on those upstart elements from which the Arévalo-Arbenz revolution had drawn its support. The CGTG and the CNCG were both abolished and a number of persons were summarily executed. Perhaps Torres Rivas's figure of 8,000 deaths is too high, but there were certainly instances of summary executions and a general climate of repression.[12] Castillo Armas called his movement the "Liberation," choosing a term which would have sympathetic reverberations in the hearts of post-World War II North Americans, though it is difficult to say who was liberated, except for United Fruit and the other expropriated landholders who regained their former holdings when Decree 900 was revoked. In fact, during the Castillo period and subsequent presidencies, the process of land reform was reversed and a greater percentage of the land devoted to commercial farming, while the average size of the small peasant proprietorship has decreased.[13] To give this regime some respectability, the new president held a plebiscite, orally and publicly, which therefore resulted in the required response. He then proceeded to rule with an entourage which has been described as a gang of "grafters and cutthroats."[14]

In July 1957, three years after he gained power, Colonel Castillo Armas was assassinated. Months of wrangling followed before a successor was elected in the person of Gen. Miguel Ydígoras Fuentes, Ubico's former minister and a losing candidate in the 1951 election, who ran with the support of the army. His period was also a stormy one. At first, he enjoyed parading himself as something of an antigringo leader and lost no opportunity to tweak Uncle Sam's beard, denouncing the United States for interference in Guatemalan affairs; but by 1960 he had discovered the advantages of cooperation and he offered his assistance in the Bay of Pigs scheme. This occasioned a revolt which, although abortive, would have very far-reaching consequences for the future of the country. Angered at the anti-Castro collaboration of the government, a group of idealistic young leftist officers rose up on 13 November 1960. Although defeated and forced to go into hiding, they sowed the seeds of an ongoing left-wing guerrilla movement that continues to this day, and of which much more will be later said.

The Ydígoras regime was, in the words of the Melvilles, "ideologically conservative, blatantly dishonest and consistently erratic."[15] This led to dissatisfaction among the ranks of the army officers, who were by no means leftists. There was a serious revolt in November 1962, which featured the bombing of Guatemala City by air force rebels. At last, in March 1963, the regime fell when Minister of Defense Col. Enrique Peralta Azurdia rumbled his tanks up to the presidential palace and seized control, abolishing the Congress, the constitution, and everything else that stood in the way of his absolute power. His reasons for this high-handed action were that the Ydígoras term was almost up, and that the president had been so foolish as to suggest that Juan José Arévalo ought to be allowed back into the country to run for the presidency again. To the army, the learned Arévalo was a dangerous communist radical whose return to power would signal a new round of land reform and unionization.

Thus, the nine years following the end of the revolution and the beginning of Castillo Armas's "Liberation" were filled with turmoil and corruption as an attempt was made to turn back the clock to the era of Ubico. Whatever the faults of Arévalo and Arbenz, and they were considerable, this was a tragedy for Guatemala. An opportunity for social change was lost and that opportunity has not come again. As one senior North American diplomat remarked to the present writer in January 1980, "no one would defend" the overthrow of Arbenz today.

Peralta Azurdia launched what he called "Operation Honesty," and he did in fact succeed in cleaning up a good deal of the corruption of the Castillo-Ydígoras period, but he also consolidated the tradition of military rule. As there were virtually no civilian organs of government, military men stepped into every phase of activity. This military was a highly professional one whose members had mostly entered the *Politécnica* in their early teens, for five years of training before being commissioned. After that, many went abroad to study in the United States or Latin America. Their loyalty was to the members of their own class or *centenario* at the *Politécnica*, to the army, and to the nation.

The United States had begun to lavish military aid on the Guatemalan army and air force in the period after 1960, and this aid was increased under Peralta, reaching $1.4 million annually by 1964. Encouraged by the United States, the army built roads, administered a school lunch program, and promoted rural health and literacy,[16] but it also severely repressed the peasantry, under the guise of its antiguerrilla campaign.

The estate-owning class, estimated by Mario Monteforte Toledo to be only 1.14 percent of the Guatemalan people, was generally content to let the military step in and take charge. The elite's share of the country's wealth was increasing, at the expense of the "popular classes" (81.86 percent of the people, by Monteforte's reckoning), while labor was effectively squelched.[17] The elite business organizations, such as the *Asociación Nacional del Café* (ANA-CAFE), the cotton growers' *Asociación Guatemalteca de Productores de Algodón* (AGUAPA), and the Chamber of Commerce, exerted considerable economic and political pressure even under Peralta.

It was plain, however, that the Peralta dictatorship could not go on forever. The oligarchy began to long for a larger political role and the United States began to apply pressure for a return to democracy. The result was a Constituent Assembly in 1965 and elections under the new constitution in March 1966, with a number of parties participating. These included the MLN, founded by Castillo Armas, which ran Col. Miguel Angel Ponciano, a former defense minister. The *Partido Institucional Democrática* (PID), backed by Peralta, ran Col. Juan de Dios Aguilar. The *Partido Revolucionario* (PR), a revamped version of Arévalo's old PAR, which had planned to run its leader, Mario Méndez Montenegro—until his presumed assassination, officially labeled a "suicide," in October 1965—ran his brother, Julio César, the rector of San Carlos University.

Col. Peralta, overly confident that indirect pressures would be sufficient to insure the victory of the PID candidate, did not resort to fraud at the polls. The result was a surprise, with Julio César Méndez Montenegro winning a plurality of the 450,000 votes cast. Thus, as no one had won a majority, the election was thrown into the Congress, which had been elected at the same time, and there the PR had a one-vote margin, giving Méndez the presidency. Evidently many Guatemalans wanted a civilian president and had good memories of the Arévalo-Arbenz revolutionary period.

It was one thing to be elected, but it was quite another to be allowed to take office. Probably only pressure from the U.S. Embassy, which was determined to install democracy in Guatemala, prevented the military from annulling the election. As it was, Méndez was forced to make a number of promises to the military in order to assume office on 1 July 1966. He was not to interfere with the military, nor investigate it; he was to keep those officers previously exiled under Peralta out of the country; and he was to name Peralta's choice, Col. Rafael Arriaga Bosque, as his minister of defense. Thus, from its very inception, "the third government of the revolution," as Méndez Montenegro liked to style it, was hopelessly shackled by the army.[18]

The army had plenty to do in this period, as the left-wing guerrilla movement continued to escalate. The movement owed its origin to the abortive coup of 13 November 1960, whose leaders, Lieutenants Marco Antonio Yon Sosa and Luis Turcios Lima, then began a guerrilla campaign known as the *Movimiento Revolucionario del 13 de Noviembre* (MR-13). The MR-13 at first had no coherent ideology other than a vague Marxism, but it developed what were styled "Trotskyite" ideas, and this led to a split in which Turcios Lima formed his own group, the *Fuerzas Armadas Rebeldes* (FAR). Turcios Lima was killed in an automobile accident in October of 1966 and the leadership of his movement passed to César Montes, while Yon Sosa was killed by a Mexican patrol along the border in June 1970, and his movement died out shortly thereafter. Other, more or less ephemeral groups also emerged, such as the *Frente Guerrillero Edgar Ibarra*; and the FAR-PGT, formed by the *Partido Guatemalteco de Trabajadores*, Guatemala's illegal Communist party.[19]

The first phase of the Marxist guerrilla movement was in the middle and late 1960s, when a number of spectacular acts of terrorism were perpetrated, including the assassination of Colonel Hauser, chief of the U.S. military group, in 1965, and the killing of U.S. Ambassador John Gordon Mein, during a botched kidnap attempt in 1968. Two years later, the German ambassador was kidnapped; a $700,000 ransom and the release of 25 prisoners were demanded and, as these terms were not met, he was killed.[20] Many prominent Guatemalans, such as Foreign Minister Alberto Fuentes Mohr, were also kidnapped.

In the period of Méndez Montenegro, the security forces were beginning to strike back. In addition to the regular army, which included commando units, such as the *Kaibiles*, there were a number of paramilitary police groups; the *Policía Militar*, drawn from the regular army and designed as a rural police; the *Policía Nacional*, with its extensive detective bureau; the *Policía Regional*, an elite force directly under the president; the *Policía Judicial*; and the *Policía de Hacienda*, a customs patrol. All of these units engaged in antiterrorist activities, often of a ruthless nature, executing the innocent along with the guilty. Particularly active against the left was Col. Carlos Arana Osorio in the department of Zacapa, between 1966 and 1970. Aided by U.S. military advisors, "Operation Guatemala" succeeded in killing an estimated 15,000 persons in that department alone and earned for Arana the title "the Jackal of Zacapa."

By 1966, anti-communist terrorist groups had also put in an appearance. These included the *Movimiento Anticomunista Nacional Organizado* (*La Mano*, often known as the *Mano Blanca*, or White Hand); the *Nueva Organización Anticomunista* (NOA); and the *Comando Anticomunista de Guatemala* (CADEG). Of these, *La Mano* became the most active and best known. The *Movimiento de Liberación Nacional* (MLN), in addition to being a legitimate political party, also participated in this anti-communist terrorism, starting in 1967.[21] These hit squads specialized in making people "disappear." Sometimes the *desaparecidos* would turn up, dead and usually tortured; at other times, their deaths remained a mystery. In March 1966, at the time of the elections, no fewer than 28 suspected members of left-wing guerrilla groups, including a niece of Yon Sosa, disappeared via *Mano*. Their bodies, rumor had it, were dumped in the ocean from an airplane. The first high point of this counterterrorism was in the presidency of Carlos Arana Osorio (1970-74), when there were more than 2,000 political murders in his first year in office. All seventeen members of the Communist Party's executive committee permanently disappeared in September 1972. In this campaign, the clandestine right-wing groups and the security forces often cooperated. Indeed, there was some evidence that *La Mano* and other organizations were simply army and police units operating under another name. They often had their headquarters in an army base. The left-wing guerrillas, on the other hand, never mustered much support in the countryside, where they had mistakenly relied on great peasant cooperation; and their urban terrorism, though spectacular, was ineffective.[22] By 1972, most groups were disbanded and the FAR, which managed to stay alive through the Arana years, was quiescent.

The left-wing guerrilla movement was destined for a revival in the mid-1970s, with the coming into existence of the Guerrilla Army of the Poor (*Ejército Guerrillero del Pobres*—EGP), which began operations on 12 December 1975, with the assassination of MLN Congressman Jorge Bernal Hernández Castellon.[23] This was followed by a guerrilla offensive by the EGP, from August 1976 to February 1977, chiefly in the department of Quiché (a largely Indian area) and in the capital, where the Sheraton Hotel, belonging to right-wing industrialist and reputed terrorist leader Jorge Kong, was bombed. The FAR also became active once more, chiefly in the backcountry of Quiché and Alta Verapaz. General Otto Spiegeler, the minister of war in the Kjell Laugerud government (1974-78), vowed to exterminate the terrorist movements, but failed, thereby weakening his own political role in Guatemala. Among those kidnapped by the EGP were the Salvadorean ambassador, Eduardo Casanova Sandoval, in May 1977; and Roberto Herrera, minister of the interior under Arana (and therefore in charge of the *Policía Nacional*), who was said to have been responsible for many of the political murders, in January 1978.[24] On the whole, the level of violence, which had fallen off in the early Laugerud years, increased dramatically in the latter part of the decade.

The politics of the 1970s featured a perfection of the system of military rule. While in El Salvador, this was accomplished through a single political party, the Guatemalan system allowed for a multiplicity of party organizations from which the army could pick and choose as the vehicle for its "official candidate."[25] The elections themselves are not necessarily dishonest in any blatant fashion (though some have been), but they are conducted in such an atmosphere of intimidation, and with the aid of such a servile press, that the desired result is almost always attained. In 1970, the army wanted as its candidate Col. Carlos Arana Osorio, and the MLN was to be his vehicle to power. The PID was persuaded to drop its plans to run Roberto Alejos, and threw its support behind Arana, in a united anti-communist front. Although the PR was ostensibly in power, under Méndez Montenegro, it lacked credibility as a political force. Its obvious subordination to the military, and the failure of its land-reform project, directed by Manuel Colom Argüeta, had compromised the "third government of the revolution." The PR's candidate in 1970 was Mario Fuentes Pieruccini, while the *Democracia Cristiana Guatemalteca* (DCG), a member of the international Christian Democratic movement, and led in Guatemala by René Armando de León Schlotter, ran Jorge Lucas Caballeros.

The election results, which were honestly counted, gave Arana a commanding plurality, with 42.9 percent of the vote, 234,625 persons having voted for the MLN-PID ticket; but as he did not win a majority, the election was again decided by Congress, where the two parties also were dominant. As mentioned above, once in power, Arana was utterly ruthless in his use of force. He used the army and police in conjunction with *La Mano* and the goon squads of the MLN.

The 1970 election was honest partly because Julio César Méndez Montenegro believed in honest elections and partly because he had calculated wrongly that the PR would benefit from such honesty. Carlos Arana Osorio had no such scruples, and the election of 1974 was a blatant farce, bringing into power the MLN-PID's military candidate, Eugenio Kjell Laugerud García, although it appears that the Christian Democratic coalition candidate had more popular support. Kjell Laugerud was not so ferocious as his predecessor, nor did he need to be, for Arana had done all the dirty work, including wiping out the entire leadership of the communist PGT.

There was general disgust with the weakness of the PR shown by the 1974 election, and in fact any of its best people had deserted the party. Francisco Villagrán Kramer (the future vice president) and Manuel Colom Argüeta, former director of the *Instituto Nacional de Transformación Agraria* (INTA) and subsequently mayor of Quatemala City (1970-74), formed a new organization, the *Unión Revolucionaria Democrática* (URD) which later transformed itself into the *Frente Unido de la Revolución* (FUR), although Villagrán Kramer later returned to the PR, from which he had been ousted by Mario Méndez Montenegro.

There were splits on the right as well. Arana Osorio had broken with the MLN to form his own personal party, the *Central Aranista Organizada* (CAO), later called the *Central Auténtico Nacional* (CAN). This multiplicity of parties led to shifting alliances, as was illustrated by the unseemly struggle over the election of officers in the Congress in June 1975. Arana sought to have his man, Luis Alfonso López, made president of that body, and when the MLN would not go along, the CAO and PID formed an alliance with the PR and DCG. That the right-wing extremist Arana could manage to get along with the two tolerated parties of the middle left surprised everyone, and in truth this *pluralismo ideológico* was only temporary, but through it Arana had his way, after, it is rumored, having bribed most of the PID and DCG members of the Congress.[26]

In other matters, Arana was not so fortunate. He had planned to make himself the power behind the throne in the Laugerud regime, but the new president outmaneuvered him. His reputed dealings with the underworld also became more notorious, and his association with the family of Elías Zimeri, a wealthy industrialist rumored to be active in the illegal arms trade, and whose San Antonio textile factory was said to be the headquarters of right-wing terrorists. In August 1975, Jorge Zimeri (Elías's son) was wounded in an assassination attempt by a rival gang and sought refuge with Arana. In April of the next year, María Olga Novella, daughter of another powerful family, was kidnapped and held for ransom—a crime which was attributed to the Zimeri family and to Roberto Arana, son of the ex-president and said to be active in the drug trade. The latter was attacked by a machine gun and wounded, in a possibly revengeful act by the Novella family, in July 1976.[27] About the same time, a police raid on the Zimeri estate netted large quantities of smuggled heavy arms.

One facet of the Laugerud years was a slow revival of labor unions. By 1976, it was estimated that some 80,000 workers were organized, up from an official count of 27,486 in 1974, but far below the more than 100,000 who had been organized in 1953. Arana had been particularly hard on the unions, persecuting even the government-supported *Confederación de Trabajadores Federados* (CTF).[28] Laugerud did not exactly welcome unionization, but he did tolerate it. He also showed some sympathy toward the plight of the peasants, encouraging the growth of the cooperative movement, even trying to create a political base among the Indians of the *Altiplano*.[29]

But all this was changed by the events of Wednesday, 4 February 1976. On that day a violent earthquake, much more severe than that which leveled Managua in 1972, struck not only the capital but many towns and villages throughout the country. An estimated 25,000 lives were lost and the physical damage was enormous. To cope with the situation, a *Comité de Reconstrucción Nacional* (CRN) was formed, including Gen. Ricardo Peralta Méndez as chairman, Finance Minister Jorge Lamport Rodil, and Miguel Angel Gaytán, head of the cooperative movement. Oscar Henriques Guerra was named executive secretary. This committee did good work, with General Peralta Méndez and Henriques Guerra especially deserving credit. The composition of the committee represented another blow to the continued ambitions of Carlos Arana, who had badly wanted to be appointed to it.[30]

The period after the quake marked a shift away from the moderate policy of the Laugerud government and toward the unions and the peasants. The need for discipline and self-sacrifice on the part of labor was not stressed; and when the unions in the capital, where there was widespread misery, struck, the president castigated them for their "political delinquency" and called them "enemies of the national reconstruction."[31] This was more in keeping with the views of Laugerud's vice president, Mario Sandoval Alarcón, secretary general of the MLN and notorious for his private army of thugs. A number of labor figures were now murdered, culminating with the death of Mario López

Larrave, dean of the law school at San Carlos, on 3 June 1977. López Larrave had been founder of the University Trade Union Center and had defended many workers in the 1976 strikes.

The major unions at this time were the conservative CTF, which was at that time a part of the ORIT and the International Labor Organization; the *Central Nacional de Trabajadores* (CNT), founded by members of the Christian Democratic Party and affiliated with the leftist Latin American Labor Confederation; and the *Federación Autónoma Sindical de Guatemala* (FASGUA), with links to the communist PGT. In April 1976, faced with government repression, the CNT and FASGUA as well as a number of smaller unions banded together to form the *Comité Nacional de Unidad Sindical* (CNUS), which today represents the most vital part of the Guatemalan labor movement.

Among the companies faced with labor troubles in the period after the quake was *Embotelladora Guatemalteca*, which had just received the Coca Cola franchise and was directed by a Texas lawyer, John Trotter. Those attempting to unionize the plant were faced with violence and intimidation. The AUROTEX textile-mill workers and those of the food-processing plant IODESA had similar experiences. When FASGUA tried to organize *Industrias Oleaginosas de Escuintla*, another food processor, owned by the Kong family, its leader, Isais Herrera Castillo, was killed, possibly by members of the Kongs' private army.[32] Although strikes in the public sector are illegal, the latter part of the Laugerud presidency was plagued by a number of them. The workers at the general hospital, San Juan de Dios, struck in 1976, and there was a strike of some 85,000 public employees in March 1978, just before the national elections.

Partly as a result of the quake, the peasants, like the urban laborers, took on a new militancy. Peasant unions are not permitted by law, but the cooperative movement, originally fostered by Laugerud, served as a basis for organization of *campesinos*. The injustices against which the peasants were protesting were low wages, the system of labor contracting, and the expropriation of their lands. Although minimum-wage laws existed, they were entirely ignored, and wages were quite low ($1.12 a day in most types of work). The contracting system amounted to temporary slavery, with the contractor rounding up peasants who were hopelessly in debt to him, often using army and police units to help. The peasants would then be sold, for the harvest, to sugar, cotton, or coffee plantations. The expropriations stemmed from the fact that many peasants, especially the Indians who considered the land the collective property of the village, had no written title to their parcels. Those who could afford lawyers could simply move in and take possession of lands which had been in the possession of *campesinos* for generations. Of course, the army and security forces would be there to prevent any armed resistance that might be organized locally, but in many cases the *hacendados* had their own private armies, and even maintained jails on their property, administering high and low justice like medieval barons.

Although Guatemala is not overpopulated, by absolute standards, a great deal of it remains inaccessible, like the Petén, and good land is at a premium. To remedy this problem, the Laugerud government began a great project to cut an east-west road from the Atlantic coast to the Mexican state of Chiapas. This road, called the *Carretera del Norte* or simply the Transversal, and built by military engineers, would open to the outside world great tracts of good land. Further, it would lead to the oil region along the Mexican border (an extension of the vast Mexican oil fields). As the project progressed, the higher officers of the army systematically began to take over the land along the road, and the great estates they established were derisively known to the local inhabitants as "the mattreses of the generals." As one priest lamented to the present writer, "The army has passed from being a defender of the landholders to being the landholder." While much of the land in the region went to the military, prominent civilian politicians also collected their share. The losers were the *campesinos*, most of them Indians. They were sometimes relocated from their villages onto so-called cooperatives where the managers kept them virtually enslaved by controlling the distribution of food.

Few raised a hand to defend the tillers of the soil. Among those who did were missionary priests, one of whom, Fr. William Woods, of the MM, died under mysterious circumstances, while another Fr. Karl Stetler, a German missionary, was expelled from the country. The Indians therefore turned more and more to cooperation with the left-wing guerrilla movements, the EGP and the FAR. Whereas almost no Indians had been involved in the guerrilla movement of the sixties, the percentage of them in the present movement is considerable.

Although many brutal killings had accompanied this process of rural transformation, the outside world only became aware of the situation with the dreadful massacre at Panzós in Quiché on 29 May 1978. The government version of the story was that some 1,000 to 1,500 Indians armed with machetes had descended upon Panzós, demanding land. They had attacked and partly disarmed the 22-man garrison led by an inexperienced young lieutenant who did not speak the local Indian dialect, Kekchí, and therefore could not communicate with the intruders. Panicked at the sight of some of his men surrendering their rifles, he ordered his remaining troops to fire, and the result was that 38 peasants were killed, including six women, while 13 peasants and seven soldiers were wounded. The lieutenant was dismissed from the service and sent abroad.

The version accepted by Amnesty International and other qualified observers is quite different. Reportedly, the Indians had announced well in advance that they would be coming to Panzós to protest that their titles to the land were not being recognized. The soldiers were then dispatched to Panzós, where they dug mass graves two days before the Indians were to arrive. When the peasants appeared, they were ruthlessly machine-gunned and over 100 of them were killed—men, women, and children cut down indiscriminately in a calculated act of frightfulness.[33]

This massacre, only the boldest of many, occurred after the election of the new president, but while Laugerud was still in office. The campaign of 1978 was greeted with great apathy on the part of the Guatemalan people. The candidate of the MLN was Gen. Enrique Peralta Azurdia, the former strongman, who promised total security, and respect for private property (not including that of ignorant peasants, of course). The Christian Democrats had toyed with the idea of running René de León Schlotter, their longtime leader, but were persuaded to join the *Frente Nacional de Unidad* (FRENU) in backing Col. Ricardo Peralta Méndez, nephew of Peralta Azurdia and a man popular for his work in earthquake relief. FRENU also contained a breakaway, leftist faction of the PR, the *Partido Revolucionario Auténtico*, and the *Frente de Participación Popular*. Peralta Méndez's program was vaguely reformist.

This decision by the Christian Democrats illustrated the weakness of their party, which had declined since its strong showing in 1974. The chief cause of this decline was a loss of public confidence in the honesty and ability of the party's leaders. The Arana bribery scandal of 1975 played a part in this. Many idealistic members had left the movement.

Although it did not have *personería jurídica*, and therefore could not participate in the elections directly, the small *Partido Socialista Democrático* (PSD) also supported the Peralta Méndez ticket. The PSD was under the leadership of one of Guatemala's most distinguished political figures, Alberto Fuentes Mohr, who had been foreign minister under Méndez Montenegro and the vice-presidential candidate of the Christian Democratic coalition in 1974. He had enjoyed the distinction of having been kidnapped by the Marxist guerrillas and by the police, both in the same year, 1970. Another distinguished figure who could not participate, for the same reason, was Manuel Colom Argüeta, the leader of the FUR, head of the agrarian-reform agency, INTA, under Méndez Montenegro, and subsequently a dynamic mayor of Guatemala City. The two most charismatic figures of the left, either Fuentes Mohr or Colom Argüeta, might have mounted a strong challenge had they been allowed to participate and had the the election been honest.

The "official candidate," or in this case "the most official candidate"—for Peralta Azurdia might have been acceptable—was the one backed by the PID, the party of the outgoing president, in alliance with the PR, which was led by the aristocrat Jorge García Granados. After some haggling, they chose Gen. Romeo Lucas García, a cousin of García Granados, over Gen. Fausto Rubio Coronado, the current agriculture minister. Francisco Villagrán Kramer, of the PR, was picked as the vice-presidential candidate after Colom Argüeta refused the position. The Aranistas also decided to back this ticket. That the PR could throw in its lot with the conservative and corrupt PID and the CAO of Arana showed clearly how far it had come from the days when it claimed to be the standard-bearer of the Arévalo-Arbenz revolution. It was now in fact a centrist, not to say conservative, party intent chiefly on picking up the political spoils which, in this case, included the vice-presidency and a couple of ministries.

Though no more fraudulent than the election of 1974, the 1978 election presented an even more unseemly spectacle. Voter apathy was widespread, as there seemed very little to choose among the three candidates, all military men and all conservative or centrist. Only 40 percent of the 1.8 million potential voters cast their ballots. As the counting began on 6 March, it was announced that Peralta Azurdia was ahead, but then, after more counting, Lucas edged in front by an announced 500 votes. At this point, Gen. Peralta Azurdia marched into the city with his private army and stormed the election tribunal. A shoot-out was only narrowly avoided when he was persuaded to withdraw as he muttered to himself, "If they want blood, blood they shall have." A few days later, Donaldo Alvarez Ruiz, the minister of the interior, nervously announced that he had discovered an MLN plot to seize the country by force, but in the end nothing came of it. The final official count gave Lucas García 262,960 votes to 221,223 for Peralta Azurdia, and 167,073 for Peralta Méndez. Thus the election was thrown into Congress, where the PID-PR and Aranistas had enough votes to name Romeo Lucas as the new president.[34]

In the elections for seats in the Congress, the MLN received 20 seats; the PID, 17; the PR, 14; the DCG, seven; and the CAO, three. The conservative Col. Abundio Maldonado was elected mayor of Guatemala City, defeating the maverick priest Luis María Ruiz Furlán, popularly known to his leftist followers as "Padre Chemita." Thus the system had functioned, as expected, to give the dominant parties control of both the presidency and the Congress.

NOTES

1. The more recent figures are from Julius Rivera, *Latin America: A Sociological Interpretation* (New York: Irvington-Halsted, 1978), pp. 198, 211.

2. Richard N. Adams, *Crucifixion by Power: Essays on Guatemalan National Social Structure, 1944-1966* (Austin: University of Texas Press, 1970), p. 178.

3. Ibid., pp. 175-76; Roger Plant, *Guatemala: An Unnatural Disaster* (London: Latin American Bureau, 1978), p. 40.

4. Plant, *Guatemala*, pp. 40-41.

5. Thomas Melville and Marjorie Melville, *Guatemala: the Politics of Land Ownership* (New York: The Free Press, 1971), p. 42.

6. Kenneth F. Johnson, *The Guatemalan Presidential Election of March 6, 1966: An Analysis* (Washington, D.C.: Institute for the Comparative Study of Political Systems, 1967), p. 3.

7. Thomas P. Anderson, "The Lesson of Guatemala," *New University Thought* 2 (Autumn 1962):54.

8. Ibid., p. 52; Plant, *Guatemala*, p. 72. Plant's figures on the size of *latifundios* are in error.

9. Adams, *Crucifixion*, p. 193; Johnson, *Guatemalan Presidential Election*, p. 3.

10. Eduardo H. Galeano, *Guatemala: Occupied Country* (New York: Monthly Review Press, 1969), pp. 53-54; Melville and Melville, *Politics of Land*, p. 77.

11. Martin C. Needler, *An Introduction to Latin American Politics: The Structure of Conflict* (Englewood Cliffs, N.J.: Prentice-Hall, 1977), p. 169.

12. Adams, *Crucifixion*, p. 496; Edelberto Torres-Rivas, "Guatemala: Crisis and Political Violence," *NACLA Report* (January-February 1980):24

13. Plant, *Guatemala*, p. 64.

14. Hubert Herring, *A History of Latin America*, 3rd ed. (New York: Alfred A. Knopf, 1968), p. 477.

15. Melville and Melville, *Politics of Land*, p. 122.

16. Adams, *Crucifixion*, p. 274.

17. Melville and Melville. *Politics of Land*, p. 1.

18. Ibid., pp. 193, 254.

19. William E. Ratliff, "Guatemala," *Yearbook on International Communist Affairs: 1970* (Stanford, Calif.: Hoover Institution Press, 1971), p. 421.

20. Ross E. Butler, "Terrorism in Latin America," in *International Terrorism: National, Regional and Global Perspectives*, ed. Yonah Alexander (New York: Praeger, 1976), pp. 48-52.

21. Plant, *Guatemala*, p. 13.

22. J. Bowyer Bell, *Transitional Terror* (Stanford, Calif.: Hoover Institution Press, 1975), pp. 49-50.

23. *Latin America* (London weekly), 2 January 1976.

24. *Latin America Political Report* (London Weekly), 13 January 1978.

25. Torres Rivas, "Guatemala: Crisis," p. 18.

26. *Latin America*, 9 January 1976, reports that DCG and PR congressmen received $5,000 each.

27. *Latin America*, 11 June 1976.

28. Plant, *Guatemala*, pp. 38, 45.

29. *Latin America*, 13 February 1976.

30. Ibid.

31. *Latin America*, 23 July 1976.

32. Plant, *Guatemala*, pp. 47, 51, 56.

33. *Latin America Political Report*, 4 August 1978; *AIUSA Report*, January 1980; *Panzós Testimonio* (Guatemala City: Centro de Investigaciones de Historia Social, 1979), pp. 27, 31.

34. *Latin America Political Report*, 10 March, 17 March, 28 April 1978.

3

Guatemala:
A Grim, Complex War

Although down somewhat in the first months of 1980, tourism continues to thrive in Guatemala. Number of visitors was up 21.9 percent in 1979 to a record of almost 350,000.[1] The elegant hotels of the capital flourished, along with bazaars and markets, while visitors traveled to such sites as the colonial ruins of Antigua, the quaint villages of the highlands, and, braving the poor transportation and lack of hotel facilities, the spectacular Maya ruins of Tikal in the Petén. But there was another Guatemala that the tourists never glimpsed, and of which they could learn little even if they read the local papers or listened to the radio. In that Guatemala, a grim and complex war to the death, with confused and shifting alliances, went on relentlessly, killing almost 2,000 persons a year.[2]

Every morning, along the streets of the capital and the country backroads, bodies were found, hands tied behind them, shot or stabbed, usually bearing the marks of torture. Often needles or razor blades had been stuck into the eyeballs; the men had been castrated; faces had been burned off with a blowtorch. This was the work of the death squads, who operated quite freely and openly in the streets. Driving about with an independent member of Congress, the present writer had their cars pointed out to him, licenseless vehicles with half a dozen men crammed in, each one armed with a sub-machine gun or automatic rifle.

In this atmosphere, no public figure went about unarmed and most of the prominent ones had several bodyguards. The powerful clans, such as the Kong, Zimeri, García Granados, Sandoval, and Arana families, had virtual private armies, often of ex-police and military personnel. In such an atmosphere, labor disputes were settled by assassination rather than by arbitration. Indeed, the line between legitimate business and gangsterism became blurred to the point where self-respecting entrepreneurs thought little of dabbling in the drug trade or arms smuggling, and politicians thought even less of aiding and abetting them in these activities. As one Guatemalan political figure lamented, "It is as if we were governed by the Mafia."

General Romeo Lucas did not invent this system, but inherited it. Being himself a product of the system, he was not destined to change it. He was sworn in on 1 July 1978, in an atmosphere of "indecision and apathy."[3] In many ways, his government was simply a continuation of that of Laugerud. Two key members of the former cabinet retained their posts in the new government, the defense minister, Gen. Otto Spiegeler Noriega and Interior Minister Donaldo Alvarez Ruiz, the secretary general of the PID. Between them, they controlled all the armed forces of the country, for the *Policía Nacional* and other such units are under the minister of the interior. Alvarez Ruiz, a hard-looking, square-built man with a perpetual frown, was a firm believer in "law and order," as he called it, and to back him up, he retained his two key henchmen from the previous government, Germán Chupina Barahona, the national police chief who had pledged to "rid the country of all leftist forces,"[4] and the chief of the detective bureau, Manuel de Jesús Valiente Telles.

The government also included Alvarez Ruiz's chief rival in the PID, Minister of Foreign Relations Rafael Castillo Valdez, a Mormon whose chief, and some unkindly said, sole, qualification for his post was his perfect English, learned from his North American wife. Other important figures in the government were Col. Julio Tulio Búcaro, the able and dynamic finance minister, and Carlos Alarcón Monsanto, minister of labor.

Another person who could not be overlooked was Vice President Francisco Villagrán Kramer. Urbane and sophisticated, he was determined, despite chronic ill health, to play a major role in the government. From the very first, he clashed with Castillo over the conduct of foreign affairs, Villagrán wishing to pursue what he called a "third-world policy," which meant forming alliances among underdeveloped countries, while Castillo favored a more traditional approach of dealing chiefly with potential investing nations. Villagrán also sought to end, by compromise, the long dispute with Great Britain over Belize, which Guatemala claimed, again irritating both Castillo and President Lucas, who found that a bellicose attitude over the issue was just the thing to distract Guatemalans from their internal plight. It finally reached the point, in the summer of 1979, that Lucas forbade Villagrán to speak on foreign policy. As the vice president also differed on internal affairs, wanting a more conciliatory attitude toward labor and the peasants, it was hard to see how Villagrán Kramer could remain in the government. Indeed, from that summer until February of 1980, he perpetually threatened his resignation. The present author had lunch with him in January 1980 and discussed his impending resignation; but the actual resignation did not come and talk of it was finally dropped altogether in March 1980. In his last interview, a few days before his assassination, Manuel Colom Argüeta, an old colleague of Villagrán Kramer, commented about him: "It's easy to join the Mafia. It's not so easy to leave it."[5] However, on 1 September 1980, from the safety of Washington, D.C., Villagrán finally resigned.

Whoever might be the elected officials of the government, it was the army which continued to exercise the greatest authority in the state. A decree was even passed in early 1979 which gave the chief of staff the right to control and register all appointments to the civil bureaucracy and to summon ministers of state before him. Particularly important among the military figures at the beginning of the Lucas presidency were General Otto Spiegeler, the minister of defense until his retirement in January 1980, and General David Cancinos Barrios, chief of staff until his assassination in June 1979. Second only in importance to the soldiers were the interests of the agricultural-export sector, led by Raúl García Granados, the brother of Jorge García Granados, the secretary general of the PR and a cousin of the president, who was said to be the real power behind the throne in the new government. Between them, soldiers and landholders arranged the elections of such men as Lucas and then saw to it that they did not overstay their hour upon the stage. To quote again from Colom Argüeta's last interview, "It is very comfortable to have a disposable president who can be traded in every four years for another 'democratically elected' one. This avoids the blemish of personal dictatorship."[6]

The government, sworn in on 1 July, did not have to wait for its first major crisis. It had to do with the bus fares in Guatemala City, where the buses are a perennial headache. Privately owned and operated, the buses are regulated by the government, which determines routes and can fix fares. In response to pressure from the companies, caught in the inflationary spiral, the government decreed a 100 percent fare increase in early October 1978. This meant that the average worker would have paid 15 percent of his wages for transportation each day—prompting the organizations of the poor to swing into action, the *Movimiento Nacional de Pobladores* and the *Comité de Defensa del Consumidor* in the lead. Protests were launched, and when these failed, CNUS and various other unions called a general strike. Within the government, some persons, such as Chupina, declared that they welcomed the strike as a chance to show the people who was boss. He lost no time in doing so, for Arnulfo Cifuentes Díaz, head of the striking telegraph workers, was promptly shot down by unidentified gunmen. In all, the strike, which began on 2 October, cost 31 lives and left 400 wounded. Perhaps the total would have been greater had not Francisco Villagrán Kramer persuaded the police to use tear gas rather than bullets in their confrontations with striking demonstrators. On 9 October, the government rescinded its fare-hike decree and the crisis began to weaken, but not before the police stormed the striker-held post office on the eleventh, arresting 400, including strike leader Marco Antonio

Hernández.[7] To finally settle the issue, the government granted a subsidy to the bus companies and ordered the buses to return to the street, under a threat of nationalization. The bus-fare confrontation demonstrated how even a relatively minor issue could shake the government to its foundations.

The forces of the opposition had a field day with the bus-fare crisis and similar problems, attacking the government for its vacillation, and inability to control events. Opposition parties included the MLN of Sandoval Alarcón, on the right, and many groups to the left; two important ones were the PSD of Alberto Fuentes Mohr and the FUR of Manuel Colom Argüeta. It was with these groups that the irrepressible Villagrán Kramer soon sought to open an all-parties dialogue, but two of the three parties in the *Frente Amplio* that had won the election, the PID and Villagrán's own PR, refused to participate. CAN, the Arana party, on the other hand, agreed, probably with an eye to upstaging its larger coalition partners. The MLN was not forthcoming either, attacking the vice president for wanting to make friends with communists. Villagrán, however, persisted, rumor having it that he was considering backing a president-vice president team of Fuentes Mohr and Colom Argüeta in the 1982 election. But on 25 January 1979, the day before his party was to receive legal recognition, Fuentes Mohr was assassinated while on his way to a meeting with Villagrán Kramer. Even by Guatemalan standards, the murder of such an important political figure was shocking, and it led to the formation of a *Frente Democrática contra Represión*, by Carlos Gallardo, an ex-Christian Democratic congressman; it combined elements from various opposition sectors including political parties and unions.

In the spring of 1979, the government also granted *personería jurídica* to the FUR, but again this proved the kiss of death, for on 22 March, Manuel Colom Argüeta was gunned down, along with his two bodyguards, on a Guatemala City street. All this of course canceled any possibility of dialogue between the government and the moderate left, especially as it was widely believed that Gen. David Cancinos Barrios, the army chief of staff, was behind the two murders. Indeed, when Cancinos himself was ambushed and killed on 10 June 1979, the EGP publicly declared that it had killed him in revenge for his ordering the murders of Fuentes and Colom. The funeral march for Colom Argüeta dwarfed even the demonstrations of sympathy that had followed the killings of López Larrave and Fuentes Mohr, with an estimated 200,000 attempting to march through the streets. Such an outpouring of sympathy might have been considered sufficient to end such political murders, but it was not. In the year that followed, six other leaders of the FUR were killed, including the secretary of the political council, Abraham Rubén Ixcamparle, shot in January 1980; and Colom's most likely successor, Jorge Everardo Jiménez Cajas, pushed off a cliff along with his five-year-old son, in March.[8] The PSD also suffered its share of violence, its secretary general, Feliciano Acevedo Oliva, being shot and stabbed to death in front of his wife and children, in July 1979.

Villagrán had appealed to Police Chief Chupina to investigate the murder of Colom Argüeta, only to be told that there was no way to investigate such political crimes. Indeed, Chupina arrested Guillermo Colom Argüeta, Manuel's brother, after Guillermo had accused him of being a party to the crime. Released, Guillermo Colom took refuge in the Venezuelan embassy and then fled the country.[9]

Not only the parties of the left, but even those of the middle, began to experience this political repression. In late May 1980, three leaders of the Christian Democratic Party were murdered in the western highlands, bringing the total murders to six in a two-week span. The DCG candidates for the forthcoming congressional election were also killed. This prompted congressional leader Guillermo Villar Aceituno, and the other two DCG members still in Congress, to declare a "holiday" from the legislature and flee the country.[10] The party's secretary general, Marco Vinicio Cerezo, also dropped out of sight for a while. By the end of 1980, more than 30 national and local DCG leaders had been killed. In February 1981, Cerezo and two other party members were set upon as they emerged from the DCG party headquarters by a group of men armed with automatic weapons. Cerezo ducked into his bulletproof car while his companions returned the fire. The attackers escaped, but the two Christian Democrats were arrested and held some weeks on charges of shooting at a police car.

If being a member of a political outgroup was dangerous, being involved in a union was suicidal, or, as Amnesty International put it: "To be a union leader or active member of a trade union in Guatemala today means risking one's life."[11] A vivid illustration of this was the continuing effort to unionize John Trotter's *Embotelladora Guatemalteca*, the Coca Cola franchise previously mentioned. Already in Laugerud's time, there had been much trouble there, and things became worse in the Lucas presidency. Starting with Pedro Quevado in December 1978, no less than three union secretaries were murdered, along with three other members. Sixteen union workers were beaten at the plant and several hundred were arrested at various times. Following the murder of the sixth person, union leader Edgar René Aldana, the CNT (a part of CNUS), which ran the union, called an emergency meeting of its 27-member executive committee, on 21 June; but the meeting place was surrounded by police and troops, who then attacked with gunfire and evidently caused some casualties before they succeeded in causing the disappearance of the entire executive committee of the CNT, including two more Coca Cola company organizers.[12] None of the CNT leaders were ever found. They were probably dropped into the ocean, like the 28 union leaders who had disappeared in March 1966. In 1979 the government, with a kind of perverse evenhandedness, had sued the bottling company for $300,000 in back taxes. The International Union of Food and Allied Workers, headquartered in Geneva, threatened a general boycott of Coca Cola products, if the parent company did not force its Guatemalan franchise to mend its ways. More direct pressure was applied by leftist terrorists, who murdered Capt. Francisco Javier Rodas, the police officer who doubled as chief of plant security, on 19 June. Finally, in September 1980, Antonio Zash Burgos bought out the interests represented by Trotter and signed a pact with the CNT.

Occasionally, despite the fact that almost all strikes were declared illegal (there having been only two legal ones since 1955), the workers succeeded in organizing and in winning concessions. The workers of the Duralita building-materials factory managed to get dismissed union members reinstated in November of 1978, by the tactic of occupying the Swiss embassy to dramatize their plight. This success had the unfortunate effect of encouraging embassy seizures, which would eventually lead to tragedy. But even where the unions were successful, the cost was high. Oliverio Casteneda de León, head of AEU (*Asociación de Estudiantes Universitarios*), the students' union at San Carlos, was machine-gunned in public at a demonstration in October 1978, and his successor, Antonio Ciani, disappeared the next month. Benvenuto Serano, leader of the bank workers' union (of CNUS) disappeared in June 1979, and on 16 November the head of the radio and press reporters' union, José León Casteñeda, was beaten to death by three men on the streets of the capital, just after he had finished his popular news commentary. These were only a few of the more prominent among the literally hundreds of organizers put to death in this way.

Another occupation that might lead to a visit from the death squads was that of activist priest. Fr. Hermógenes López Coarchita was killed in June 1978 at San José Pinula, probably for opposing the Arana family's scheme to take over all the water rights in the area. In 1980, three missionaries who had been outspoken defenders of the peasantry were similarly victims: Conrado de la Cruz (Filipino) disappeared in Guatemala City in May; Walter Voordrecke (Belgian) was assassinated by gunmen in Santa Lucia the same month; and José María Cran Sierra (Spanish) was murdered in June at Chapul in the Quiché highlands. Even before the assassination of the three missionaries, there had been so much violence against churchmen that many of the bishops became enraged over the complacent attitude of Cardinal Casariego, whose lack of a stand on human rights prompted seven bishops to threaten their resignation in June 1979.

But who was doing all the killing and what did it mean in political terms? U.S. Ambassador Frank Ortiz, who had come down from Washington in June 1979, explained to the present writer that much of the killing was that of "common criminals" by death squads made up of various police units, done as a way of ending petty crime; and it was certainly true that all too often, an unfortunate who was released from jail was found the next morning with all the marks of a death-squad execution. As for the rest, the ambassador suggested that various private armies were at work and that the whole thing was beyond the control of the government. This view is disputed by other observers not connected to the government, and even by Vice President Villagrán

Kramer. The National Lawyers Guild declared, "There is no doubt such clandestine forces exist [the death squads] and operate without government interference."[13] They stated that the death squads were made up of military and police personnel given specific hit lists. As Manuel Colom Argüeta commented in his last interview, "Every murder is that of a key person." This is also the view of Amnesty International, of the Guatemalan Human Rights Commission (founded in December 1979), and of the *Frente Democrática contra Represión.*

A dramatic instance which seems to substantiate charges of government cooperation in the activities of the death squads was the attempted assassination of student leader Manuel Valvert at San Carlos, which was bungled in June 1980. One of the three hit men escaped, but students seized the other two, who turned out to be a member of the *Policia de Hacienda* and a member of the S-2 intelligence section of the army. The S-2 man was taken to the main gate of the university, doused with gasoline, and publicly burned to death.[14] Valvert, who had been wounded in the attempt on his life and could not have taken part in this burning, was then arrested at his hospital bed, and charged with the crime. Eventually he was allowed to go into exile in Costa Rica, in return for the release of Nestle executive José Antonio de Lima, who had been held by the FAR. After that, the situation at San Carlos continued to deteriorate. On 14 July 1980, right-wing terrorists sprayed a bus stop at the university with machine-gun bullets, in retaliation for the killing of police Col. Miguel Angel Natareno. Five persons were killed and 11 wounded. By the end of the year, 86 university professors, 389 students, and a number of other persons at the university had been killed. The rector, Saúl Osorio, fled into exile and the institution was practically closed.

Although the government's hand in death-squad activity might be denied, it would be hard to deny its heavy-handedness in two cases that rocked the country. The first of these was the Calvario church incident in October 1979. In this case a number of peasants from Quiché occupied a church in the capital, protesting the arrest of nine of their fellow villagers from the highlands who had in turn been protesting the seizure of their lands, in the same manner as the peasants of Panzós. Msgr. Jerón Peronia, the rector of the church and a churchman of the old school, called for the police, who came and systematically beat and then arrested the *campesinos.* Two hours later, the body of the peasants' leader, Miguel Angel Archilla, was discovered in the street. This occurred on Friday, 12 October. The peasants were to be arraigned the following Monday and their lawyer was Yolanda Urízar Martínez de Aguilar, whose husband had been a well-known labor lawyer until his recent death, along with their son, in a mysterious automobile accident. Not being able to attend the hearing, the lawyer sent her 16-year-old daughter, Yolanda de la Luz Aguilar, and her friend Freddy Valiente (a relative of the chief of detectives), to look after the peasants. The two young people were arrested by detectives and although Freddy was released, Yolanda was taken to the police station and beaten, according to her testimony, by Manuel de Jesús Valiente. She then had her head covered by a *capucho*, a black plastic bag, which was filled with insecticide. She was repeatedly raped by the police and only released several days later after protests by, among others, her great uncle, Msgr. Jerón Peronia. The girl was, for a time, blinded from the insecticide and she and her mother both fled the country.

Another takeover case, and one with even more drastic consequences, was that of the Spanish embassy, also seized by peasants from Quiché, likewise demonstrating against repression and the seizure of their lands. As in the case of the Swiss embassy seizure, the Spanish embassy was chosen precisely because it was the embassy of a democratic country that might be sympathetic to the cause of the peasants. The seizure came after a week of protests, including the temporary seizure of a radio station, by those same peasants, to broadcast their message. The *toma* took place on 31 January, and Spanish Ambassador Máximo Cajal y López was quite properly sympathetic, and willing to temporize with the armed *campesinos*. Police Chief Chupina was not, and despite the pleas of the ambassador that he should be allowed to work out some solution, the building was stormed by riot police the same day. The 30 peasants had herded the embassy personnel and others, including two distinguished Guatemalans, former Vice President Eduardo Cáceres Lehnhoff and former Foreign Minister Adolfo Molina Orantes, both of whom happened to be visiting, into a small room. As the police came in shooting, one of the peasants dropped the molotov cocktail he had been holding. In the resultant holocaust, 39 persons burned to death, including all but one of the peasants. The one peasant survivor was badly burned and taken to San Juan de Dios Hospital, where he was seized, dragged off, and murdered by a death squad the same day.[15] Both of the distinguished Guatemalans were killed but, unfortunately for the government, the Spanish ambassador himself escaped, by some miracle, and he promptly accused the police of excessive violence. In protest, Spain immediately closed its embassy.

One reason for this savage violence was the fear of the leftist guerrillas. Indeed, it was claimed that half the peasants in the Spanish embassy massacre could be linked to the EGP. Certainly, the FAR and EGP had been active, and they had been joined in September 1979 by another organization: OPRA (*Organización del Pueblo en Armas*). The region of Quiché and Alta Verapaz continued to be subject to hit-and-run guerrilla raids, and Nebaj was temporarily occupied by guerrillas in January 1979. Despite the use of helicopters and sophisticated weaponry, the army seemed to make little headway against these attacks. Spectacular kidnappings were also the order of the day. Elizabeth Lippmann, daughter of a rich planter, was seized by leftist guerrillas in May 1979 and released for a huge ransom in July. Vice Foreign Minister Alfonso Alonso Lima was similarly seized for two weeks. But the greatest coup of all was the seizure of Jorge Raúl García Granados, son of Raúl García Granados (the leader of the landholders' group), and nephew of Jorge García

Granados (the PR chief), and of President Lucas himself, on 7 October 1979. He was finally freed on 18 January of the next year, after between $4 million and $12 million was paid.

There were also a number of assassinations and ambushes by left-wing terrorists, chiefly of army and police personnel, including that of Juan Antonio Lima, the deputy chief of the police strike force, in January 1980. In revenge for the Spanish embassy massacre, the EGP attacked a military convoy in Quiché, killing 13 soldiers, as well as making unsuccessful attempts on the lives of Chupina and Alvarez Ruiz. Soldiers were also killed at Uspatán in March of that year. In November 1979, the newly formed OPRA had clashed with troops near the Mexican border and temporarily seized a village in the department of San Marcos. The communist PGT also surfaced as a terrorist movement, killing industrialist Alberto Habie, the president of the *Consejo de Agricultores, Comerciantes, Industriales y Financieros* (CACIF)—the coordinating body for the private sector—and architect Otto Diemeck, who was on the staff of San Carlos.

The continued resurgence of the guerrillas had been the death blow to the political hopes of General Spiegeler, who went into retirement in January 1980. Originally, it had been planned that Cancinos would replace him; but as Cancinos himself was murdered, it was, instead, his successor as army chief of staff, Gen. Aníbal Guevara, who ended up as minister of defense, being succeeded as chief of staff by Gen. Juan Mendoza. General Guevara soon announced that he had the guerrilla situation "practically under control," but nothing could have been further from the truth.[16]

Faced with an intractable guerrilla war, the government in 1980 moderated its stand toward labor, even while engaging in such tactics as causing the disappearance of the CNT executive committee. A new labor code has been framed in 1979 by the government, to replace the 25-year-old statutes, and it was extremely antilabor, making it almost impossible to form a union. Suddenly, in May 1980, this legal plan was withdrawn from consideration and returned to committee for redrafting. Further, Labor Minister Alarcón Monsanto announced in March a new minimum wage, for agricultural workers, of $3.25 a day (up from $1.12), to counter a growing two-week-old strike of sugarcane workers and cotton pickers on the south coast. This caused loud protests from the landholders' group, the *Asociación General de Agricultores*, which had expected at most a doubling of the wage. Similarly, the next month, the government raised minimum industrial wages, by occupation, with the highest-paid trade, the bottlers, getting $4.12 under the new scale and the lowest-paid, the sand and gravel workers, getting $3.36.[17] This was the carrot part of the carrot-and-stick approach toward labor problems, the stick being obviously represented by such things as the seizure of the CNT executive committee.

Two noteworthy things about these increases in minimum wages were that they raised the bottling-industry workers the most, and thus affected the situation at the Coca Cola plant, and that they happened just before the national municipal elections, and thus influenced voters. These elections had been postponed from 23 March, for one month, because of accusations that the government coalition was planning to use force and fraud in the contests. FUR threatened to boycott them, as did the DCG. MLN did not go so far, but charged the government with coercion. The one-month suspension was then agreed to in order to work out a plan for the various parties to monitor the event. Possibly because of the wage boosts, the government parties did very well when the elections were finally held in an atmosphere of relative honesty and relaxation, and under supervision of the OAS. The PR and the PID, running together, picked up 171 of the 280 mayoralties, while the Aranista party, CAN, got a surprising 35. The MLN continued its political decline, winning only 28.[18]

Perhaps the decline of the MLN could be laid to the increasing recognition of its gangsterlike tactics. In a dramatic instance of these, the wealthy Raúl Castillo Love had been kidnapped in April 1979, and held for a $1-million ransom.

The government soon seized two MLN former members of Congress, Adolfo Bran Sánchez and José Vicente Navas Villatoro, ex-bodyguard for Carlos Arana, and accused them of the deed. In May a third kidnapper was taken, Gustavo Adolfo Mairene, who admitted that the kidnapping was part of the fund-raising efforts of Sandoval Alarcón for the 1982 presidential campaign, when he planned to be the candidate of his party. In his aforementioned last interview, Colom Argüeta had styled Sandoval "a buffoon straight out of the middle ages," but this seemed a bit much even for him. Indeed, there was, in some circles, the suspicion that Donaldo Alvarez Ruiz had managed to rig the incident, with the intention of hurting Sandoval. Within the MLN, there was a growing factionalism, and an attack on the house of Bran Sánchez on 3 May 1979 was probably the work of members of his own party. These internal dissensions became more public in November when the leaders of the MLN met to map out their strategy for the 1980 local and congressional elections. "Let us not be carried away by a war psychosis," Congressman Jorge Torres Ocampo urged the other party leaders.[19]

Economically, the country continued to prosper during the early Lucas period, with agricultural exports doing well; but the hope of the future was the oil industry. During the 1970s, Petromaya, S.A., a division of Basic Resources International, had done very well for itself, exploiting the Rubelsanto oil fields in the northwest. Indeed, it was charged by Finance Minister Julio Tulio Búcaro that it was doing entirely too well, a charge in which Villagrán Kramer concurred. The problem was that although the Petroleum Law of 1975 specified that oil companies must share 55 percent of their revenues with the state, Basic Resources continued to operate legally under an earlier statute, which required that only 12.5 percent of the profits had to go to the state. Eventually, Basic agreed to raise the state's share to 51 percent, but this still fell short of the stipulations of the 1975 law. Other companies which began exploration in the late 1970s, Getty, Texaco, and Hispanoil, were bound by the 1975 rules. Búcaro and Villagrán therefore began to press for a revision of Basic's charter, Búcaro further charging that Basic was engaging in manipulative practices to defraud the government of revenue. Basic, faced with these threats, began to shake up its management and become more cooperative with the government. The company's position was further improved when Ashland Oil, a far larger firm, went into partnership with Basic in new drilling ventures. With the completion of the pipeline to Santo Tomás, near Puerto Barrios on the Atlantic coast, and of the storage facilities there, large exports began in the summer of 1980.[20]

The biggest economic headaches were still unemployment and under-employment. Colonel Búcaro estimated to the present writer that it was necessary to invest $10,000 to get one new job in the private sector. To do this, he suggested a number of schemes; but he disagreed with the proposal, by Economics Minister Valentin Solórzano, to extend $22 million in credit to the housing industry to stimulate the construction of low-cost units. Instead, the finance minister stressed the need for continued foreign investment, particularly by the United States, which accounts for 75 percent of all outside investment in the country. For this reason, Búcaro opposed exchange controls, not fearing capital flight nearly as much as he feared damaging the investment climate. One heartening development to which he could point was the proposal Hanover Brands made to expand its vegetable-processing works with an investment of $300,000.[21]

But continued U.S. investment was closely tied to good political relations between the two countries, and these relations appeared to be deteriorating markedly under the Lucas administration. Although Ambassador Frank Ortiz, who had come in the summer of 1979, appeared sympathetic to the Lucas government, there began to be strong indications, in the fall of that year, that Ortiz's views were not necessarily shared in Washington. Both William Bowdler, the then deputy undersecretary of state for Central American affairs, and Viron Vaky, assistant secretary of state for inter-American affairs, whom Bowdler was about to replace, visited Guatemala and then made very negative statements. Vaky, a well-known human rights advocate, urged that the United States support change in Guatemala rather than a maintenance of the status quo, while Bowdler likewise urged the government to democratize and reform. These comments received unfavorable publicity in the Guatemalan press, and the head of the *Asociación Guatemalteca de Agricultores* accused Bowdler of interfering in the country's internal affairs.[22] Guatemalan hackles were further raised when Deputy Assistant Secretary of State John Bushnell reportedly told representatives of several major U.S. companies, including Exxon and Shell, "Any U.S. effort to maintain the status quo could only buy time, and would make the final outcome even worse for the United States." He suggested a hands-off attitude similar to that the

United States had maintained in the last stages of the Nicaraguan civil war. Although Ortiz later declared Bushnell had been partly misquoted, there were angry rebukes from the Guatemalan business community.[23]

Although the USAID continued to put money into Guatemala, including $5.6 million in December 1979, to resettle some 4,000 *campesinos* in the Transversal, all military aid had been cut off. This was in response to repressive activities by the armed forces. These, despite Ambassador Ortiz's claims to the contrary, were getting worse. The Guatemalan Jesuits stated, in January 1980, that the level of repression was as high as it had ever been in the history of the country, which brought down upon their heads a threat of extermination from the *Ejercito Secreta Anticommunists*. Further, human rights activists, such as William Wipfler of the National Council of Churches, began to denounce the "public relations role" of Ambassador Ortiz himself.[24]

Ironically enough, even while the U.S. ambassador was being attacked by human rights groups, false rumors spread, through the Guatemalan press in June 1980, saying that he was masterminding a coup similar to the one in El Salvador the previous October. Younger army officers were to oust Lucas, the rumors had it, and replace him with Villagrán Kramer, and a junta of Christian Democrats and such persons as Julio Tulio Búcaro. The embassy emphatically denied the rumors. Close on their heels, however, came word that after only 11 months, Ortiz himself was to be replaced.

The replacement of Frank Ortiz signaled a dramatic shift in U.S. policy that had very serious implications for the internal affairs of the country. The tragedy of Ortiz, a career diplomat, was that he had tried to do his job as he conceived it, but this had forced him into very close relations with the Lucas government, which he thought he could persuade to reform itself. His task was rather like that of someone trying to teach a fox not to catch chickens.

With the number of political killings reaching 20 a day by mid-July 1980,[25] the Carter administration, with the situation in El Salvador and Nicaragua also in mind, had decided that supporting the Lucas government was not in the best interests of the United States. The Carter administration's choice of a successor for Ortiz underscored this. George Landau, the former ambassador to Chile who had raised a storm over human rights violations in that country, and over Chile's failure to prosecute the murderers of Letelier, was to be given the post. This was clearly designed to raise the hackles of the Guatemalan government, and did so. President Lucas publicly announced that he hoped for a Reagan victory in the November 1980 presidential election and refused to accept Landau's appointment. When Reagan did indeed win, there was general rejoicing among Lucas's circle, and an assumption that military aid would be restored. Such a restoration would be very timely, as the guerrilla campaign was escalating at the start of 1981, with the Indian part of the population playing an increasingly active role.

While anxiously watching the North American political campaign, Guatemala was doing some early maneuvering of its own toward the election of

1982. The MLN, already rent by factionalism, saw a new group break away, the *Partido Nacional Renovadora* (PNR), under the leadership of Alejandro Maldonado Aguirre. Maldonado's plan was to create an alliance with a group called the *Frente de Unidad Nacional* (FUN), led by that old campaigner Peralta Azurdia, and with the CAN of Arana. Maldonado would then have been the candidate of this coalition. Certainly, the combined backing of Arana and Peralta would have gone a long way toward making him a powerful candidate.

But many were wondering whether there would indeed be elections in 1982 and whether anyone would dare to run if there were, for the level of political assassination made any active candidate a sitting duck. This was underscored by the fate of Julio Segura Trujillo, a prominent economist and head of the National Planning Board, who had been attempting to organize a coalition of the PSD, the PR, the DCG, and possibly FUR, to back the candidacy of his brother-in-law, Julio Tulio Búcaro. In September 1980, while visiting a shopping center, Segura was gunned down along with his bodyguard. He had no known enemies on the left, and the deed was probably the work of some of his associates within the government and meant as a warning to Búcaro to stay out of the presidential contest.

In July 1981, several major parties finally made their move, creating a *Frente Democráticio Popular*, to run Defense Minister Aníbal Guevara. This front consisted of the PR, the PID, FUN, and one wing of the DCG. It was expected that Maldonado Aguirre's PNR would eventually join them. The MLN continued to back Sandoval Alarcón for the presidency. The choice of Guevara, a military man, disappointed many who had hoped that a civilian would be the official candidate, and thus probable winner, in the 1982 election.

NOTES

1. *Central America Reports*, 10 December 1979.
2. *Amnesty International Reports*, January 1980; *Central America Reports*, 17 September 1979.
3. *Latin America Political Report*, 4 August, 17 November 1978.
4. *Latin America Political Report*, 17 November 1978.
5. *Latin America Political Report*, 30 March 1979.
6. *Latin America Political Report*, 6 April 1979. See also Edelberto Torres-Rivas, "Crisis and Political Violence," *NACLA Report* 14 (January-February 1980).
7. *Latin America Political Report*, 13 October, 20 October, 1978.
8. *This Week Central America and Panama*, 28 January, 10 March 1980.
9. *Central America Reports*, 16 July 1979.
10. *This Week Central America and Panama*, 2 and 16 June 1980.
11. *Amnesty Action*, January 1980.
12. *Central America Update*, June 1980.
13. This was in a statement issued by the guild in about January 1980, undated and unsigned.
14. *This Week Central America and Panama*, 16 June 1980.

15. *This Week Central America and Panama*, 4 and 11 February 1980.

16. *This Week Central America and Panama*, 12 March, 26 May 1980; *Latin America Political Report*, 29 June 1979; *Latin America Weekly Report*, 25 January 1980; *New York Times*, 10 February 1980.

17. *This Week Central America and Panama*, 10 March, 14 April 1980.

18. *This Week Central America and Panama*, 28 April 1980.

19. *Central America Reports*, 21 May 1979, 26 November 1979; *Latin America Report*, 1 June 1979.

20. *This Week Central America and Panama*, 21 January, 18 February 1980.

21. *This Week Central America and Panama*, 18 February 1980.

22. *Central America Reports*, 8 August, 24 September 1979.

23. *This Week Central America and Panama*, 18 February 1980.

24. *Nicaragua and Central America Report*, 1 December 1979; *Latin America Update*, November/December 1979.

25. *Latin America Regional Report*, 11 July 1980.

4

Guatemala Analysis: The Battle Lines Are Drawn

Guatemala, in 1981, resembled a particularly backward medieval principality, where lawless barons roamed about virtually unchecked by any central authority, and where the central authority itself seldom had much regard for its own laws. Given this political climate, it was not surprising that the country functioned badly, the only surprise being that it functioned at all. Obviously, complex forces were working to maintain an uneasy balance, while at the same time, others were working toward the ultimate destabilization of the country.

THE POLITICAL SPECTRUM

Essentially there are two types of political organizations in Guatemala: those which seek to work within the establishment framework of government, enjoy or attempt to attain *personería jurídica*, and present candidates for office; and those which lie outside the accepted framework and attempt to achieve their ends chiefly by force. In this latter group are such right-wing terrorist organizations as the ESA, and such leftist terrorist-guerrilla movements as the EGP, OPRA, FAR, and the PGT (which has recently taken on a terrorist identity). It would be a mistake, however, to assume that those groups which lie within the first category always seek a peaceful, political solution to their problems. As has been illustrated earlier, CAN, MLN, and other political groups maintain private armies of their own and often carry out death-squad-type activities, kidnapping, and other crimes.

On the extreme right stands the MLN, which ex-Vice President Mario Sandoval Alarcón still hopes will be his vehicle to the presidency. Although it has links to the business community, it chiefly represents the interests of the agricultural oligarchy. It would be wrong to think of the Aranista movement, represented by CAN, as being less linked than the MLN to the preservation of the old order. The differences are, rather, those of personalities. Carlos Arana Osorio simply did not get along with Sandoval. Although Arana himself could not be president again, he intended to continue in his role as king maker, with Maldonado being the heir apparent. If these two organizations were ever to combine, they would present a formidable challenge to the right-center part of the spectrum.

This right-center category might be said to include the other two parties which operate with the Aranistas in the Lucas government, the PID and the PR. These groups are obviously not without landholder support, for Jorge García Granados, the secretary general of the PR, is a great landholder; but they may be said to chiefly represent the progressive commercial interests which seek to broaden the economic base of the country through new industries and through an improved communications network. They have ties with CACIF and with the relatively progressive businessmen's group known as the *Amigos del País*. Both of these parties were rent by internal dissension. Within the PID, the struggle was a personal one between Interior Minister Alvarez Ruiz and Foreign Minister Castillo Valdez. Inside the PR (which had abandoned the last shred of its old revolutionary image, with the defection of Villagrán Kramer), there was considerable dissatisfaction with the leadership of García Granados.

In Guatemala, the middle, or centrist, position beloved by North American diplomats, was occupied by the DCG, but the Christian Democrats were in disarray, not so much because of internal problems, but because it was simply unhealthy to be identified with the party. With so many leaders assassinated, and the party's offices in Guatemala City closed after July 1980, the Christian Democrats appeared to have been at least temporarily eliminated as an effective political force. Further, public confidence in the integrity and ability of the party appeared to be very low, with many of the younger, brighter members of the DCG abandoning it.

Political assassination had, by the end of 1980, also completely demoralized the parties of the progressive, democratic left, such as the FUR and PSD. The charismatic leaders of these movements had been eliminated in 1979, at the very time they gained legal recognition. Dissension and schisms, common problems of left-wing parties in Guatemala, plagued both of these groups. Only the emergence of some particularly attractive political candidate might rally them, but it appeared increasingly unlikely that such a candidate would emerge. Julio Tulio Búcaro might have been such a candidate, but the murder of his brother-in-law and campaign manager, Julio Seguro, coupled with the defeat in Congress of his package of higher taxes, in early December 1980, weakened his chances considerably. Most Guatemalans of the left appeared ready to abandon the political scene entirely and to see a solution only in armed conflict against the established order.

Thus, Guatemala, as it began the new decade, had several strong movements of the right or right center, but a very weak middle, represented by the Christian Democrats, and a democratic left virtually eliminated by terrorism. The 1982 election, if such an election could be held at all in the climate of violence likely to exist, would feature several conservative alternatives, like the last election, rather than giving the Guatemalan people a real choice between opposing ideologies.

SOCIAL CLASSES AND FORCES

By far the largest single group in Guatemala, as it is throughout Central America, is the peasantry. But these *campesinos* (and perhaps the Spanish word which means simply "country people" designates them better than the misleading European term "peasants") do not represent a homogeneous whole. At the economic top of the scale are many who own a few *manzanas* of land and largely support themselves from their holdings. They are a substantial part of the *ladino campesinos* as a whole, perhaps 40 percent, but a dwindling faction as landholding has become concentrated, and, so far at least, land settlement programs, such as that in the Petén, have had meager results. The larger part of the *ladinos* have little land or none at all. They shift from harvest to harvest, and if they had any doubts about shifting, the labor contractor, often backed by the local military, is able to draft them for the next harvest, in a manner not much different from that of the early Spanish *repartimiento* system. As Blaise Bonpane comments, "Farm workers are routinely kidnapped, forced into military service, robbed of their lands and murdered."[1]

In a way, the Indian component of the peasantry, some 40 percent, is better off. The village communal society regulates land distribution, an infrastructure of support lessens many imposed burdens, and there is a feeling of solidarity. But, especially in recent decades, the Indians have been as mercilessly exploited in commercial agriculture as their *ladino* counterparts, and perhaps more so, for the Europeanized Guatemalan regards Indians as a breed apart and hardly human. As Bonpane points out, "It is not a crime to kill an Indian in Guatemala." The *ladino* peasant has long been susceptible to left-wing propaganda, and Arbenz made such peasants the basis of his regime; but only in the last two years have the Indians responded likewise, thanks largely to the mammoth task, undertaken by the EGP, of speeches and radio broadcasts given in the many local dialects. As a result, the Indians are showing a new militancy and are a force to be reckoned with.[2] A peasant, largely Indian, group called the *Comité de Unidad Campesina* has been formed, and cooperates with the EGP.

Organized labor, which grew tremendously under Arbenz, only to shrink under the persecutions of more conservative regimes, still can be considered an important political force. But with the recent massive death-squad activity against unionists, a new type of unionism has emerged. No longer are there union halls and meeting places where the leaders congregate. The fate of the CNT leaders ended that. Instead, unionists work underground, no longer seeking simply economic goals or better working conditions, but, rather, trying to instill a stronger class consciousness and revolutionary potential. The unions are forging links to the peasant-mass organizations and to the EGP.[3]

Some sections of the nonagrarian lower middle class are also beginning to be radicalized, especially such groups as teachers and journalists. Three hundred and twenty-six elementary and secondary school teachers lost their lives in the 1980 political violence, along with 12 journalists.[4]

The wealthier landholders and the commercial and manufacturing sector— in short, those groups represented in CACIF—do not want left-wing revolution, but many of them have grave doubts about the actions of the Lucas government. This is often expressed in capital flight and, in many cases, in physical removal to the politically healthy climate of Miami. On the whole, this sector of the population remains staunchly conservative, remembering only too well how it fared in the days of Jacobo Arbenz; but it increasingly deplores the corruption of the government and the iron control that the military maintains over all significant national activity.

The military is only too well aware of its bad repute within the country, and efforts are underway to change the image of the soldier from that of the enemy into that of the friend and teacher. To that end, an ambitious literacy campaign has been undertaken, making use of soldiers as teachers. Further, the army declared in August 1980 that it would end its traditional policy of impressing peasants, as they came out of theaters or bars, and whisking them off to remote barracks where relatives might not hear of them for six months to a year. Instead, the facade of a universal military service is to be abandoned and enlistment is to be made "voluntary," with the pay of recruits raised to 50 dollars a month.[5] It remains to be seen whether this reform actually changes the method of recruitment.

After the 1980 presidential elections in the United States, the army was hoping to greatly increase its firepower and efficiency. The 14,000-man force expected that Reagan advisor Roger Fontaine's comment that they "will be given what aid they need" came directly from the new president. High on the shopping list were new medium-range transports to replace the antiquated DC-3s and Cobra gunships, so useful in guerrilla warfare. In the economic and financial spheres, the power not only of individual colonels and generals, but of the military as an institution, might be expected to grow. One indication of how great this power could be was the announcement by the *Instituto de Previsión Militar*, the army pension fund, of the building of a cement factory at El Progresso, at the cost of $360 million.[6]

Another institution of traditional importance was the Catholic church. But in speaking of the Guatemalan church, it is well to remember that the long period of "liberalism" from Barrios to Ubico virtually broke the power of the institution. At the close of World War II, the church hardly existed outside Guatemala City and was as bankrupt economically as it was spiritually. As part of the plan to combat communism in the years after the takeover by Castillo Armas, the North American hierarchy, in cooperation with the U.S. government, launched a massive missionary campaign. Every religious order of any importance sent contingents of its members into the country. The result was a great revival of the church as a religious institution, although to this day more than half the priests and nuns are foreigners.

While the church has revived spiritually, it has remained very tentative in dealing with the political sphere. But in recent years, it has become increasingly polarized between those who follow the conservative line, led by the aged Cardinal Mario Casariego and by papal nuncio Emanuele Gerada, and those, chiefly missionaries, who follow the Medellín line of liberation theology. Although himself essentially a moderate, Msgr. Juan Gerardi, bishop of El Quiché, had been forced into a leadership role by his heading of the National Bishops' Conference and by the fact that his diocese was the scene of so much civil strife. He finally, in late 1980, took the dramatic step of evacuating all the clergy from the region, after the murder of several religious. For his pains, he was greeted in late November 1980, upon his return from a visit to Rome, by security forces which exiled him from the country.

FACTORS MAKING FOR STABILITY

The Guatemalan political system may be defined as a disguised military dictatorship in which the election of a "disposable president" (to use Colom Argüeta's phrase) is held every four years. The list of acceptable candidates for the presidency is drawn either from military men or from those satisfactory to the military. Those unacceptable are discouraged from participating, through the denial of *personería jurídica*, or, that failing, through threat of death. The most acceptable candidate to the senior military commanders can generally count on the support of a coalition of parties going from center right to far right. Once in power, the president is expected to maintain military men in key positions, such as the ministries of defense, the interior, and, in the case of President Lucas, the ministry of finance.

The chief functional imperative of this system is that it respond to the articulation of opinions of the military council, the chief of staff, the defense minister, and other military leaders. But the input of the army is only one of several voices to which the government must pay heed. The political parties are not simply vehicles of a particular candidate, but generally have a constituency of their own. In several cases, they represent in part the interests of a single powerful clan—the PR representing García Granados; CAN, Arana; and MLN, Sandoval; but even so, they also represent the interests of a number of financial backers, party workers, and, sometimes, less powerful clans. Each party in a victorious coalition can expect a share of the spoils, and each active party member can expect to share in these spoils in proportion to his role in the party and the party's influence in the coalition.

It might be inquired, then, why any party to the right of center would fail to sense who was the favored candidate and fail to join the coalition. In some cases a party might be excluded through personal animosities, such as those between Arana Osorio and Sandoval Alarcón, or a party might feel that there is more than one acceptable candidate and that the balloting might be relatively free and honest. Probably both these factors played a role in the decision of the MLN to back Peralta Azurdia in 1978. The backing of either a very strong party, such as the MLN in 1970, or of a coalition of strong parties is an imperative for the maintenance of the system.

Agricultural and commercial interests must also be conciliated, and they play their role in the aggregation of interests necessary to perpetuate the system. These express their input through their individual grower's associations, such as that of coffee and cotton growers, and like groups; through the Chamber of Commerce, and other business groups; such as the *Amigos del País;* and, most importantly through CACIF, representing all the large agricultural and business groups. Failure to consult the interests of those sectors which control the wealth of the country, especially export sectors, would bring down a presidency and possibly the system.

When one puts together the military and security forces, the party workers on every level, and the various economic sectors able to articulate their demands, then one finds that the base of support of the government is not so narrow as might appear at first glance; yet it is not likely that more than 5 percent of the populace actively support the current regime. The very low turnout in the 1978 presidential election suggests as much. But, like any government, that of Guatemala relies on passive acceptance by the vast majority; and it is precisely this passive acceptance which appears to be eroding. There is little articulation of public opinion favoring continuation of the present political order.

DESTABILIZING FACTORS

The ubiquitous activities of the so-called death squads are at once a symptom of the lack of popular support and an accelerating factor in the erosion of such support. By death-squad activity is meant that broad range of murder and

and terrorism that engulfs everyone from petty criminals to union leaders and political figures of the opposition. These murders are conducted almost openly and with little interference from the authorities. Insofar as they are political crimes, they represent the frantic efforts of certain persons in the regime—particularly within the security forces, often linked to powerful private armies—to cleanse the country of subversives. They have succeeded in almost totally disrupting all parties to the left of center, even the centrist Christian Democrats; and they have cowed the press into silence. But they have, in the long run, contributed greatly to alienating the average citizen from a regime which he increasingly perceives as a cynical collection of political gangsters. The ESA, which is the most powerful of the right-wing terrorist groups, is certainly feared, but it is hated even more. Further, the extent of this political suppression severely limits the type and amount of feedback the government receives concerning its policy. Since it has so severely restricted input, the government is unable to judge the actual reactions of the citizenry to its policies and must stumble along in the dark, until illumination comes in the form of a massive strike, riot, or even a revolution.

The antithesis of the death-squad activity is the guerrilla-terrorist movement which has existed sporadically in Guatemala since the days of Yon Sosa. The main groups in operation in 1980 were the EGP, the FAR (which is the oldest), and the OPRA. But the communist PGT has recently emerged as a terrorist group, assassinating business figures and politicos of the right, in a mirror image of the death-squad activity. The new enthusiasm shown by the long-passive Maya for the EGP marks a distinct turning point. There were, at the close of 1980, an estimated 5,000 guerrillas in the field, either full or part time. This is a formidable force for the 14,000-man national army and the security forces to handle, for the guerrilla has many natural advantages over the soldier. To maintain such a force also requires a vast infrastructure among the people of the area through which the guerrilla bands roam. This infrastructure can only in part be achieved through terror or intimidation. A large part of it must come through the acceptance by the populace of the guerrilla bands. Castro's movement in Cuba succeeded because of its extensive infrastructure; Ché Guevara's movement in Bolivia failed because it failed to develop one. The very harshness with which the military treats the people of the guerrilla areas often tends to make them supportive of the antigovernment forces and is, therefore, counterproductive. The guerrillas alone probably could not bring down the regime, but combined with massive popular discontent, they might well prove more than the government could handle.

The Guatemalan governmental system has presented an image of strength and rigidity for the past 15 years; but, in reality, the structure is extremely brittle. It has resisted direct assault, but if it were to begin to crumble, it might shiver into pieces with astonishing rapidity. This is not a prediction, but it is a suggestion of what might possibly be expected in the future. There is a serious need for the government to broaden its base of support; and the terrorization of parties of the democratic left and center, the suppression of legitimate unionism, and the massacres of peasants are not good ways to achieve this goal.

The Economic Factor

One important source of political stability in Guatemala has been the surprising resilience of the economy, occurring despite the political turmoil and massive capital flight. The debt situation of the country was the best of any Latin American state. The real growth rate of the economy was 4.5 percent in 1979 and 3.5 percent in 1980, with manufacturing being up 6 percent in 1979. The 1980 gross domestic product was $8.05 billion and the per capita income was up dramatically to about $1,200, although this was badly distributed, with 2 percent of the populace receiving 25 percent and the lower 50 percent receiving only 10 percent.[7]

The agricultural-export sector has been a very important source of Guatemala's wealth, and it did especially well in 1979 and 1980 (see Table 4.1). As can be seen from the table, the value of coffee, sugar, and cardamom made impressive gains from 1979 to 1980.

Oil, however, remained the hope of the future. In addition to Petromaya (Basic Resources Corporation), Hispanoil, Getty, Monsanto, Braspetro (of Brazil), Texas Eastern, Texaco, Amoco, and the French giant, Elf-Aquitaine, were all exploring in Guatemala for the precious substance. With the exception of Petromaya, all were bound by the 1975 law, which meant that a substantial proportion of their finds would go to the government. Petromaya, after much haggling, agreed that it, too, was under the 1975 law, and would therefore pay $11.2 million in back taxes. It further agreed to a reduction, in the size of its concession, by one-half to a still impressive 200,000 hectares.

TABLE 4.1. Guatemalan Agricultural Exports for 1979-80

Commodity	1979		1980	
	Volume	Value	Volume	Value
Coffee	Q3,100.2	$432.0	Q3,000	$495.0
Cotton	3,295.8	188.1	3,000	180.0
Sugar	3,407.8	34.5	3,400	68.0
Bananas	5,356.5	18.4	5,500	20.0
Beef	343.4	41.4	350	41.3
Cardamom	74.9	49.2	78	55.0

Note: Volume is in thousands of quintals; value, in millions of dollars. Cardamom seed is used in the manufacture of aromatics.
Source: This Week Central America and Panama, 8 September 1980.

The position of Basic Resources in the oil hunt was greatly enhanced in July 1980 when Elf-Aquitaine went into partnership with it.[8] So far, only a limited amount of oil has been shipped out, and this has been more symbolic than anything else, for Guatemala must still import oil. But with reserves estimated as high as 5 billion barrels of oil, the situation might be expected to change radically.

Oil is not the only power resource in Guatemala. Blessed with large lakes and fast-running rivers, Guatemala in 1980 launched an ambitious $1.7-billion hydroelectric project designed to replace oil, which in 1980 supplied 70 percent of the electrical power.[9] Unfortunately, like so much else in Guatemala, the project appeared to be dragging its feet, thanks largely to technical difficulties.

Tourism, long a standby for the economy, was understandably down some 30 percent in 1980, thanks to greater worldwide publicity about the violence; the income from tourism was $67 million below predictions, and 15,000 workers in tourist-related industries were out of work by November 1980.[10] Despite this, the government was going ahead with the building of two new jetports. One was to be created at the famous ruins of Tikal in the Petén, at a cost of $25 million. A hotel complex was to replace the current shoddy accommodations at the site. The second airport was to replace La Aurora, which serves Guatemala City and is located virtually in the city. The argument that La Aurora was dangerous was underscored in January 1981 when a propjet crashed on takeoff into an empty school. But the location picked for the replacement raised some eyebrows. It would be built at Masagua, on the Pacific coast, 80 kilometers from the capital. Not only would this mean an hour-an-a-half ride from the capital, but it would mean a road that would be almost indefensible from a military point of view, as El Salvador was discovering with its newly opened Cuscatlán jetport, also far from the capital. The generals, it need hardly be said, had already managed to make some sound real estate investments in the Masagua area before the choice of the site was publicly announced.

Another communications project of great importance to the economy is the proposed Periférico Nacional highway, which, as the name implies, would be a ring road around the country, stretching to 1,400 kilometers and costing $1.2 billion. Desarrollo de Autopistas y Carreteras de Guatemala, S.A., was to begin the project in 1981 with the construction of a six-lane road from the capital to San José on the Pacific coast. When finished (about 1990), the road would link up with the Transversal highway and give the country splendid communications with previously remote regions.

Despite the capital flight, there was still some private investment in 1980, such as the new mushroom-processing and canning plant to be built by ALUSA; and toward the end of the year, the government was increasingly able to obtain loans from such agencies as the Inter-American Development Bank, one instance being a $51-million loan for a hospital-building program. This was a sign both of confidence in the Guatemalan economy and the continued stability of its regime.

FOREIGN AFFAIRS

The election of Ronald Reagan in the United States, as previously indicated, warmed the frosty relationship that had existed between the two countries in the Carter years. That could facilitate international loans, over which the United States has a large say, and could help reequip the army. However, Guatemalan relations with Great Britain over Belize continued to be very bitter. An almost endless round of conferences did little to resolve the issue. Resolutions of both the United Nations, and the Organization of American States had called for Belize to become an independent state, and Great Britain had announced its intention to give the country its independence in 1981, whether Guatemala liked it or not; Guatemala would not like it, but the issue was more for home consumption than anything else. The people in Belize certainly had no desire to become a part of strife-filled Guatemala, and they would continue to have a British military presence. The battalions of regulars and the Harrier aircraft in Belize would be more than a match for the entire Guatemalan army and air force, even if the Guatemalans could extricate themselves from their own guerrilla war. A tentative agreement was worked out between Britain and Guatemala in April 1981, only to break down almost immediately.

Guatemala retained close ties with the junta in El Salvador, and relations with the revolutionary regime in Nicaragua were virtually nonexistent. Plainly, the government thought of the Salvadorean civil war as its own civil war and regarded the Nicaraguans as interfering in that struggle as creating a front for Cuba and the Soviet Union.

Options for U.S. Policy toward Guatemala

The left-wing guerrillas are so disaffected from the United States that a policy of backing them appears to be out of the question; and if they were to come to power, relations would be likely to be cool for some time to come. They would be likely to draw closer to Cuba and Nicaragua. This leaves the United States with four basic options in regard to the existing governmental order.

One of these would be to encourage all parties, including those of the democratic left and center, to participate in the electoral process and to encourage the government to allow their participation and curb death-squad activity. This might considerably strengthen the legitimacy of the regime in the eyes of the Guatemalan people. The election of 1982 would be crucial in this regard, as a test of the broadening of the democratic process. In this option, the United States would encourage a free election and discourage the imposition of military candidates upon the various political parties. Whoever then won that contest might be encouraged to make dramatic social reforms, especially in the area of land reform, to undercut the basis of support of the radical left. This was essentially the policy that Ortiz pursued in his months as ambassador. He pursued it through a carrot-and-stick approach, but had scant success in convincing his host government, with whom he became too closely identified.

A second option would be to put the anti-communist aspect of the government first, ignore the human rights factor, and give unconditional backing to the regime as currently constituted. This has the virtue of simplicity and is perhaps more realistic in that it realizes that there is little likelihood of reforming the current governmental system. Its obvious drawback is that if the regime were to collapse anyway, the Guatemalans, like the Nicaraguans, would be so anti-North American that it would make relations very difficult, if not impossible.

A third possibility would be to try to nudge the government toward very modest changes, while largely backing the existing governmental order, even militarily. Such a minimalist program might simply aim to encourage some civilians or moderate military men to stand in the 1982 election, and to encourage the dialogue already attempted by the DCG between the government and the democratic opposition. The social order would be expected to change very slowly.

A fourth possibility would be a total hands-off approach, as was advocated by many in the Carter White House. In this case, because of its human rights violations, the government of Guatemala would be left to save itself. In the event of an eventual left-wing victory, this might considerably aid the United States in eventually achieving some sort of accommodation with the new order. But if the existing regime were to hang on, it would view the United States with disfavor.

In any event, Chapters 2-4 ought to have made clear that the realities of Guatemalan politics are extremely complex and that the situation is much more fragile and filled with difficulties than might appear on the surface. The political problems of Guatemala have deep roots, and they may be around for some time to come.

NOTES

1. Blaise Bonpane, "Beware the Wrath of the Formerly Docile," *In These Times*, 26 May 1980.
2. Ibid.
3. *Latin America Regional Report*, 19 September 1980.
4. *This Week Central America and Panama*, 24 November 1980.
5. *This Week Central America and Panama*, 4 August 1980.
6. *This Week Central America and Panama*, 17 and 24 November 1980.
7. *This Week Central America and Panama*, 4 and 18 August 1980.
8. *Latin America Regional Report*, 19 September 1980.
9. *This Week Central America and Panama*, 24 November 1980.
10. *This Week Central America and Panama*, 4 August 1980.

PART II
EL SALVADOR

5

El Salvador:
50 Years of Solitude

El Salvador, smallest of the Central American republics, comprises barely 8,000 square miles of land, the exact figure not being determinable because the border with Honduras remains undefined. Despite this small size, no bigger than New Jersey or Massachusetts, the country is the second most populous state in the region, with some 5 million inhabitants in 1980, giving it a density of over 600 persons per square mile and making it the most densely populated state on either American continent. This population is growing rapidly, having expanded between 1970 and 1975 at the annual rate of 3.7 percent, which means that it would double in 20 years.[1] El Salvador is a land of volcanic peaks, the highest of which rises to over 6,000 feet, and of large crater lakes; but it also has broad valleys of rich volcanic soil suitable for farming, and, along the eastern part of its Pacific shore, a littoral plain of great natural fertility. Unlike the other Central American republics, it has no Atlantic coastline, being hemmed in on the north by Honduras.

Indigo was the chief crop of colonial times, but in the late nineteenth century, coffee, grown on the volcanic slopes of the mountains, has become king. In recent decades, sugar, grown in the central valleys, and cotton, a product of the littoral plain, have also assumed importance. Cattle raising has been common since colonial days; and food crops, such as maize, beans, and tropical fruits, are grown in abundance. Until after World War II, there was no industry to speak of, and even by the end of the seventies, there were only a few dozen factories, concentrated in the capital and producing a variety of goods from textiles to electronic components. The major foreign investor in such industry was Japan, until the level of violence forced it to withdraw in the late seventies.

The large Indian population of the precolonial era blended into the Hispanic conquerors, producing a mestizo population. Until 1932, there were a number of Pipil Indian communities in the western part of the country, but they were largely exterminated or disbursed following their unsuccessful, Marxist-inspired uprising of that year.[2] The small oligarchy, which traditionally owned some 60 percent of the land, tended to be ethnically European.

This oligarchy represents less than .2 percent of the populace, and it has always been known as the 14 families (*los catorce*), although no one can agree as to which families make up the 14. While the number is a myth, it indicates the perception of the common man that a very small group of very wealthy persons dominates the nation, and in fact certain names, such as Dueñas, Regalado, and Escalón, occur again and again in the economic and political history of the country. For the last 50 years, however, this oligarchy has not really ruled the country, its political demise having come about through a series of violent events.

In 1931, Pío Romero Bosque, an aristocratic president linked to the ruling circles, held what probably was the only free election in the country's history. Out of this emerged as president an urbane reformer, Arturo Araujo. Something of a socialist, Araujo promised social justice to all at the very time that the world depression was causing the price of coffee to plummet and driving the country toward bankruptcy. To make matters worse, the small *Partido Comunista de El Salvador* (PCES), under the charismatic Agustín Farabundo Martí, was stirring up trouble both among urban workers and among the Indian peasants of the western part of the country, whose lands were being gradually seized by the oligarchs. The army, alarmed that Araujo might be a forerunner of Martí, rose up in December 1931 and deposed the president, substituting a man of its own, Gen. Maximiliano Hernández Martínez, the vice president and war minister. General Martínez (as he preferred to be called) captured Farabundo Martí before the latter could launch his intended revolt in January 1932; but the revolt occurred anyway, chiefly among the Indians of the Izalco region, thousands of whom armed with machetes, seized a number of towns and villages. The regular army had little trouble dispersing them; and afterward, to prevent this from ever happening again, it rounded up between 10,000 and 30,000 of the peasants and killed them in cold blood. Martí and most of the principal leaders of the PCES were publicly executed. The frightful massacre of 1932 is a shadow that hangs over Salvadorean politics in much the same way as the events of 1954 hang over Guatemala's. The hatred the peasants had for the oligarchs was confirmed and the fear the upper classes had of another *machetazo* became deeply ingrained.

General Martínez proved an efficient, if somewhat chilling, ruler. Known as *El Brujo*—the witch doctor—he dabbled in the occult, but kept his feet on the ground when it came to dealing with the economy, thereby pulling his country firmly through the depression. The great landholders, in a bargain which became permanent, forfeited to him and to the military the lion's share of political power and offices, while retaining for themselves the larger part of the wealth and social prestige. As in Guatemala, the alliance was an uneasy one, with the oligarchs looking down on the middle-class soldiers as their social inferiors and with the military holding the effete landholders in contempt for their inability to rule.

Like Ubico, Martínez was the victim of the renewed idealism spawned by World War II and was driven from office in 1944. There followed a brief period of rule by a civilian-military junta, but when it suggested reforms, it was overthrown by Col. Osmín Aguirre y Salinas, who seized power and held it until the election of his crony, Gen. Salvador Casteneda Castro, who took office in March 1945. The latter in turn was removed by a majors' revolt of December 1948, when a group of younger, reform-minded officers seized power. The rhetoric was about reform, but in fact little was accomplished under the presidency of Lt. Col. Oscar Osorio, while his hand-picked successor, Col. José María Lemus, turned out to be a cruel and vicious tyrant whose ouster, by still another group of reformist junior officers, in October 1960, troubled nobody. But 1960 was 1944 over again. The junta of liberal civilians and progressive officers was regarded with suspicion by the oligarchy and the military conservatives, who accused it of flirting with Fidel Castro's new regime in Cuba. Col. Julio Adalberto Rivera ousted the junta in a coup of 25 January 1961, and soon had himself made president.

Rivera created a system which was destined to last until 15 October 1979. Borrowing from Mexico the idea of a single, dominant party, he created the *Partido de Conciliación Nacional* (PCN), which would run the official candidate every five years and do whatever was necessary to assure victory at the polls. But, in the early years of the system, the opposition parties were allowed to hold a number of mayoralties, including even that of the capital city, San Salvador, and to win a number of seats in the unicameral National Assembly. Thus it was that Colonel Rivera was succeeded by Col. Fidel Sánchez Hernández, and he by Col. Arturo Armando Molina, and he by Gen. Carlos Humberto Romero.

A number of opposition parties were allowed to exist, the most prominent of which was the Christian Democratic Party (*Partido Demócrata Cristiano—* PDC), under the leadership of engineer José Napoleón Duarte, mayor of San Salvador from 1964 to 1970, a highly visible, but not very powerful, post.[3] A group of moderate socialists associated with the National University of El Salvador founded the *Movimiento Nacional Revolucionario* (MNR). In the seventies, the MNR would be led by Guillermo Manuel "Memo" Ungo. The communist PCES, illegal since its uprising in 1932, formed a surrogate party, the *Unión Democrática Nacionalista* (UDN), while on the extreme right a group of disgruntled oligarchs founded the *Partido Popular Salvadoreño* (PPS).

The election of 1967, which picked Rivera's immediate successor, had not been too difficult to arrange. Neither the rector of the National University Fabio Castillo of the PAR nor Secretary General Abraham Rodríguez, who was the candidate of the PDC, commanded any great popular following, while Fidel Sánchez Hernández was a man of impressive military bearing and self-confidence. Further, he had the advantage of running in the midst of the border crisis between El Salvador and Honduras, which created popular enthusiasm for the military. Unfortunately, two years after he took office, this border dispute got out of hand when Honduras, faced with problems of land reform, decided to expel some of the 300,000 illegal Salvadorean immigrants who had taken up residence in that country. What followed was a tragedy, with as many as 25,000 Salvadoreans streaming back across the border in May and June 1979. Eventually, some 80,000 were expelled. Because the crisis of 1979 happened to occur at the same time as the bitterly contested World Cup soccer matches between the two countries (which certainly helped raise tempers), the war which El Salvador launched on 14 July has become known erroneously as the "Soccer War." In fact, the war was over the problem of immigration, itself the product of overpopulation of the land, and over Honduras's holding of a negative balance of payment in regard to El Salvador, both being in the Central American Common Market. The war created a wave of patriotic furor; and when his armies advanced a few miles into Honduras, President Sánchez proclaimed a victory, even though the OAS soon forced him to withdraw his troops. A splendid victory parade through the streets of San Salvador served to mask the fact that nothing had been done to stop the expulsions.[4]

In the long run, the consequences of the war were disastrous. The refugees, although merely a drop in the bucket as compared to a natural increase of the population, served to swell the ranks of the indigent.[5] Further, the profitable Honduran market was lost for over a decade. These became contributing factors to the economic decline of El Salvador during the seventies. Ultimately, the army also lost face over its handling of the crisis and its phony victory.

The war served to turn the country in upon itself and its problems. These were massive enough, for the population was outrunning the food supply, while the large landholders continued to take land out of food production and put it into cash crops. Only the people of Haiti had a lower caloric intake in the Western world. So desperate was the desire for farm land that peasants even commandeered vacant lots in the capital, in the hopes of getting in a harvest of maize before they were run off.[6] By the early seventies, unemployment was 20 percent and underemployment 40 percent, and the annual inflation rate had reached 60 percent by 1974.[7] Faced with problems of this magnitude the government decided on a course of capitalist-industrial modernization backed by repression of discontent.[8] This was despite the fact that a National Agrarian Reform Congress in January 1970 had called for the expropriation of the large estates as the only possible solution to the country's problems.

The elections for seats in the National Assembly and for the 250 or so mayoralties in March 1970, were conducted with more fraud than any previous ones under the system devised by Rivera. The PDC mayoralties shrank from 78 to eight, while their numbers in the National Assembly fell from 19 to 16. The PPS lost all its mayoralties.[9] This set the stage for the presidential elections of 20 February 1972. By that time, the country was obviously in a recession, and the leftist opposition, composed of the PDC, the MNR, and the communist UDN, had decided to form a united front under the banner of the *Unión Nacional Opositora* (UNO). The majority party in the UNO was the Christian Democratic Party and it put forward its best-known figure for the presidency, José Napoleón Duarte, as the collective candidate of the UNO.

In the balloting, it appeared that Duarte easily outdistanced the colorless Colonel Molina by 72,000 votes, but the electoral commission took charge and declared Molina ahead by some 100,000 votes.[10] There were two minor candidates; so the election went to the PCN-dominated Assembly, which declared Molina the winner.

At this point, history threatened to repeat itself. As in 1948 and 1960, a group of reform-minded younger officers decided that the time had come to end the faltering PCN regime, relying upon popular discontent over the electoral fraud and over the stagnant economy to give them a power base. Col. Benjamín Mejía was the leader. He and most of the other participants in the movement had fought in the war with Honduras and had seen the mismanagement and waste with which the war was conducted. The coup was launched on 25 March and for two days it appeared it would be successful, President Sánchez Hernández having been seized at his residence and the capital appearing to be firmly in rebel hands. But the *Guardia Nacional*, the *Policía Nacional*, and other elite units, including the air force, remained loyal to the regime, and by the 28 March, Mejía and his forces had been forced to lay down their arms. The revolt cost some 200 lives and caused widespread damage in San Salvador.[11]

One immediate casualty of the revolt was the position of Duarte, the defeated candidate, who had been contacted at the last moment and persuaded to join the revolt and to make propaganda broadcasts for the rebels. He was arrested, tortured, and shipped off to exile in Venezuela. Except for a brief return in 1974, he was destined to remain in exile until after the 1979 coup.

Electoral fraud persisted in the elections after 1972. In the mayoral and legislative elections of 1974, the PCN helped itself to 36 of the 52 Assembly seats, allowing the UNO 15, although the PDC continued to hang onto a few mayoralties, including that of San Salvador.[12] This so discouraged the UNO members that they were divided over participation in the 1976 elections for the same offices. At last, they decided to withdraw from the ballots, an action which greatly displeased President Molina. "If they tried that in a fascist regime," he declared, "they would be forced to participate in the elections." Subsequently, he refused them permission to withdraw, thus forcing them to participate in the elections.[13] With the UNO urging nonparticipation, and fraud being rampant, it is hardly surprising that the PCN took every seat in the legislature and every mayoralty, a process which it would repeat in the local elections of 1978, when only the PCN and the tiny PPS would participate.

Not only did Molina continue the high-handed electoral actions of the government, but he proved bungling and inept as president. Seeking to boost the faltering tourist industry, he decided to play host to the Miss Universe Pageant in July 1975. Upon this grotesque display, the government spent some $1.5 million, the result being massive popular protests. A huge rally of workers and university students on 30 July was fired on by the *Guardia Nacional*, leaving 12 dead and many wounded. Molina then blamed the incident on "a communist plot."[14] The next year, in August, the president took the country by surprise by launching a land-reform scheme, designed to quell peasant protests. His plan involved 57,000 hectares (about 140,000 acres), or 3.7 percent of the nation's arable land. The aim was to benefit about 20,000 peasant families with small plots. So great was the concentration of landholding that 60 percent of this land was owned by a mere 100 families. The plan, which was actually workable and moderate, drew a torrent of criticism from the private-enterprise lobby (*Asociación Nacional de Empresa Privada*—ANEP) and from FARO (*Frente Agraria Región Oriental*), a large landholder organization. Their protests did not stop at words, the landholders arming themselves and threatening to resist expropriation throughout the eastern part of the country.[15] ANEP represented a very strong element in the PCN and Molina soon realized that he would be undercutting his own power base if he were to go through with the reform. He therefore shelved the whole enterprise after a few token plots had been distributed. It was destined to be the last effort at reform under the PCN.

With elections becoming such an obvious travesty, it is somewhat surprising that the UNO parties agreed to participate in the 1977 contest for the presidency. Molina and the PCN had picked the defense minister, Gen. Carlos Humberto Romero, whose name was linked to the scandal in which the army chief of staff, Col. Manuel Alfonso Rodríguez, had been arrested and convicted in the United States of gunrunning. Romero, however, had the advantage of controlling the armed forces and also of being the head of ORDEN (*Organización Democrática Nacionalista*), a so-called civic organization founded in the sixties by Gen. José Alberto Medrano, the *Guardia* commander under Sánchez Hernández. ORDEN was in fact a paramilitary group of thugs and police informers, with a boasted membership of 80,000, that specialized in aiding the *Guardia* and other police organizations in putting down rural discontent.

Faced with an election which would probably be manifestly unfree, the UNO decided to pick a symbolic candidate, a hero of the Honduran war, Col.

Ernesto Claramount Rozeville. Claramount had no great political following but he was known to be upright and courageous. His candidacy frightened the PCN into extraordinary measures for this contest of 20 February 1977. A shortwave network was set up between PCN headquarters and the various polling places. In the polls themselves, the opposition was discouraged from scrutiny by armed ORDEN men. As the contest progressed, cryptic messages emanating from the PCN offices urged backers to "put more sugar in the urn than coffee," meaning, of course, to stuff the ballot boxes for General Romero. The outcome was a foregone conclusion, although it appears certain Claramount would have won in an honest contest. The *Manchester Guardian* (13 March 1977) called the election "a shoddy affair," even by the standards of the area.

Widespread protests followed the election; and on 28 February, Claramount and the UNO held a massive demonstration in the Plaza de Libertad, which the cathedral and the National Palace both face. Although the assembly was peaceful, the government brought in the *Policía Nacional*, troops, and members of ORDEN, who stormed the square. Claramount and several other leaders sought sanctuary in the cathedral, but more than 200 persons were killed, cut down on the street by machine-gun fire. The government minimized the incident, admitting only six deaths, but after the massacre was over, they had to use fire hoses to wash away the blood.[16] Claramount Rozeville was then arrested and sent into exile along with several major figures of the opposition union.

The election of 1977 simply reenforced the idea that no meaningful change could come about through constitutional means, but even as early as the spring of 1972, following the electoral farce of that year, a number of persons had turned from ballots to bullets. In 1970 a group of young communists, dissatisfied with the conservative stance taken by their party under its new secretary general, Shafik Jorge Handal, had broken away under the former secretary general, Salvador Cayetano Carpio, and formed the *Fuerzas Populares de Liberación* (FPL), to prepare for eventual armed struggle. The events of February and March 1972 gave them the signal to swing into action. These events also caused a small group within the PCES to form its own force for armed conflict, the People's Revolutionary Army (*Ejército Revolucionario del Pueblo*—ERP), under the leadership of the communist poet Roque Dalton García. Another guerrilla group which appeared in 1975 was the *Fuerzas Armadas de Resistencia Nacional*—FARN). The ERP was never easy in its relations with the Communist Party, and in May 1975, Roque Dalton was assassinated by his fellow members, who then broke with the PCES. The ideology of these movements has fluctuated, but the FARN has been considered Maoist while the FPL has styled itself Maoist-Guevarist. The ERP has also expressed its admiration for the Castro-Guevara school of revolutionary warfare, but more recently has styled itself Trotskyist.

While these have proved to be the major ongoing guerrilla movements, a number of others enjoyed at least an ephemeral existence, such as that of the

Workers' Revolutionary Organization and the thirtieth-of-July movement. The activities of all these guerrilla movements included bank robberies; bombings; seizures of radio stations, to broadcast propaganda; kidnappings for ransom; embassy takeovers, and assassination. The robberies and kidnappings often yielded large amounts of cash, with which the guerrillas bought arms and explosives. The first major assassination was that of the secretary of the presidency, Raymundo Pineda Rodrigo, in April 1974, by the Farabundo Martí Brigade of the FPL. Among others who were killed were Foreign Minister Mauricio Borgonovo Pohl, after being kidnapped in April 1977 by the FPL; tourism director Robert Poma, whose body was also found in May; ex-President Osmín Aguirre y Salinas, in July of that year; and, a month later, the government-imposed rector of the National University, Carlos Alfaro Castillo. Late 1978 and early 1979 saw the kidnapping or assassination of a number of foreigners.

Even more alarming to the government was the growth of the so-called Popular Forces. *Campesino* unions had been officially banned since 1932, although the government had formed its own peasant association, the *Unión Comunal Salvadoreña* (UCS), around 1970, to stave off peasant discontent and work toward a token redistribution of the land. Despite the official ban on real peasant organizations, two major ones had come into existence in the early seventies: the *Unión de Trabajadores del Campo* (UTC) and the Catholic church-sponsored *Federación Cristiana de Campesinos Salvadoreños* (FECCAS). Both of these groups worked with the landless and nearly landless peasantry to demand better wages and working conditions on the great estates and, ultimately, a redistribution of the land. In 1974 the *Frente de Acción Popular Unida* (FAPU) was formed, bringing together some small peasant associations; the *Federación Nacional Sindical de Trabajadores Salvadoreños* (FENASTRAS), the second largest Salvadorean labor organization; and some teachers' and students' groups, for collective popular action. This was the first of the popular movements, and its significance lay in the fact that it brought together persons from several walks of life, with a common interest in destroying the established order. The next year, FECCAS and UTC founded the powerful *Bloque Popular Revolucionario* (BPR), along similar lines, bringing into it labor unions and the country's foremost teacher organization, the *Asociación Nacional de Educadores Salvadoreños* (ANDES). These movements grew to the point where the *Bloque* alone had over 80,000 members. On the urban scene, they were able to challenge more conservative labor groups, such as the PCES-backed *Federación Unida de Sindicatos Salvadoreños* (FUSS).[17]

Although not ideological at first, the popular movements were radicalized by the unwillingness of the government to undertake meaningful change. The BPR denounced Molina's land-reform scheme of August 1976 as meaningless, while, interestingly enough, the PCES praised it as a step toward peaceful change. The BPR advocated boycotting the local elections of 1978, declaring that it had lost all faith in the electoral process; and in May 1979, Secretary General Facundo Guardado y Guardado labeled the *Bloque* "Marxist-Leninist," though he hastened to add that it had to adapt these principles to the local conditions.[18]

The response of the Molina and Romero governments to the challenge posed by the terrorist groups and the popular movements was heavy-handed repression. For this purpose, they had available a regular army of some 8,000 men, plus about 5,000 men in various military-police organizations, including the dreaded *Guardia Nacional* (an elite rural police force), the *Policía Nacional* (the *Guardia's* urban counterpart), the *Policía de Aduana* (customs police), and the *Policía de Hacienda* (treasury police), all heavily armed. In addition to these regular units, there existed ORDEN. Further, taking their cue from the highly successful activities of the extreme right in Guatemala, a group of conservative Salvadoreans had formed a right-wing terrorist organization known as the White Warrior Union (*Unión Guerrera Blanca*—UGB), to assassinate those believed associated with the left-wing guerrilla groups or the popular movements. Like its Guatemalan counterparts, the UGB was rumored to work closely with the security forces, especially with the *Policía Nacional*, and with Col. René Chacón, the chief of army intelligence under Molina.

As the Marxist guerrillas were extremely elusive, it was the peasantry associated with the BPR and FAPU who were most frequently targeted for repression. Sometimes whole villages would be surrounded and seized, with many of their inhabitants being killed or brutalized. This happened most notably at Cayetana in November 1974, at Aguilares in May 1977, and at San Pedro Perulapán in March 1978. Many individuals were also seized by the security forces, and disappeared. By 1979, there was an impressive list of *desaparecidos*, comprising people from every social class from peasants to such professionals as lawyer Lil Milagro Ramírez and medical doctor Hugo Torres.[19] Most of them were never found.

The changing nature of the Catholic church since the 1969 conference of Latin American bishops at Medellín was more evident in El Salvador than in Guatemala. By the mid-seventies, a new spirit of social activism was abroad and many priests and nuns were working with the popular movements. They now became obvious targets for the UGB and the government. Fr. Rutilio Grande, a Jesuit working with FECCAS in the Aguilares region, was shot down by UGB agents on 12 March 1977. On 11 May, four days after the discovery of the body of kidnapped Foreign Minister Borgonovo Pohl, the UGB assassinated a parish priest, Fr. Alfonso Navarro, on the outskirts of the capital. In all, seven priests were killed by the UGB or the security forces between 1977 and 1979.

The killings of Fathers Grande and Navarro brought down upon the government the wrath of a new and formidable opponent, Msgr. Oscar Arnulfo Romero y Galdámez, who had been consecrated archbishop of San Salvador, replacing the aged Msgr. Luis Chávez y González, in the spring of 1977. Archbishop Romero had been known as a cautious, conservative cleric, and seemed destined to continue the tradition of the church being the handmaiden of the state, but he had absorbed the ideas of Medellín and he became radicalized by the execution of his two priests. From that time on, he used his considerable authority, and his eloquent sermons from the cathedral every Sunday—which were relayed all over the country by the church-owned radio station, YSAX—to denounce the right-wing terrorism and to back, though not uncritically, the popular movements. His eloquent pleas for social justice and human rights were much more significant than left-wing guerrilla activity in bringing down the fall of the PCN regime. In his policy, he enjoyed the support of most of the missionary clergy, and perhaps two-thirds of the native clergy, but the hierarchy was bitterly divided; Bishop Arnoldo Aparicio, heading the conservative wing, opposed the views of the archbishop, with the backing of the papal nuncio, Msgr. Emanuele Gerada.

The UGB, realizing the hostility of the missionaries, directed its attention to the powerful Jesuit order, which had some 40 active members in the country and which ran the *Universidad Centroamericana* (UCA), José Simeón Cañas, since the government's 1972 seizure of the National University, the only free university in the country. Following the deaths of Grande and Navarro, the Jesuits were given until 20 July 1977 to get out or be killed, according to a UGB manifesto. As many of the Jesuits were North Americans, this angered the embassy and occasioned diplomatic pressure by Ambassador Frank Devine upon the new president, Carlos Humberto Romero (not a relative of the archbishop's). President Romero, not wishing to annoy the United States at the beginning of his administration, forced the UGB to behave, and the date passed without incident.

General Romero appeared at first to adopt a more conciliatory posture than his predecessor. Not only was the UGB restrained, but the state of siege, imposed on 28 February 1977, was lifted in July of that year. However, on 24 November 1977, a new law was put into effect, the so-called *Ley de Orden* (the full title of which was: The Law for the Defense and Guarantee of Public Order), which gave the government sweeping powers to prevent dissent. It provided penalties for "those who in any form conspire or attempt to commit an offense against the constitutional regime and the peace of the State."[20] Much of the normal judicial protection was also done away with in the law, giving the government what was in effect a permanent state of siege. It was finally repealed in March 1979, after strong protests from human rights groups and the U.S. embassy. Under Romero, disappearances continued much as they had under Molina, but the government could at least boast that no more priests had been killed until the death of Fr. Ernesto Barrera on 28 November 1978. His execution was followed by four more through August 1979. In fact, the level of government violence began a continual rise under Romero.

A new wrinkle was put into the guerrilla activities of the left when Swedish businessman Kjell Bjork was kidnapped, on 14 August 1978, by the

FARN, which released him after a considerable ransom. This success spurred imitations and the FPL kidnapped a Japanese businessman, Fujio Matsumoto, but killed him when he tried to escape. Two British bankers, Ian Massie and Michael Chatterton, were seized in November and not released until July 1979. The pace of assassinations was also maintained, with the FPL killing the mayor of the second largest city, Santa Ana, and the Israeli honorary consul in the very month the *Ley de Orden* was repealed.

In an effort to improve his deteriorating relations with Monsignor Romero, President Romero had agreed to enter into high-level discussions, appointing Vice President Julio Ernesto Astacio and two other government members to confer with Msgr. Ricardo Urioste and other members appointed by the archbishop; but by the spring of 1978, the talks had broken down and the "war of the two Romeros," as it is known in Salvadorean history, went on.

An even more significant confrontation was building with the popular movements. FAPU, beginning a new tactic, seized the Red Cross headquarters at the end of December 1978, as well as the Mexican embassy, holding a total of 120 hostages and demanding the release of political prisoners and *desaparecidos*. This was tolerated until 16 January, when the FAPU militants allowed themselves to be removed by the *Guardia* on the condition of their being released unharmed. In March 1979, there was a massive series of strikes, and the BPR launched a series of demonstrations on behalf of the strikers, often tangling with the security forces in the process. In April, the government conducted an anti-*Bloque* sweep in Cuscatlán, with soldiers killing a number of peasants and raping the women. In retaliation, the BPR occupied the Venezuelan, Costa Rican, Panamanian, and Swiss embassies, while FAPU again seized the Red Cross headquarters. They were soon forced to withdraw and on 2 April, Facundo Guardado, the secretary general of the BPR, was arrested along with several other leaders of the movement. *Bloque* documents captured at that time, according to Defense Minister Gen. Federico Castillo Yanes, indicated a plan to "create a climate of social agitation, to destabilize the country economically and finally to violently take power."[21]

Immediately after the seizure of Guardado, his supporters occupied the cathedral of San Salvador, although they had no quarrel with the archbishop, in order to dramatize the arrest. The *Policia Nacional* was content to surround the structure (a vast, unfinished pile of masonry in the heart of the capital) until the BPR militants swarmed out onto the steps of the cathedral on 8 May, in a noisy, taunting protest. The police then opened fire, killing 24 *Bloque* supporters. This massacre was filmed by foreign TV correspondents and appeared on news programs all over the world. The BPR then seized the Venezuelan, French, and Costa Rican embassies once more, evacuating them and the cathedral in early June. In the meantime, on 22 May, a group of women and children supporting the BPR attempted to march into the Venezuelan embassy, bringing food for the militants holding the building. The police fired on the marchers and killed 14.

This second San Salvador massacre within a month caused a great increase in discontent. The *Bloque* had become increasingly militant and Marxist and had formed ties with the terrorist FPL, in imitation of FAPU, which had for some time been in league with the FARN. Further, a new organization had been formed that was much more in favor of direct action than either of the older groups. This was the *Ligas Populares, 28 de Febrero* (named for the date of the 1977 massacre), which began to use the ERP as its terrorist arm. In retaliation for the Venezuelan embassy massacre, the FPL murdered Minister of Education Carlos Antonio Herrera on 23 May and then Swiss diplomat Hugo Wey on the thirtieth. The very day of the cathedral massacre, the government had reimposed the state of siege, which lasted until 24 July, but the killings went on, chiefly by the UGB, ORDEN, and the security forces. In May, there were 188 political murders, and in June, 137— more than in the entire year 1978.[22] The numbers continued to grow and, in all, perhaps 600 persons lost their lives in political violence in that year. In July, ANDES, a part of the BPR, called a general strike of teachers for one week and seized the ministry of education.

President Romero felt control slipping from his grasp. On 17 May, he had made what he considered a gesture of conciliation to all political parties, the peasant organizations, the unions, and the church, offering to enter into a "national dialogue"; but this offer fell upon deaf ears. He further announced in July that all political exiles could return, but few took advantage of this suspect offer. One who did was Antonio Morales Erlich, the PDC secretary general, and Duarte's right-hand man, who used his return to demand an end to the death squads, and that a new national election be held before any dialogue.

This idea of a new national election, years ahead of the scheduled date, had emanated from the U.S. embassy, where signs of the government's collapse were viewed with alarm. But President Romero stubbornly refused this pressure and preferred to go bumbling on toward disaster. On 6 September, his own brother, José Javier Romero, was shot down at his house in Apopa, by left-wing terrorists, signaling a new round of killings by both sides.

Clearly something had to be done, and many of the younger army officers began to regard a coup by progressive moderates as the only way to avoid a civil war. They were working against the background of events in Nicaragua, where the forces of Somoza had just surrendered and the Marxist Sandinista movement was now in control. They approached the U.S. embassy and evidently received an encouraging response from Ambassador Frank Devine. They also sought support from among the intellectuals at the Catholic University (UCA), from the provincial, Fr. César Jérez, and other members of the Jesuit order. In fact, the coup is often referred to in El Salvador as the "coup of the Jesuits." The officers, led by Capt. Francisco Mena Sandoval, launched their movement on 15 October 1979, easily seizing control of the major tactical positions around the capital. Most of the senior garrison commanders who did not participate in the "military movement," as it was called, at least agreed to remain neutral. Even the *Guardia* offered no real resistance and the coup was virtually bloodless. General Romero meekly surrendered and flew into exile the next day.

The coup was hailed even in some conservative circles and welcomed by the U.S. embassy as a move toward stability. Even Archbishop Romero gave it his cautious approval and adopted a wait-and-see attitude. The leftist forces, however, remained suspicious, and the troubles of El Salvador, far from being at an end, were only beginning.

NOTES

1. Julius Rivera, *Latin America: A Sociological Interpretation* (New York: Irvington-Halsted, 1978), pp. 198-200.

2. For a full account see: Thomas P. Anderson, *Matanza: El Salvador's Communist Revolt of 1932* (Lincoln: University of Nebraska Press, 1971).

3. Stephen Webre, *José Napoleón Duarte and the Christian Democratic Party in Salvadoran Politics: 1960-1972* (Baton Rouge: Louisiana State University Press, 1979), p. 82.

4. For the problems associated with the war, see Thomas P. Anderson, *The War of the Dispossessed: Honduras and El Salvador, 1969* (Lincoln: University of Nebraska Press, 1980) and William H. Durham, *Scarcity and Survival in Central America: Ecological Origins of the Soccer War* (Stanford, Calif.: Stanford University Press, 1979).

5. Durham, *Scarcity and Survival*, p. 167.

6. David Browing, *El Salvador: Landscape and Society* (London: Oxford University Press, 1971), p. 262.

7. *Latin America*, 9 August 1974.

8. Nicolás Mariscal, "Regímenes Politicos en El Salvador," *Estudios Centroamericanos* 34 (March 1979):145.

9. Webre, *José Napoleón Duarte*, p. 136.

10. Eddy Jiménez, *La Guerra no Fue de Fútbol* (Havana: Casa de las Americas, 1974), p. 157.

11. Ibid.; Webre, *José Napoleón Duarte*, pp. 176-78.

12. Webre, *José Napoleón Duarte*, p. 187.

13. Thomas P. Anderson, "El Salvador," *Yearbook on International Communist Affairs: 1977* (Stanford, Calif.: Hoover Institution Press, 1978), p. 449.

14. *Latin America*, 22 August 1975.

15. Broadcast of YSKL (San Salvador), as reported by Foreign Broadcast Information Service, 24 August 1976.

16. *Latin America*, 4 and 11 March 1977.

17. In the mid-1970s, FENASTRAS had about 13,000 workers, to 8,500 for FUSS. The Federated Union of Construction and Transportation (FESICONTRANS) was the largest Salvadorean union, with 20,000.

18. Interview in *Jornal do Brasil*, 21 May 1979, as reported by FBIS, 25 May 1979.

19. Robert F. Drinan, John J. McAward, and Thomas P. Anderson, *Human Rights in El Salvador—1978: Report of Findings of an Investigatory Mission* (Boston: Unitarian Universalist Service Committee, 1978), pp. 43-50.

20. Ibid., full text, pp. 54-61.

21. *Central America Reports*, 21 May 1979.

22. *Latin America Political Report*, 3 August 1979.

6

El Salvador:
The Junta de Chompipes
and After

The coup of October 1979, blessed as it was by the church, the Catholic University, the army and, presumably, the U.S. embassy, had been a long time brewing in military circles. The first senior officer to be informed of the plot had been Col. Jaime Abdul Gutiérrez, head of the *escuela militar*, who had agreed to support it. Much later, the able Col. Adolfo Arnoldo Majano Ramos, commander of the military arsenal, who had studied for the military at Texas A&M and at Fort Benning, Georgia, was also brought in.

As soon as ex-President Romero had been hustled out of the country, a new government was formed, but neither Mena Sandoval nor any of the other young Turks among the military would take part in it. They preferred to maintain their purity of concept, and not become tainted with the sordid, day-to-day business of government that would follow the *"insurrección militar,"* as they were fond of calling the coup. However, the officers of the army and security forces did create a *Consejo Militar Superior*, theoretically under the minister of defense, to act as a watchdog over the new government. This government was to be led by a five-member junta, including both Gutiérrez and Majano along with three civilians. One choice for this body was Mario Andino, a San Salvador businessman who worked for Phelps Dodge and who had strong connections in ANEP, but the other two were mildly to the left of center: Román Mayorga Quirós, the slim, 30-ish rector of the UCA, and the leader of the MNR, Guillermo Ungo. These last two were highly respected in the country and thought capable of conciliating the so-called Popular Forces, that is, BPR, FAPU, and LP-28.

The cabinet reflected the same mixture of liberal and conservative elements as did the junta, with such men as Luis Nelson Segovia, as minister of justice, and Manuel E. Hinds, the economics minister, representing ANEP, while the UCA and the PDC were represented by the scholarly Héctor Dada Hirezi, as foreign minister, and Salvador Samayoa, as minister of education. Another PDC member was Rubén Zamora Rivas, as minister of the presidency. There was even one communist, Gabriel Gallegos Valdés, the new minister of labor, officially representing the UDN. The most fateful choice was that of a military conservative, Col. José Guillermo García, as minister of defense. This choice was made with the intention of conciliating those officers who only reluctantly accepted the coup and who were afraid that it would eventually lead to a government by the Popular Forces.

The country over which the new government was to preside was in sad financial shape. The gross domestic product fell 3.5 percent in 1979. During the course of the year, 20 factories closed, laying off 12,000 workers, and a massive flight of capital took place.[1] The country was also suffering from a severe balance-of-payments problem, especially within the Central American Common Market. Economics Minister Hinds and Finance Minister Ernesto Arbizú soon found that these problems were practically insoluble.

Worse still, the country was deeply divided politically. The army was resentful and suspicious of the Popular Forces, and these forces were equally mistrustful of the intentions of the military. As a gesture of conciliation, the new government appointed a commission, headed by Attorney General Roberto Suárez, to hunt for *desaparecidos* and other political prisoners.

Few were found alive; but mass graves were uncovered, with many bodies bearing visible marks of torture.[2] Indignation over such discoveries led to instances of private vengeance, such as the shooting of Col. José Antonio Castillo, the army's chief of investigations and an alleged torturer under Romero, on 28 October.[3]

Many in the Popular Forces refused even to believe that the government was sincere in its efforts to hunt for Romero's victims or to punish those guilty of the repression; and to spur the government to greater efforts in this regard, the *Ligas* and FAPU occupied a number of ministries on 24 October, seizing two ministers of state, one of them, ironically, Gabriel Gallegos of the UDN. Two days later saw the triumphal return of José Napoleón Duarte from Caracas. No less than 30,000 supporters of the long-exiled PDC leader went to Ilopango Airport, but they were met by an equal number of demonstrators from the Popular Forces. In the ensuing clash, Duarte's car was burned and there were a number of injuries.[4] This event caught the government, and most foreign observers, by surprise. It had always been assumed that the PDC in general, and Duarte in particular, spoke for most Salvadoreans in their struggle against the military dictatorship, but the PDC had waited too long in the wings; its leaders had been in other countries, or engaged in academic debates at the Catholic University. While they had complacently assumed that the people would eventually turn to them for leadership, many of the people, through the *Bloque*, FAPU, the *Ligas*, and other organizations, were choosing less aristocratic leaders.

On 29 October, while several ministries were still in the hands of protest-ers, the *Bloque* and other organizations resorted to street demonstrations on behalf of the *desaparecidos*. The *Policía Nacional* and the *Guardia* responded with gunfire, leaving 25 dead, a massacre worthy of the Romero era. By the end of October, it was quite plain that the major left-wing groups were not going to accept the rule of the new junta. Before long, the line of the Popular Forces became clear, the BPR declaring that the 15 October coup had been used by "Yankee imperialism to deviate our revolution from its true course," and FAPU accusing the United States of "trying to restrain the advances of our people."[5]

While the left refused to accept the junta, the army and security forces seemed determined to ignore it, returning very soon to their old policies of making people disappear and attacking villages suspected of harboring radicals. This was why such conciliatory gestures of the junta as the raising of minimum agricultural wages by 14 to 38.5 percent in November had little effect upon the attitude of the peasantry, for the peasants saw every gesture of reform coupled with acts of repression.

The aggressive stance of the Popular Forces seemed calculated to spur the security forces on to ever-greater excesses. In mid-December, ANEP and other conservative bodies organized a massive protest march of middle-class women in the capital; it was called the Pro-Peace and Work Crusade, and meant to call up images of the "march of the empty pots and pans" in Chile. As the marchers reached a park a few blocks from the center of San Salvador, they were set upon by leftists from the BPR who tossed fire bombs into the crowd, killing several participants and disbursing the marchers.[6] The BPR, the LP-28, and FAPU also offered many provocations in the backcountry, seizing estates and refusing to move off them. This, combined with military indignation over the assault on the marchers, led to the El Congo massacre on 18 December. Here, as in similar incidents during the Romero regime, the army surrounded the village and began the slaughter of peasants, whom it claimed were members of the *Ligas*. Leaders of the Popular Forces told the present writer that they believed 125 persons were killed, though this figure may be exaggerated. A similar event took place at Opico about the same time.

Since much of the continuing violence was due to gross overreaction on the part of the government forces, it is hardly surprising that some members of the junta sought to restrain them. Román Mayorga and Memo Ungo were insistent that the army had to be brought under civilian control, but they received little support from Mario Andino or the moderate Colonel Majano, and none at all from Colonel Gutiérrez, who joined with Defense Minister García in seeing the entire question in terms of a "communist menace." Even if the junta had been less divided, it could have done little, for the *Consejo Militar Superior*, elected by the army and security forces themselves, had taken it upon itself to give all the orders to the troops, and listened to no one in the government but García. Shafik Handal, the PCES leader, commented, "What we have are two governments."[7] This indeed was true.

However, in the long run, a country can have but one government, and this began to be talked of by the members of the cabinet by mid-December. Somehow they would have to bring the army under civilian control. Several cabinet members decided that the best course was to threaten resignation. These included Dada, Rubén and Mario Zamora, Samayoa, and Gallegos, who brought their project to Mayorga and Ungo. The two junta leftists, however, realized that such a resignation would be considered simply a confession of the government's impotence in dealing with its armed forces. They persuaded the cabinet members to defer their resignations until after the junta had a chance to consult with the military leaders. The consultation took place on 27 December 1979 and included the junta, members of the cabinet, including García and the members of the *Consejo*, along with the chiefs of the eight major *cuarteles*, or garrisons, and of the various security forces. The military men were haughtily arrogant. "We have been running this country for fifty years, and we are quite prepared to keep on running it," Col. Eugenio Vides Casanova, the chief of the *Guardia Nacional*, is reported to have declared. In the end, nothing was accomplished other than a clarification of the positions of the various junta members and the soldiers.

If the five junta members had stood together and if they had had the nerve to sack García, they might have succeeded in overawing the soldiers, but Gutiérrez was strongly rightist and a firm supporter of García, while Majano's military background also inclined him in that direction. The weakness and indecision of the junta, by this time, were well known, and from November on, the populace had been referring to it jokingly as the "*junta de chompipes*," that is, the junta of turkeys, for the members would be cooked and served up by Christmas time.

They survived Christmas, only to fall at New Year's. The left-wing members of the junta and the cabinet, following the meeting of the twenty-seventh, decided to force the issue by making a number of explicit demands upon the army: that the army recognize that its orders were to come from the junta, through the minister of defense; that Andino (who had constantly backed the soldiers) be forced out of the government; that all promotions, transfers, and removals of officers be made by the junta; that no military meetings be called without permission of the junta; and that the army accept the fact that the constitution was no longer in force. This last point was included because the military had been claiming various privileges under the old constitution, and because ANEP and other rightist groups were claiming that no sweeping reforms could be made because the constitution forbade them. These demands were made on the twenty-ninth and were read publicly on the radio by Héctor Dada. Everyone now knew that a moment of truth had been reached and Archbishop Romero spoke, in his sermon of the thirtieth, of the gravity of the "internal crisis."

The day after the holiday, Msgr. Romero y Galdámez brought the military and civilian leaders together at his less-than-palatial residence, the sprawling seminary of San José de la Montaña. A sweltering all-day session followed, while several observers waited outside to hear the outcome. The meeting broke up with grim faces all around, and, noticing that after everyone else had gone, Román Mayorga's car was still there, observers inquired about him, to be told by Msgr. Ricardo Urioste, the vicar general, that he had collapsed physically and was asleep inside.

It was not only Mayorga that collapsed. The entire government now fell, Ungo and Mayorga resigning from the junta, and all of the cabinet, except García, following suit. Ungo and Mayorga then flew into exile, the former vowing to form an exile group similar to *Los Doce* in Nicaragua (before the fall of Somoza), and the latter simply vowing never to return to his homeland. It was a sorry ending for a government that had started in October with such promise.

There were three days of interregnum, with crowds burning buses in the streets of the capital and a number of violent clashes between the military and the Popular Forces; and then a new government was announced that was startlingly like the old, for, behind the backs of Mayorga and Ungo, the military had been secretly negotiating with the leaders of the PDC since 27 December. The PDC leaders, José Napoleón Duarte, Secretary General Antonio Morales Erlich, and Héctor Dada, had agreed to form a new government in which the issue of civilian control over the army would be politely ignored. Thus, the Christian Democratic members of the cabinet had resigned with the blithe assurance that they would be back at their posts, or at different ones, within a few days. To many Salvadoreans who had admired Duarte and his party, this seemed a sellout of their principles, and a dirty trick to play upon such old friends as Ungo and Mayorga. Others, however, saw it as a move to bring peace and stability, which could only come from giving the security forces a relatively free hand. The attorney general, Roberto Suárez, declared to this writer that he thought the demands made by the first junta had been "a conspiracy against the army." And he pointed out that it was impossible to try political criminals without the assurance that the military could protect judges and witnesses.

The second junta had the same two military members as the first, but Andino was returned to Phelps Dodge, having had his moment of glory. In his slot now was José Ramón Avalos Navarrette, a San Salvador physician belonging to no particular party, while the other two members were Morales Erlich and Héctor Dada, whose place as foreign minister was taken by corporation lawyer Fidel Chávez Mena, another leader of the PDC. Other Christian Democrats to enter the cabinet included Ovidio Hernández Delgado, as interior minister, and the leader of the younger, left-leaning PDC members, Oscar Menjívar, as minister of economics. The name most conspicuously absent from the ranks of the government was that of José Napoleón Duarte, who ostentatiously flew off to Guatemala soon after the first junta fell. It was said that he was deliberately waiting in the wings until presidential elections could be held, so that he could run without the taint of having been personally involved in the second junta.

In Guatemala, Duarte was extremely free with interviews, declaring to the local press that the first junta fell because it had mistakenly tried to undertake reforms before restoring political democracy and holding elections. But now, he declared, "the danger of civil war was past." A few days later, he told Alan Riding, of the *New York Times*, that the army had turned to the PDC "because we are the only instrument left through which it can reach the people"; and that the public trusted the Christian Democrats because "twenty years of party work have left a memory of faith in us, and," he modestly added, "I am the symbol of that memory."[8]

While the PDC was reorganizing the government, the Popular Forces were also busy reorganizing. Significant in this reorganization was the dramatic change in the situation of the communist PCES and its front group, the UDN. The PCES had long been a moribund and conservative body of about 200. Its leaders, such as Secretary General Shafik Jorge Handal, seemed to spend a great deal of time junketing about Eastern Europe at the expense of the Soviet Union; indeed, cynics remarked that the only reason for membership in the PCES was to take the vodka-and-caviar trips abroad. Although the party was illegal, it had been tolerated by the PCN governments simply because it was ineffective, and it was constantly derided by the left. A FARN manifesto of December 1978 had declared of it that "each day increases its decadence and diminishes its influence in the popular movement. . . . " Similarly, the BPR called it "revisionist" and accused it of betraying the Salvadorean people. The PCES defended itself against such barbs by labeling the more radical movements "adventurist" and declaring their militant tactics were "bound to fail."[9]

But as the Popular Forces grew in power during 1979, the communists were considering an abrupt about-face. This occurred at the Seventh Party Congress, which met in May 1979. Handal himself now proclaimed that armed revolt was both necessary and possible and declared it a heresy to believe otherwise. This revolutionary attitude did not stop the PCES from accepting posts on the first junta, having been expelled by the Christian Democrats in January, they now firmly joined the Popular Forces. In early January 1980, the representatives of the UDN, including its secretary general, Mario Aguinada Carranza, met with the leaders of LP-28, José Carlos Guillermo Argueta Romero and José Guillermo Canenguez Pérez. Also present were Juan Angel Chacón Vásquez, who had replaced Facundo Guardado, in September, as secretary general of the BPR, and Alberto Ramos, the secretary general of FAPU. The meeting took place at the National University, which, since October, had once again become a center of radical activity. The leaders of the four movements declared themselves to be united in a new umbrella organization, the *Coordinadora Revolucionaria de las Masas* (CRM). A short while later, the CRM published its "Duties and Objectives of the Revolution," which were: to overthrow the reactionary military dictatorship and Yankee imperialism; to end the dominance of the landed oligarchy and nationalize land and industry; to assure the democratic rights of the people; to raise cultural standards and stimulate popular organizations and create a new, revolutionary armed forces.

The respective guerrilla movements associated with the three mass organizations, BPR's FPL, FAPU's FARN, and LP-28's ERP, also agreed to coordinate their efforts; and for the sake of symmetry, the PCES now declared itself to be the revolutionary arm of the UDN, seizing several radio stations, by armed force, to broadcast this startling message. The coordination of the guerrilla movements proved easier to proclaim than to achieve. The BPR favored a "prolonged popular war" based on the Nicaraguan model; the Trotskyite ERP called for an immediate insurrection; and FARN, whose chief was Salvador Cayetano Carpio, the ex-secretary general of the PCES, favored a wait-and-see policy. For a while, the ERP even broke with the others and went its own way.

The *Coordinadora* targeted 22 January as an opportunity to flex its muscles. This day was the anniversary of Agustín Farabundo Martí's abortive revolt in 1932, and a great parade of the Popular Forces was held. Estimates of the number of marchers vary from 80,000 to 200,000, but at eight abreast, it took them more than three hours to file by. As the procession reached the Plaza de la Libertad, it was suddenly fired upon from the windows of the Palacio Nacional. About 20 persons were killed either by gunfire or in the ensuing panic, and the incident set the seal on the bad relations between the second junta and the CRM. As the polarization of Salvadorean society grew, there were increasing numbers of defections to the left, including that of Salvador Samayoa, the former education minister, who now declared himself an FLP guerrilla, and of Morales Erlich's own son, José Antonio Morales Carbonelli, who joined the same organization.

The right was also stirring. ORDEN had been officially disbanded as one of the first acts of the junta in October 1979, but someone forgot to tell its members, who continued to work closely with the security forces. Further, Major Roberto D'Aubuisson, who had been deputy chief of military intelligence in the time of Romero, now emerged as a major spokesman of the extreme right, and as a link between the officers who had been driven into exile, such as his old boss, Col. Roberto Santivañas, and the current military leaders. Behind D'Aubuisson, many professed to see the machinations of the old intriguer, Gen. Chele Medrano, the ex-*Guardia* chief and founder of ORDEN, who was living in retirement in San Salvador. In early February, Medrano and D'Aubuisson proclaimed an organization called the *Frente Democrático Nacionalista* (FDN), which was to be ORDEN under a new name. About the same time as they proclaimed FDN's existence, D'Aubuisson declared on TV that Mario Zamora Rivas, the attorney general of welfare, was, like Samayoa, working for the FPL, to which Zamora responded with a libel suit. On 22 February, while the PDC leader was conducting a meeting at his house, with such persons as Napoleón Duarte and Héctor Dada, they were raided by masked right-wing vigilantes of the UGB. Mario Zamora was singled out, taken into the bathroom, and shot dead. As a result of this incident, both Rubén Zamora Rivas, brother of the murdered man and a member of the PDC central committee, and Héctor Dada resigned from the party and the government, which they criticized for not being able even to protect its own members and for its failure to arrest D'Aubuisson for Zamora's murder. The government, Dada proclaimed, was "without popular support."[10]

The loss of Héctor Dada Hirezi was a stunning blow, for he was the PDC's leading intellectual and a man greatly respected among nonparty members. Further, it compelled Duarte to change his game plan and take Dada's place on the junta, a move which clearly showed the desperation of the PDC.

Late January and February saw vigorous action from the left as well as the right. A series of attacks was staged on military and police installations, and the PDC headquarters was seized by LP-28 on 30 January, along with 17 hostages, including the daughter of Morales Erlich. Several ministries, the Catholic University, the Spanish and Panamanian embassies, and the water-works were also seized by terrorists, so that by 17 February, there were no less than 455 persons being held hostage. Some of these hostage situations were ended by negotiation, but the PDC headquarters in central San Salvador was stormed by the police and four members of the LP-28 were killed. Another ten CRM members were killed in a "victory march" following government concessions which had led to the release of the hostages at the education ministry. These were only the most conspicuous casualties as violence by the army and security forces, on one hand, and guerrillas, on the other, continued in the countryside.

In the midst of these events, the U.S. ambassador was replaced. Frank Devine, who had taken so long to give up on reforming the Romero government, gave way to Robert White, the former ambassador to Paraguay and a noted human rights advocate. White had come down in late December to take a look at the situation, but before he could return there, Devine, who already had other commitments, was forced to leave. This necessitated William Bowdler's sending James Cheek, formerly with the Nicaraguan embassy and now deputy assistant secretary of state for Central American affairs, to take temporary charge in mid-February. Cheek, I have been told, heard that there was a plot by D'Aubuisson and certain active officers to overthrow the junta on 24 February, and he took vigorous action to forestall this possibility, arguing, with Colonel García and other officers, that this would lead to civil war. The coup was barely forestalled, making an irony of the comment

Bowdler had made, after visiting the country in January: "There is no crisis in El Salvador, only a process of transition. . . . "[11] When White arrived on the scene on 15 March, he evacuated all embassy dependents, lest this process of transition get out of hand. He, like Devine and Cheek before him, believed that the junta was the best hope for El Salvador, though he declared that some elements in the army were "the enemy within." He appeared to believe that the PDC could rally moderate elements and avoid civil war. At the same time, he saw no way of entering into a dialogue with the Popular Forces, who were determinedly anti-Yankee, and whom he considered "politically naive" and cut off from outside realities.

One reason that the embassy was successful in staving off the February coup was that it could hold over the heads of the soldiers the $4.7 million in military aid, including trucks, radios, tear gas, which was promised as part of a $50-million U.S. aid package. This military aid was welcomed by the soldiers, engaged as they were in an endless and growing guerrilla war; but it was regarded with suspicion by the Christian Democrats on the junta, as a possible kiss of death for the hopes of making a democratic El Salvador. Archbishop Romero was adamantly opposed, and had told William Bowdler so in no uncertain terms during their chilly meeting. Indeed, even the State Department was divided on the issue, but the national security adviser in Washington was apparently strongly behind it.[12]

Two events in March 1980 further complicated the situation in the country. First, there had long been a clamor for land reform, and during the first junta, Enrique Alvarez Córdoba, as agriculture minister, had made efforts in that direction, only to become bogged down in red tape. The second junta had taken up the question and wrestled with it through January and February; then, in the wake of the barely aborted coup, it decided to act with dramatic suddenness, announcing the seizure of 25 percent of all the arable land. This consisted of 376 plantations belonging to 244 owners and encompassing 224,083 hectares, or almost half a million acres. That so few had owned so much was itself dramatic proof of the need for land reform. Eventually, declared the junta, no one would be allowed to own more than 100 hectares (about 250 acres). This was, therefore, only the first stage of the projected reform. The seized land was to be paid for under a tax valuation, in government bonds maturing over 25 years, with special incentives given for use of these bonds as collateral in obtaining government-backed loans for industrial development. The estates, declared the decree of 6 March, were to be maintained as agricultural units and not to be returned to subsistence agriculture. Peasant families would receive individual lots but would be encouraged to farm in cooperation with the other families who received shares, and to use the tractors and other farm machinery that were seized along with the estates. Simultaneously, the government nationalized all Salvadorean-owned banks, sparing the foreign banks in the country. This would facilitate the granting of industrialization loans with the agricultural bonds as collateral. According to the banking decree, the state would keep 51 percent of the stock in each bank, but the rest would be sold within a year, half to the banks' employees and half to the general public, with the proviso that no one could own more than 2 percent of such stock.[13]

After having been accused of inaction, the government had now moved so rapidly as to create immense confusion. As no other body capable of taking on the task existed, the job of actually occupying the estates fell to the army and security forces. It was they who moved in and impounded everything in sight, including even television sets. They were also to be the ones to distribute the land, and they used this power in two ways. First, they sometimes favored their old friends in ORDEN by giving them plots whether they were entitled to them or not. Secondly, ORDEN men were posted at the stations where peasants were to register for lots, and were used to finger members of the Popular Forces or the guerrilla movements, who were then killed or whisked off by the military. Ten days after the reform went into effect, peasant discontent led to the CRM's calling of a massive general strike, which was only partially successful, and to large-scale land seizures by armed peasants of the BPR. These seizures resulted in clashes in which some 60 persons died. However, after the initial problems, the *Instituto Salvadoreño de Transformación Agraria* (ISTA), under peasant leader Rodolfo Viera, took hold and tried to do a good job of land reform. In this he was aided by the *asesor* (really the general manager) of ISTA, Leonel Gómez Vides, who was the real organizer of the land-reform movement. Viera and Gómez were constantly at odds with the government, even fomenting a strike of their own technicians in June 1980, in order to end corruption in the program. Whenever possible, they sought to neutralize the efforts of ORDEN.

By spring of 1980, the general level of violence had become appalling. Amnesty International estimated that 2,000 persons were killed between January and April, a figure that dwarfed even the political violence in Guatemala.[14] But the assassination that caught the eye of the world was that of the government's most prominent critic, Msgr. Oscar Arnulfo Romero y Galdámez, archbishop of San Salvador. Throughout all the strife of the late seventies, the archbishop had stood out as the conscience of his country, fearlessly denouncing President Romero, urging the two juntas to reform, and castigating the army for its continued atrocities. He had been becoming more and more despairing of the PDC and its role in the government, and more and more inclined to see armed revolt as the only solution. In his sermon of 2 February, he had declared, "When all peaceful means have been exhausted, the Church considers insurrection moral and justified"—a hint that such an impasse had now been reached. On 17 February, he had written President Carter a moving letter opposing aid to the junta, especially military aid, stating that the government resorted to repression and violence and that this had "resulted" in a much greater toll of dead and wounded than in previous military regimes. On 23 March, seeing the violence that was attending the land reform, he addressed the soldiers of El Salvador directly in his broadcasted Sunday sermon, urging them to defy their officers and obey a "higher law" by not firing on unarmed civilians. This was virtual treason in the eyes of the military and the archbishop, of course, knew that his life was in danger. "They can kill me," he had once said, "but it should be very clear that they cannot kill the voice of justice."[15] On the evening of Monday, 24 March, he went, as was his regular custom, to say mass at Divine Providence Hospital, in the capital. There, at the very elevation of the mass, he was shot once in the chest, and slumped, dying over the altar. A nun who rushed to his side claimed that his last words forgave his assassin. No group ever took responsibility for this deed, though it was widely blamed upon D'Aubuisson or UGB. It was probably the work of a professional hit man. The *Guardia* immediately celebrated the death of the prelate by a savage attack on his hometown of Ciudad Barrios that left ten dead.[16]

The death of Archbishop Romero, who was replaced by his old friend Msgr. Arturo Rivera y Damas, signaled the beginning of a rapid escalation in the violence. The memorial service for the slain prelate was held at the unfinished cathedral in downtown San Salvador, on Sunday, 30 March, and attended by dignitaries from all over the world and an immense swarm of Salvadoreans, guarded by the Popular Forces. Suddenly a bomb was thrown from the Palacio Nacional and shooting began. The crowd stampeded and over 30 persons were killed, either by gunfire or by being crushed against the fence surrounding the Cathedral. The government claimed it was the work of the left, but most observers disagreed. Over 100 persons were killed in the second week of April alone in clashes between the guerrillas and the troops, and the numbers increased to over 200 a week in late May.[17] This meant that the civil war so long talked of was at hand. Yet the CRM kept postponing the date of its final drive to oust the junta from control. In the first week of May, the CRM announced that "the final offensive" was near, but nothing happened. In mid-June the rumor was that the all-out guerrilla drive of the FARN, FPL, and the PCES was to start between 16 and 20 June, but again nothing of the sort happened. One reason was that the military was keeping the guerrillas off balance through its own activities; another was the lack of training and arms; and perhaps the most important was the lack of coordination among the various guerrilla groups. The ERP was so disaffected from the rest at this point that it had withdrawn into seclusion.

While unable to launch an offensive, the Popular Forces were able to found a virtual government. This had first been tried in late December when Fabio Castillo was named head of a *Movimiento de Liberación Popular*, but the movement was stillborn and absorbed into the CRM, which in March spoke of forming "a democratic, revolutionary government." What then emerged was the *Frente Democrático Revolucionario* (FDR), comprising the CRM and the *Frente Democrático* (FD). The FD was composed of the MNR of Memo Ungo; dissident members of the PDC, such as Oscar Menjívar, who had resigned his ministry, Enrique Alvarez, and Héctor Dada; and represent-atives of private business, such as Luis Buitrago. The leadership of the FDR was to be a group of seven—one each from UDN, FAPU, BPR, and LP-28, plus three members of the FD. Enrique Alvarez was elected secretary general, and René Medellínas, foreign relations secretary. The FDR had no sooner organized than it sent Alvarez, along with Juan Angel Chacón of the BPR and Memo Ungo, on a mission to both Latin America and Europe, to drum up support for their cause and to denounce the junta as the puppet of the military. The response from European Social Democrats was surprisingly encouraging and no doubt stemmed in part from their own long rivalry with the Christian Democrats.[18] The party's Second International, meeting on 13 June in Oslo, and at the urging of the Swedish Socialist Party, promised aid to the FDR. At home, the FDR called for a new general strike on 24 and 25 June, which was about 80 percent effective.[19]

Still, the military situation of the left did not improve, and this was due to events which began in early May. On the second, the irrepressible Major D'Aubuisson, who had been going about, from *cuartel* to *cuartel*, giving lectures on the communist intentions of the junta and of the new U.S. ambas-sador, launched another abortive coup. This time he was arrested, whereupon his right-wing supporters surrounded the official residence of Ambassador Robert White and held him a virtual prisoner from 9 to 12 May; then they were finally dispersed by State Department security agents and marines firing tear gas. While D'Aubuisson's coup fizzled, a kind of minicoup took place within the ranks of the military itself. Someone had to be the official com-mander in chief of the military forces, and until this point, it had been Majano, who favored a policy of nonconfrontation with the Popular Forces, wherever possible. As the situation deteriorated, more and more officers became dis-satisfied with this approach. A team of U.S. Army guerrilla-warfare experts had visited the country in December and advocated a much more aggressive line. Plainly, argued many officers, if the government were not to fall to the likes of D'Aubuisson, public confidence in the army had to be maintained. Thus, a new election for commander in chief was decided upon, in early May, by the *Consejo Militar Superior*. In this ballot of all the army and security officers, Gutiérrez was chosen commander over Majano, a change which greatly pleased Defense Minister García. It should be noted, however, that within the army, more officers had voted for Majano than for his rival on the junta, but among the other forces, Gutiérrez won overwhelmingly.

While the army was undergoing a shakeup, the extreme right was also reorganizing. In June, D'Aubuisson, Medrano, and their associates put to-gether something they called the *Ejército Secreta Anticomunista* (ESA), long the name of a Guatemalan terrorist group. The ESA was to combine the UGB, ORDEN (FDN), *Mano Blanca*, long thought extinct, the *Escuadrón de la Muerte* (literally the Death Squad), the *Organización para la Liberación del Comunismo*, the *Brigada Anticomunista Salvadoreña*, and two transnational groups: the *Legión del Caribe* and the *Frente Anticomunista Centroamericana*. Plainly, the right, encouraged by the replacement of Majano, was gearing up for a long struggle.

Freed from Majano's restraining influence, the military now prepared to take the offensive. On 9 May, talks were held with Honduran and Guatemalan officers at Nueva Octopeque, to insure their cooperation; and then the first great sweep was launched in the mountainous northern department of Chalatenango, long a stronghold of the BPR and where, via the border with Honduras, arms and even Cuban advisors were rumored to have come. Everyone in the path of this sweep was considered a guerrilla, as had so often happened in Vietnam, and they were driven mercilessly toward the Sumpil River, a muddy stream marking the de facto Honduran border. There, at El Carrizal, on 14 May, a horde of peasants attempted to cross, only to be met by Honduran soldiers firing from across the river. The two armies then began a general slaughter, which claimed, according to figures put out by official church sources in both Honduras and El Salvador and based on the eyewitness accounts of priests, between 300 and 600 persons. The governments of both countries denied that any such incident had taken place, but the church stuck by its testimony.[20] Shortly after this incident, on 26 June, the military invaded the National University and killed perhaps 50 students in taking it over. There the government announced it had found some 300 bodies of guerrillas killed in earlier fighting, though there was some suspicion they might simply have been cadavers for the medical school. The army also claimed to have discovered tunnels going from the university to a neighboring shantytown controlled by the FPL. The military ransacked the school and burned books. On 29 June, bombs were set off by terrorists at the UCA.

Although the sweep into Chalatenango had certainly damaged the guerrilla movements in the area, they bounced back in late May, seizing three villages and declaring them "liberated territory," in a move reminiscent of the Sandinistas in the last stages of the Nicaraguan civil war; but the estimated 3,000 guerrillas could not hold them permanently and were forced to withdraw. In the wake of this, some 2,500 peasants fled into Honduras, this time without interference.[21] Early in June, the army and members of ORDEN made another sweep, east of San Salvador, with a force of about 3,000 men, again killing a large number of alleged guerrillas.

In this period, Major D'Aubuisson was freed by a military court and immediately went underground to continue stirring up trouble, while Salvador Samayoa, who had joined the FPL in January, was captured in San Salvador. This capture occasioned the partially successful general strike, which failed to immediately win Samayoa's freedom, although he was eventually released, and fled into exile.

Despite the various reverses suffered by the leftist forces, including the massacre of doctors, and wounded victims in a clandestine medical center at Santa Ana in July, Salvador Cayetano Carpio, of the FPL, could still proclaim: "This war that has already lasted ten years is reaching its final stages. We don't think the establishment of a popular, revolutionary government is very far away."[22] And there were, by midsummer, certain reasons for his optimism. First, the ERP rejoined the fold, accepting the direction of a new, unified guerrilla command under the title of *Dirección Revolucionaria Unificada Farabundo Martí*, which later in the year was proclaimed the *Frente Farabundo Martí de Liberación Nacional* (FMLN), in imitation of the Nicaraguan example.[23] Secondly, it appeared that Nicaragua was willing to at least look the other way while its citizens slipped across the border into El Salvador, by way of the Gulf of Fonseca. These persons, styled "deserters" from the Sandinista army, appeared to enjoy certain backing in their own country, which proclaimed in mid-May a week of solidarity with the people of El Salvador.[24] Even Costa Rica and Panama appeared to be getting into the act, as they had during the Nicaraguan civil war. In a bizarre incident, a plane belonging to the Panamanian air force crashed in El Salvador in June 1980 while bringing in supplies and arms for the leftist guerrillas. This aid, said the late Panamanian *Guardia* commander and strongman, Omar Torrijos, had been given without his knowledge. Apparently the supplies themselves had been picked up in Costa Rica, bringing into question that government's neutrality in the struggle.[25] The civil war in El Salvador thus appeared to be becoming internationalized in the same manner that the war in Nicaragua had been internationalized.

The root problem remained that of the military and its relation to the whole of Salvadorean society. As long as the soldiers indeed called the shots for the government, there could be no accommodation between the junta and the CRM. Only if the junta could bring the soldiers to heel, could it convince the Popular Forces to lay down their arms and accept positions in the government. While the army ruled, the CRM could continue to charge that the curious mixture of reform and repression practiced by the government was designed simply to destroy the left. But the military still had the guns. No matter how idealistic the land-reform program and other schemes of the government, they always ran into the fact that only the soldiers could make them effective through armed force, and this armed force would always favor ORDEN and similar groups that were anathema to the *Coordinadora*. This was the basic reason why the junta had lost the support of Héctor Dada, Rubén Zamora, and Salvador Samayoa. With the departure of such men from the government, the moderate middle had virtually ceased to exist. Even more than Guatemala, El Salvador was polarized into warring camps.

On the other hand, for all its proclamations of new solidarity groups, and the beginnings of aid from abroad, the left was unable to bring about its much-talked-of offensive to resolve the situation in the Nicaraguan fashion, by driving the army out of the country. The truth was that El Salvador was little suited to a guerrilla campaign, being small and isolated, while the Salvadorean military was far stronger than the corrupt and confused *Guardia Nacional* that had supported Somoza. The key to the situation, therefore, seemed to lay with U.S. Ambassador Robert White. Perhaps White might have tilted the scales in favor of the CRM, but he could hardly do so when the CRM, and later the FDR, refused to believe in the good intentions of the United States. Further, White's own position was soon undermined. As the presidential contest in the United States tilted toward the Republican candidate, it became apparent that White's policies would probably be out of step with the new administration. After the election victory, a hit list that circulated included White as an ambassador who would have to be replaced. From that time on, he was ineffective, and when he was relieved of duties on 2 February 1981, it was indeed anticlimactic.

The tempo of the civil war picked up in August 1980 and continued through the rest of the year and into January 1981, when a final offensive of the FMLN was announced for 10 January. This offensive was no more final than the one which had been launched on 15 August of the preceding year. It was to coincide with a general strike, which also fizzled. Yet several things that happened in this January 1981 offensive were indeed new. The garrison of Santa Ana, the nation's second city, defected under the leadership of Capt. Francisco Mena Sandoval, who had led the October coup. Mena burned the *cuartel*, and marched a good part of his men off to join the FMLN. Further, the capitals of the departments of Chalatenago and Marazán (San Francisco Gotera) were temporarily seized by the leftist forces. Traveling along the Honduras-El Salvador border from San Marcos to La Virtud in January, this writer was told, by sources close to the guerrilla command, that they now had a large supply of heavy weapons, which had not been true in August 1980.

The growing intensity of the war brought about a stream of refugees. Relief authorities estimated that 20,000 had crossed into Honduras by the end of 1980, and another 10,000 or more were said to be in Guatemala. These refugees, with whom I spoke in January 1981, were in pitiful shape. Food was sufficient, thanks to Catholic and Protestant relief groups in Honduras, but disease was rampant, and shelter, in that chilly, mountainous region, was nonexistent. They universally agreed that they were fleeing from the military forces of the Salvadorean government, which had burned their villages and commited the atrocities customary on such occasions. At first, it seemed baffling that the government would so deliberately alienate its own people, but soon it became clear that the idea was to destroy the infrastructure of support which maintained the guerrilla army. With the northern part of El Salvador depopulated, the guerrillas would have no source of food or hiding places. Yet the psychological costs of such a campaign of terror were enormous and very likely to create more guerrillas.

While the war escalated to the point where an estimated 10,000 persons had lost their lives in 1980, other events were making the situation increasingly difficult. Colonel Majano's situation was further eroded when, on 1 September, Colonel García, the defense minister, issued order number ten, transferring a number of key Majano supporters from positions of power to attaché posts abroad. This was done without the consent of the junta, and with only Colonel Gutiérrez's prior knowledge, clearly indicating who was boss. Majano Ramos at once began to make the circuit of the garrisons, appealing to the officers not to obey this new order of battle. He made particular efforts at El Zapote, the artillery *cuartel* which overlooks the presidential palace, and which favored his cause. It appeared as if a civil war within a civil war was imminent, but Duarte and Morales Erlich mediated the situation and on 4 September, a compromise was worked out. Order number ten would stand, but García promised not to do such a thing again without consulting the junta, a promise he could easily make now that the deed was done. Further, Majano gained slight concessions: Col. Julio Agustín Trujillo of El Zapote would step down from control of that key post, but he would not be forced to accept the attaché post in Caracas, while Maj. Francisco Samayoa would be named attaché to the United States rather than to far-off Chile.[26]

Amid the general slaughter, some individual deaths continued to be of importance. Ernesto Jovel, leader of the FARN, was killed accidentally in September 1980, at a time when his group was temporarily disaffected from the other guerrilla movements. In October, a leader of the Salvadorean Human Rights Commission, María Magdalena Henríquez, was killed, and the group promptly voted to disband, as it could no longer function effectively. The rector of the National University, Felix Ulloa, was machine-gunned on the twenty-eighth of the month and, his murder, like that of Mrs. Henríquez, was attributed to right-wing groups. On 3 November, a powerful bomb was blown up outside ISTA as a car carrying Colonel Majano passed by. He was not hurt, but great damage was done to the land-reform center and many employees were wounded.

A spectacular massacre took place on 6 November. The directors of the FDR were meeting clandestinely in the Jesuit secondary school located a few blocks from the U.S. embassy in central San Salvador. Two hundred uniformed men cordoned off the area and the FDR leaders were seized. The tortured bodies of President Enrique Alvarez Córdova, Juan Angel Chacón Vásquez, head of the BPR, Manuel Franco (UDN), Enrique Barrera (MNR), and Humberto Mendoza (FAPU) were recovered the next day. The deaths of so many prominent leaders stunned the left wing, but a new FDR directorate was soon announced, including Eduardo Calles (president), Leoncio Pichinte (LP-28), Juan José Martell, Carlos Gómez (of the new Popular Liberation Movement—MPL), Francisco Rebollo (BPR), José Napoleón Rodríguez Ruiz (FAPU), and Manuel Quintanilla (UDN).[27] The massacre raised several interesting questions: How did it happen that the leaders of the FDR had felt it safe to meet in the enemy-held capital without bodyguards? Were they betrayed by someone, a Jesuit perhaps, whom they trusted? How could such an operation as their seizure be carried out in broad daylight, in such a location, without military cooperation?

While world opinion was still trying to absorb this event, a more shocking massacre took place. Three North American nuns and a female Catholic lay worker were murdered on their way back to the city from Cuscatlán Airport, on 3 December 1980. They had been tortured and probably raped and their bodies dumped into a shallow grave. The targets of the attack appear to have been two Maryknoll sisters, Ita Ford and Maura Clarke, who were returning to their posts in Chalatenango, where they had often been accused of aiding the guerrilla movement. Dorothy Kazel (an Ursaline) and Jean Donovan just happened to have been there at the wrong time. The group had passed through three military checkpoints on the long road from the new airport and it is, again, difficult to imagine that their murder was not done with the knowledge of some elements of the security forces. U.S. military aid was temporarily suspended while an investigation was conducted, but the investigation never went very far and the aid began to flow just in time to coincide with the guerrilla offensive of 10 January 1981.

On the evening of 3 January 1981, while dining at the posh San Salvador Sheraton, Rodolfo Viera, director of ISTA, and two North American advisors, Mark Pearlman and Michael Hammer of AIFLD, were cut down. Viera, a large, happy-go-lucky peasant of charismatic personality, had lent great prestige to the land-reform program. His death was attributed, even by José Napoleón Duarte, to the right. The general manager of ISTA, Gómez Vides, was to have been at that fatal dinner, but failed to get the message. However, on the fourteenth, he was arrested, accused of being a guerrilla *comandante*, and then released, only to be visited by two truckloads of death-squad members that evening. Miraculously escaping, he was spirited out of the country. With the murder of Viera and the exiling of Gómez Vides, the land reform came to a virtual halt.

The murders of the FDR leaders and the North American missionaries brought to a head the long-simmering governmental crisis. Disgusted with the lack of restraint shown by the military, Colonel Majano resigned from the junta on 7 December. He was offered the attaché post in Madrid, which he declined, and promptly went into hiding.[28] The two PDC members on the junta then demanded that the army find "a political solution" to the problem of government structure. The military then agreed that there should be a civilian provisional president. According to Rubén Zamora, the PDC leadership then suggested that Foreign Minister Fidel Chávez Mena ought to get the post, as one of the few leaders still commanding some popular respect, but Duarte was insistent that he himself must have the presidency. Further, PDC demands for a complete restructuring of the high command were shunted aside, thanks to the strong opposition of *Guardia* commander Vides Casanova. The compromise at last worked out made Duarte provisional president, but Col. Jaime Abdul Gutiérrez became vice president and retained the title of commander in chief of the military forces. As if to further underscore who was in charge, García retained his post of defense minister, but to mollify the

PDC, his deputy, Col. Nicolás Carranza, was shifted to the presidency of the telephone company, ANTEL.

The FDR seemed to have solidified its structure but it did make one significant change in January 1981, with the setting up of a virtual government in exile, known as a political commission. This was headed by Guillermo Manuel Ungo as president, and also included Mario Aguinada (UDN), Salvador Samayoa, Angel Guadalupe Martínez (BPR), José Napoleón Rodríguez Ruiz (FAPU), Fabio Castillo, and Rubén Zamora.

In January 1981, they seemed to be enjoying increased foreign support. An invasion by a ship from Nicaragua was partially turned back in mid-January, and the government claimed over 100 invaders had been killed. Such an attack could hardly have been launched without government knowledge in Nicaragua. In West Germany, at the end of the month, there were riots of support in Frankfort and other cities, with attacks on North American institutions. In Panama, former government minister Hugo Spadáfore announced the formation of an International Brigade to fight in El Salvador. The grim parallel to the Spanish Civil War was not unintentional.

NOTES

1. *This Week Central America and Panama*, 21 January 1980.
2. *This Week Central America and Panama*, 3 December 1979; *Update Latin America*, November/December 1979.
3. *Latin America Weekly Review*, 2 November 1979.
4. Ibid.
5. *La Prensa Gráfica* and *El Independiente* (both of San Salvador), 29 February 1980.
6. *Central America Reports*, 17 December 1979.
7. *Vancouver Sun*, 14 November 1979
8. *Prensa Libre* (Guatemala City), 4 January 1980; *New York Times*, 18 January 1980.
9. *New York Times*, 2 December 1978; *El Salvador Reports*, August 1978.
10. *Latin America*, 4 March 1980.
11. *Latin America*, 1 February 1980.
12. *This Week Central America and Panama*, 25 February 1980; *New York Times*, 8 March 1980.
13. *This Week Central America and Panama*, 17 March 1980; *New York Times*, 8 March, 1980.
14. *AIUSA Matchbox*, May 1980.
15. *This Week Central America and Panama*, 31 March 1980; *New York Times*, 26 March 1980.
16. *New York Times*, 1 April 1980.
17. *New York Times*, 16 April 1980; *Latin America Regional Reports, Central America and Mexico*, 11 July 1980.
18. *Central America Update*, June 1980.
19. *Latin America Regional Report, Central America and Mexico*, 11 July 1980.
20. Ibid; *Central America Update*, June 1980.
21. *This Week Central America and Panama*, 26 May 1980.
22. *New York Times*, 2 April 1980.

23. *La Tribuna* (Tegucigalpa), 20 June 1980.

24. *This Week Central America and Panama,* 21 April 1980; *New York Times,* 23 April 1980.

25. *The News* (San José, Costa Rica), 27 June 1980.

26. *Latin America Regional Report, Central America and Mexico,* 24 October 1980.

27. *Central America Update,* December 1980.

28. *Washington Post,* 9 December 1980; *Boston Globe,* 17 December 1980.

7

El Salvador Analysis: Civil War

To try to analyze the chaotic and changing situation in El Salvador in a calculated and mechanistic manner would be futile. The best one can do is to describe the situation as it existed at the beginning of 1981. No doubt, by the time this analysis is published, the situation will have changed drastically. To predict the nature of such changes is also out of the question.

THE POLITICAL SPECTRUM

There is not even a general agreement on the relative positions of the contending forces on a right-to-left continuum. The view held in the U.S. embassy during the tenure of Robert White was that Duarte, Morales Erlich, and what was left of the PDC represented the moderate middle of the spectrum, and that they were engaged in a heroic effort to stave off a victory by either the extreme right, represented by Major D'Aubuisson, or a radical "Pol Pot left." Thus, President Duarte is apparently trying to master forces beyond his control, and only the timely intervention of the United States can save him. The need is for U.S. aid, especially military aid, for this will help maintain his grip on the army, in which, to be sure, there are some radical-right elements, especially in Vides Casanova's *Guardia*, but which is essentially on Duarte's side. The left, in this view, is made up of extreme Marxist radicals who create bloodbaths and who could be expected to do far worse should they come to power. Men such as Guillermo Ungo and Rubén Zamora appear in this scenario as mere window dressing. They would be disposed of in the moment of victory when the left would throw off the mask of moderation and present itself, fangs and all, to the world.

A rival view of reality holds that Duarte and the civilian members of the government are the pawns of a military dominated by the extreme right, under the leadership of Colonel García, and that this military works hand in glove with ORDEN and the ESA. Those who hold this view also declare that the real as well as the apparent leadership of the left is vested in Guillermo Ungo, and the circle of leftist intellectuals around him, such as Rubén Zamora, Salvador Samayoa, and Fabio Castillo. When and if victory comes to the left, and this thesis holds, they will establish a just and moderate regime, Marxist, to be sure, but independent. As Rubén Zamora recently told this writer, "We cannot reproduce Cuba in El Salvador." Only an hour earlier, in the same San José hotel room, Antonio Morales Erlich had declared, "We are creating a social order unknown in Latin America." There are thus rival visions of what would happen if and when either of the contending parties should win out.

Those who hold that President Duarte is a mere puppet of Colonel García have no trouble in believing that Ungo is indeed master of his fate, while those who believe that Duarte represents a struggling moderate position profess to see, behind Guillermo Ungo, the glittering eyes of fanatic peasant nihilists. These rival views are not really mutually exclusive, for both Duarte and Ungo could be moderate independent leaders, or both could be mere front men for fanatics. The problem of how each perceives the other has made negotiations or dialogue very difficult. The government attempted to talk with Enrique Alvarez and the then leaders of the left in June 1980, but the talks broke down, because, Morales Erlich contends, "The left thought it was going to win." The left, of course, accused the government of offering unacceptable terms. Duarte's junta offered a general amnesty in October 1980, but few real guerrillas appeared,[1] for the peasantry remained suspicious of the government's intentions.

The failure to reach a compromise solution to the continuing civil war underscores what Nicolás Mariscal, the distinguished Salvadorean priest-scholar, called the "irreconcilable polarization" of Salvadorean society.[2] On the extreme right, the major group has been, for more than a decade, ORDEN. Once numbering an estimated 80,000 active members, its numbers have undoubtedly shrunk since it lost its *personería jurídica* and became the target of extensive guerrilla attacks. A typical anti-ORDEN campaign was that carried out at San Pedro Perulapán in October 1980, when 60 peasants were lined up and shot by leftist guerrillas on the grounds that they were ORDEN members.[3] In the late seventies, the UGB emerged as a Guatemalan-type death squad. This has now become, along with several rather shadowy organizations, a part of the ESA. ORDEN, since its inception in 1967, was closely linked to the *Guardia Nacional*, whose then commander, General Medrano, was its instigator. The UGB likewise maintained links to the security forces, principally the *Policía Nacional*, many of whose members were said to have "moon-lighted" as UGB thugs, and to the army's G-2 section, especially during the Molina presidency. These connections remained at the end of the decade, despite the fact that such radical rightists as D'Aubuisson and Santivañas had been officially purged from the ranks of the military in the coup of 1979. The radical right also maintained links with the private-enterprise group ANEP and with FARO and other landholders' groups. This segment of the political spectrum appeared to barely tolerate Duarte's government. Ultraconservative business leaders with whom I spoke, in February 1981, were anxious to replace the existing government with an open military dictatorship that would restore order and put an end to such pretensions as the land-reform program. They saw Duarte's situation as a parallel to that of Arturo Araujo in 1931, prior to the time that he was ousted and replaced with General Maximiliano Her-nández Martínez. That famous dictator, long anathema to all circles of Salvadorean society, has suddenly begun to be remembered fondly, and the group which took credit for the assassination of the FDR leaders called itself the "Maximiliano Hernández brigade."

Whether Colonel Gutiérrez, or perhaps Colonel García, would be willing to be cast in General Martínez's role was open to conjecture at the start of 1981. If one could believe reports by the U.S. embassy, they in fact represented the moderate element within the military and were working to persuade their more militant colleagues not to launch a coup. In embassy views, as men-tioned above, the civilian middle was what was left of the PDC, plus the more progressive elements in the business community, as represented by Avalos on the junta. But most of the business community that could be labeled moderate had fled abroad, and that which remained was silent out of fear of the death squads.

If there was a moderate left, it was represented by the MDN leaders in exile, led by Memo Ungo, and by the dissident Christian Democrats, led by such men as Rubén Zamora and Oscar Menjívar. Indeed, the number of PDC leaders in exile probably outnumbered those in power. To the right, they appeared as mere stalking horses for the far left, playing the same role as did the unfortunate Alfonso Robelo in Nicaragua. Farther to the left, and ap-parently in a process of radicalization, was the UDN, the communist front group. Its clandestine arm, the PCES, had emerged as a frankly terrorist movement, paralleling the transformation of the PGT in Guatemala. The *Bloque* and FAPU were likewise moving leftward since their identification with the terrorist-guerrilla groups FPL and FARN. But these groups, while radical, hardly qualified as a "Pol Pot" left. Such well-known leaders as Shafik Handal, of the PCES, and Salvador Cayetano Carpio, of the FPL, were old political hands who could at least be considered sane, though cer-tainly not moderate. If there were a "Pol Pot" left, it was probably represented by the *Ligas Populares* and by their guerrilla arm, the ERP, a self-proclaimed

Trotskyite group believing in permanent, violent revolution. What influence such a group might have on a government of the left was purely conjectural.

SOCIAL CLASSES AND FORCES

As in every Central American country, in El Salvador, by far the largest sector, some 70 percent of the population, is made up of *campesinos*. However, as was pointed out in the case of Guatemala, this term covers a multitude of social groups, sometimes with opposing interests. Some three decades ago, more than half of the peasant families owned some land, though they might supplement their income by participating in the seasonal harvests. About 25 percent were *colonos*, who received a *milpa*, or parcel of land, from the landholder (*terrateniente*).[4] This situation has changed dramatically over the last several decades. The *colono*, or year-round farm hand, has largely disappeared, thanks to a better transportation network, which makes it possible to bring in all the hands one needs for a harvest. The percentage of those owning some land also decreased, due to a rapidly growing rural population as well as the steady encroachment of the great estates upon the lands of the peasants. The purely migratory, utterly landless peasant became increasingly the norm in El Salvador. If some revolutions are revolutions of rising expectations, that of El Salvador can be said to be one of lowered expectations and increasing desperation.

As the eroded land could no longer support the increasing demands made upon it, a new social factor emerged, the urban destitute. Every major Central American city has its share of such people, but the numbers in San Salvador became truly appalling. Careful research has shown that many of these shanty-town dwellers were not newly arrived *campesinos*, but themselves part of an urban population explosion, parallel to that in the countryside.[5] They were a visible reminder to the rich of the existence of the poor, for they often affixed their lean-tos against the walls of mansions, but they were also a constant reminder of the threat of an urban uprising. In recent years the BPR, through the Association of Slum Dwellers, managed to organize these people. Urban guerrillas can melt into the shantytown at a moment's notice and thus greatly increase the task of the security forces.

Ten years ago, when Guatemala had guerrilla movements and El Salvador had none, it was fashionable to explain this by the existence in El Salvador of a hard-working, ambitious middle class. Indeed, the broad spectrum of the middle class, ranging from teachers and clerks to bankers and physicians, was impressive. Symbols of this were such large and affluent barrios as *Colonia Escalón* and *San Benito*. But, as Karl Marx could have told them, the bourgeoisie is the most revolutionary of all classes. Each year, the universities turned out too many ambitious, but unemployable young men and women from hard-working, aspiring families. At the top, the wealthy 14 families held onto the social and economic power and only a career in the military could lead to real political power. Out of this frustration, intellectuals such as David Alejandro Luna and Roque Dalton García became revolutionaries. To decide which stratum of the middle class produced most leaders of the revolutionary movement would be impossible, given the current state of affairs; but indeed it did so, as an examination of the key posts in the FDR would clearly show.

One segment of the aspiring middle class must be singled out for special comment: those young men of ambition who went not to universities, but to the whitewashed buildings and broad playing fields of the *Escuela Militar*. A chasm grew between them and the rest of their stratum of society. Their loyalty was to their profession and to their *tanda*, or class at the academy. Thanks to their training, they became intensely patriotic—or perhaps "nationalistic" is a more accurate term—highly anti-communist, and superbly overconfident in the training they had received. If they remained with the regular battalions of the army, the soldiers with whom they worked were impressed peasants. Outside of maneuvers and occasional assignments abroad, their days would be spent in strong-walled *cuarteles* with battlements and looming towers. Envied were those who took up with elite units, such as the *Guardia Nacional*, the *Policía de Hacienda*, or the Rangers. The officers and the career enlistees lived in a world apart, with special privileges such as PXs and free housing. They were despised by the wealthy, who needed their protection; and they in turn despised every nonmilitary part of the Salvadorean world. Ferocious in their dealings with the oppressed and weak, they conjured up their own nemesis in terrorism and guerrilla warfare. No country of the region, not even Guatemala or Nicaragua, could be so truly said to be occupied by its own army. The habitually sad, yet defiant expression of the professional officer perhaps reflected this fact.

Among those who formed the top stratum of Salvadorean society, there seemed to exist a sharper distinction between urban and rural wealth than existed in other countries of the region. Within the rural sector, Abel Cuenca had distinguished between those landholders who represented the old, pre-coffee wealth (the *latifundistas*) and those who were of more recent wealth, usually from coffee (*terratenientes*).[6] Such distinctions might indeed be useful under some circumstances, but in terms of their political effect, both groups were much the same. These groups, through FARO and other growers' associations, long resisted any effort at the reform of the land, and effectively killed the well-thought-out land-reform scheme of the Molina government in 1976. That was perhaps the last opportunity to effect peaceful social reform, and its demise indicated the suicidal propensity of the landholding groups. The chaotic land reform of 1980 swept away a great many of the noncoffee holdings and raised savage indignation among the former owners, most of whom had not received their promised compensation bonds a year later. It was, in fact, unlikely that they would ever be properly compensated, for the government was totally disorganized, as well as broke. Many in the business community were not unhappy to see the *latifundistas* being roughly handled, but they expressed their indignation over the nationalization of banking, which had accompanied the land reform, and over the general impossibility of doing business in the war-torn country. But the large landholders and the business leaders had come to the conclusion, by the beginning of 1981, that what was needed was a strong military dictatorship. "We will fall into bankruptcy if we do not move sharply to the right," declared ANEP President Eduardo Palomo.[7]

A dominant factor over the last several years has been the role of the church. Until the assassination in March of 1981, Msgr. Romero y Galdámez was the acknowledged spokesman for those opposed to repressive policies. His chief vehicle of protest was the Sunday sermon delivered weekly from the cathedral in San Salvador and broadcast over the church radio station, YSAX. His successor, Msgr. Rivera y Damas, has followed a much more ambiguous course. He has continued the tradition of the Sunday sermons, but they are much less political in tone and do not attract the audience that listened to the previous archbishop. However, in a sermon delivered on 26 October 1980, Rivera attacked the army's "war of extermination and genocide against a defenseless civilian population."[8] It was thought that this uncharacteristically strong statement had been written for him by Ricardo Urioste, the vicar general, or by Fabian Amaya, who represented the most antigovernment element among the priests of the diocese. After that, both Urioste and Amaya left the country, and they were unlikely to return unless the government changed hands. With their departure, the National Commission of the Popular Church, a militant group backing the Popular Forces, lost influence. In a statement delivered in mid-December, Archbishop Rivera forbade priests and nuns from making political statements "in the name of the Church," a statement clearly aimed at the National Commission. In the meantime, the radio voice of the church had been at least temporarily silenced. On 19 November 1980, troops invaded San José de la Montaña, ransacked the offices of *Orientación*, the paper of the archdiocese, and then destroyed the equipment and offices of YSAX, which stands next door.[9]

Factors Making for Stability

Given the enormous demographic and economic problems of the country, which would appear catastrophic even if perfect peace reigned over the land, it seemed surprising that, as the year 1981 dawned, the government and the society were able to function at all. In part, this was a tribute to the resilience and power of the military, which, although it had received very little outside aid during the seventies, and although it was rent by the purge which followed the 1979 coup, still managed to present a fairly united front against the guerrilla groups and against the external world in general. However, the security forces suffered an estimated 1,000 killed in 1980, and these must have been predominantly from the elite units.

In part, the continued stability of the regime was also due to the incompetence of the left and its multiple divisions. The FMLN showed little signs of being as unified as the FSLN had been in its fight against Somoza. Within the FDR, organizational and doctrinal disputes raged on, regardless of their effect on the military struggle. A strong, charismatic leader was decidedly lacking. Guillermo Ungo might be upright, but he was known as a dull speaker and a less-than-charismatic personality.

Further, certain interests continued to feel that they were represented by the junta under President Duarte. These included at least a segment of the San Salvador business community. This group, while fearing a leftist dictatorship, above all things, felt little inclination to support an outright rightist, military dictator. But, as the economic situation worsened, this group, never very large, was likely to dwindle. A part of the church, led by Bishop Aparicio, also continued to be a part of the aggression of interests supporting the Duarte regime, although the UCA and the Jesuits were resolutely hostile. A large number of peasants, particularly those in the UCS, who had benefited from the first stage of the land-reform program, might also be expected to offer at least implicit support to the government. Despite efforts of the left to paint the government as totally lacking in support, there were indeed elements, other than the army, whose interests were served by maintaining the junta in power.

Perhaps the most significant stabilizing factor was the continued support of the United States, expressed in money as well as words, and the support of the Venezuelan government, but to a lesser extent. Ambassador Robert White had been the symbol of North American support, and though he was replaced, the policies he expressed might linger, though with a declining insistence on human rights.

Destabilizing Factors

A raging civil war was the most obvious factor leading to destabilization of the government, but even if the guerrilla forces could not win militarily, the economic disruption, the chaos, and the killing engendered by the conflict threatened to lead to such general dissatisfaction that an outright military dictatorship could easily result.

It was easier to point out which groups and forces did not support the government than to discover its sources of support. A vocal element of the church was on the side of the opposition, despite the fact that the government had a Christian Democratic flavor to it. While some peasants who might have benefited from the land reform favored the regime, probably most of the *campesinos* opposed it, especially those who had been uprooted from their lands by the war and driven into either the departmental capitals or exile in Honduras or Guatemala. By and large, the *campesinos* would have welcomed a victory of the left. If some in the world of business believed that the regime was the best possible under the circumstances, others talked openly, by January 1981, of a military dictatorship which would deal strongly with the guerrilla problem, the death squads, and the economy. Landlord interests were also anxious to see a rightist regime cancel the land reform. These included not only the *latifundistas*, whose land was expropriated in stage one, but also the *minifundistas*, threatened by the Land to the Tiller program, and the coffee growers, who had largely escaped the first wave of expropriations but were waiting for a new one.

Meanwhile, despite the death of 10,000 persons in the civil war, the population inexorably continued to grow, outrunning the food supply. The problem was complicated by the taking out of production of land, in the sweeps through guerrilla territory by the army, and by the estimated 85,000 refugees who swelled the urban centers.

ECONOMIC FACTORS

The economic situation by the beginning of 1981 was about as bad as it could possibly be. Starvation was commonplace. The gross national product had fallen 3.5 percent in 1979, and plunged 10 percent in 1980. Coffee production for the harvest of 1980-81 was down 25 percent from the harvest of 1975. Sugar production declined by 40 percent in 1980 from the production of 1979 and there was a 30 percent drop in cotton production.[10] However, the government believed that, with the land-reform program causing more acreage to be put into foodstuffs, there would be a considerable gain in the production of beans and rice. Table 7.1 gives the government's projections in mid-1980. Even this forecast, which was probably not achieved, indicated a drop in the most important crop of all: corn. Cattle production was also down, as many expropriated ranchers drove their herds across the nearest border.

In a population of just 5 million, it was estimated that there were 300,000 out of work by the middle of 1980, and the government projected a deficit of

TABLE 7.1. Expected Production of Salvadorean Food Crops in 1980

Item	Projected Targets	1978-79 Totals
Corn	478,000	499,900
Beans	46,000	42,300
Rice	55,200	50,000

Note: Figures are in metric tons.
Source: This Week Central America and Panama, 23 June 1980.

200,000 housing units by 1982. Duarte therefore announced, in June 1980, the start of a massive "emergency public works project," costing up to $900 million, to create over 50,000 jobs in the construction industry. The United States was to back this project with a pledge of $49.8 million in grants and credits, while Venezuela was to supply a $10-million loan. The government also planned to reopen 25 closed factories at a cost of $156 million. This again would require massive loans at a time when foreign exchange reserves were practically nil, inflation was running at 20 percent, government tax revenues were off 17.7 percent, and the nation's oil bill was skyrocketing from $70.4 million in 1978 to $148 million in 1980.[11]

Thanks to the backing of the United States, there was some evidence that the required funding might come, in part, from nongovernmental sources. The International Monetary Fund (IMF), over which the United States exercises considerable influence, announced in August 1980 that it was planning a "soft loan" of $25.4 million to El Salvador. This loan would be soft in that its interest structure would not be designed for the IMF to make a profit on the interest, nor indeed to break even. There would be no payments for five years after the loan was given, and then the scale of repayments would be slow and at the hardly usurious rate of 0.5 percent interest. In short, this was a gift. Similarly, the Inter-American Development Bank, in January 1981, agreed to loan El Salvador $45.5 million, under a 40-year repayment plan with a grad-uated interest rate of 1 to 2 percent.[12] In the next couple of years, the government of El Salvador hoped to receive a total of $400 million in such soft loans. This would be $80 per Salvadorean, or slightly more than the average per capita income of the *campesinos*.

Coupled with what the country could expect from the U.S. government and other foreign backers, enough money might be infused into the system in the short run to keep the economy afloat. But the long-range prospects were parlous, civil war or no civil war. Assuming that the United States succeeded in keeping a friendly government in power, it could probably count on El Salvador as a bottomless pit of economic need for the foreseeable future.

FOREIGN AFFAIRS

As the civil war continued, both sides made strong bids for outside support. The junta sent Morales Erlich on a tour of a number of capitals, in late 1980, to ask for aid and understanding. The government of Venezuela, of which Christian Democratic leader Luis Herrera Campins is head, warmly supported the government of El Salvador, as did Costa Rica, also partly governed by Christian Democrats. The European affiliates of that party were also sympathetic to the cause of the junta. Adolfo Rey Prendes, the mayor of San Salvador and a prominent PDC leader, visited the United States in mid-January 1981 and appealed to foreign countries to "let the Salvadorean people resolve their own problems," but made an exception concerning the United States because its intervention was "strengthening democracy."[13] While Guatemala and Honduras continued to offer warm backing to the government, there were student protests against this policy in both countries, though these would likely have little effect on the governments.

The FDR leaders and members of the guerrilla forces traveled frequently to Cuba for training and advice. Nicaragua, while perhaps not actively promoting aid to the FDR, certainly turned a blind eye toward the use of its airstrips and ports as a conduit for arms shipments. "The Nicaraguan government has never hidden its full support for the revolutionary aspirations of the Salvadorean people," said Daniel Ortega, in a speech in Managua in December 1980. Mexico's president, José López Portillo was still, at the end of the year, resisting pressures for making a total rupture with the Salvadorean government, despite a protest march of 30,000 and some anti-North American rioting. Trying to maintain a certain distance from the conflict, Foreign Minister Jorge Castaneda declared in Mexico City that his country opposed "all intervention" in the affairs of El Salvador. The government of the Dominican Republic and President Antonio Guzmán were also under severe popular pressure to support the FDR.[14] In Europe, the strongest support for the FDR continued to come from the German government of Helmut Schmidt, aside from that given, of course, by the communist-bloc countries.

Options for U.S. Policy toward El Salvador

In November 1980, a remarkable document circulated in Washington circles that was known as the El Salvador dissent paper. Strictly speaking, this title was inaccurate, for State Department dissent papers, prepared by lower-ranking officials who disagree with their chiefs' policies, are official documents, filed through the dissent channel and signed by the authors. This document was anonymous and was probably prepared by a number of persons in the State Department, the Defense Department, and the CIA. It suggested that the policy of supporting the junta was bankrupt; that El Salvador was really in the hands of military extremists linked to the right-wing terrorist groups; and that the United States ought to consider making peace with the insurgents, or, at the very least, not supporting the current government with military and financial aid. Such a policy of withdrawal would certainly lead to a victory for the FDR, but, as the document argues, would this be so bad? Many governments analysts are convinced that it would be. With Nicaragua and El Salvador both in leftist hands, the "dominoes" would be lined up, they say. Honduras and Guatemala would "fall" and be "lost," disappearing from the maps in the State Department, in much the same way as China once did. The oil of Guatemala would go with them and the Mexico fields in Chiapas would be threatened.

To counter the publicity received by the dissent document, the State Department released a white paper on El Salvador in February, claiming that the country was a textbook case of armed communist aggression. Appended to the document were a collection of papers said to have been captured from the guerrillas in El Salvador. The papers included a detailed itinerary of Shafik Handal's visits to the communist world and a series of papers dealing with Cuban arms shipments via Nicaragua. Many newspapers, including the *New York Times* and the *Washington Post*, were quick to point out that these documents did not really support the conclusions which the Reagan administration had drawn. Indeed, the government was eventually forced to admit many inaccuracies in the white paper, though it continued to claim that these did not affect the general truth of the document.

If one rules out the option suggested by the dissent document, two possibilities still remain. The United States could continue the carefully charted course of supporting the junta while, at the same time, deploring human rights excesses and trying to make the government see that the best way to lose the civil war would be by antagonizing its own people. Aid, including arms, would be given, but there would be some gentle arm twisting to induce the government to bring the death squads under control and end the scorched-earth policy in the northern part of the country. This was essentially the plan in effect during 1980.

The other alternative would be to give unconditional support to the military. Such a policy at least would have the virtue of simplicity and would appeal to those who imagine themselves to be realists and who concern themselves only with the best interests of the United States, as they conceive these interests. The most obvious drawback to this plan would be the catastrophic consequences of its failure. If the security forces were to lose after all, an implacably hostile El Salvador, plus an equally hostile Nicaragua, would be the assured result.

That such a tiny nation should generate problems of such magnitude at first appears absurd, but one must remember that El Salvador is not some far-off land. San Salvador is considerably closer to Washington, D.C., than is Los Angeles. Whatever role the United States assumes, it must remember that this is not some distant corner of Asia but our own backyard.

NOTES

1. *This Week Central America and Panama,* 6 October 1980.
2. Nicholás Mariscal, "Regimenes Políticos en El Salvador," *Estudios Centroamericanos* 34 (March 1979):p. 149.
3. *This Week Central America and Panama,* 15 August 1980.
4. Richard N. Adams, *Cultural Surveys of Panama, Nicaragua, Guatemala, El Salvador and Honduras* (Washington, D.C.: Pan American Sanitary Bureau, 1957), pp. 431-35.
5. Alastair White, *El Salvador* (New York: Praeger, 1973), p. 148.

6. Abel Cuenca, *El Salvador: una democracia cafetalera*, (San Salvador: n.d.), pp. 13-16.

7. *This Week Central America and Panama*, 2 June 1980.

8. *This Week Central America and Panama*, 5 November 1980.

9. *Hartford Courant*, 29 December 1980; *Update Latin America*, November/December 1980.

10. *This Week Central America and Panama*, 23 and 30 June 1980.

11. *Latin America Regional Report, Central America and Mexico*, 19 September 1980.

12. *This Week Central America and Panama*, 1 September 1980, 5 January 1981.

13. *Boston Globe*, 31 January 1981.

14. Ibid.

PART III
HONDURAS

8

Honduras:
The Essential Banana Republic

Honduras has been generally regarded as the poorest and most backward of the Central American republics. Lying to the north of El Salvador, it encompasses more than five times the territory of that country; and a small section juts southward to the Gulf of Fonseca, giving Honduras a Pacific coastline and separating El Salvador from Nicaragua. Most of the country is made up of rolling green ridges, rising to a maximum elevation of over 9,000 feet, but there is an extensive littoral plain along the Atlantic coast that was almost uninhabitable until the conquest of malaria and yellow fever in the early part of the present century. Traditionally, the populace remained in the hills, living on haciendas or in the sleepy villages, one of which, Tegucigalpa, became the capital of the republic. However, the introduction of banana culture, coinciding with the introduction of modern medicine, opened up the north coast in a kind of "banana rush."

This event brought about North American interest in the land. Samuel Zemurray, an entrepreneur from Selma, Alabama, became the first to recognize the possibilities of the banana. He eventually sold his Cuyamel company to the larger United Fruit, only to be forced to come out of retirement and take over United itself when it faced bankruptcy during the depression. United Fruit (or United Brands as it has been known since 1972) is still the largest employer in the country, incorporated as the Tela Railroad Company. Standard Fruit, the other giant of the industry, also has extensive holdings.

The banana interests often played politics in the country. Zemurray himself overthrew President Miguel Savila in 1910 and replaced him with the more responsive Manuel Bonilla. But the North Americans did not create Honduras's political instability. From the declaration of independence from the rest of Central America, in 1839, to 1900, there were 64 separate presidencies as well as a number of juntas. Few of these regimes entered or exited according to the constitution. The record in the twentieth century has hardly been better, and for almost the entire decade of the seventies, the country was ruled by a succession of military strongmen with no pretense of constitutionality. The picture of Honduras that thus emerges is that of the pure essence of a banana republic, poor, Yankee dominated, and chronically misgoverned from the castle that serves as the presidential palace in the overgrown village of Tegucigalpa. This, however, would be a superficial view of the situation. In fact, Honduras has followed an interesting course of political development and, at the beginning of the eighties, was receiving considerable attention from the U.S. State Department as a potential island of moderate democracy in the midst of turbulent Central America.

The Hondurans have always regarded their bad government with a kind of bemused whimsy, even referring to their capital as "Tegucigolpe," because of the frequency of *golpes de estado*. They can point out that in many ways they are freer than their neighbors. No 14 families rule in this land. Landholding is concentrated, but not quite to the extent it is in El Salvador or Guatemala. In 1970, 38 percent of farmland was held by 0.8 percent of the farmers.[1] There are many important *hacendados*, generally living on their remote estates, styling themselves colonels and dominating the local political scene; but they do not govern the country, although they can influence events through their powerful *Federación Nacional de Agricultores y Ganaderos de Honduras* (FENAGH). Many *campesinos* have some land of their own, though these plots are often pitifully small. In the 1960s, two out of three farms were of less than two acres in size and half of the rural families made no more than $250 a year. The national per capita income in 1973 was only $350.[2] Despite the small extent of their holdings, possession of land gives them a feeling of self-worth and independence.

Another important factor in asserting the rights of the *campesinos* has been their long-term unionization, a factor without parallel in Guatemala or El Salvador. This was achieved through massive strikes against the Tela Railroad Company (United Front) and against Standard Fruit in April 1954. President Juan Manuel Gálvez branded the strikers "communists" but proved powerless to stop the walkout, which quickly spread to other industries and agricultural enterprises. In the end, after months of haggling and considerable violence, United and the other companies had to bow, and two major banana workers' unions emerged: the *Sindicato de Trabajadores de Tela Railroad Company* (SITRATERCO) and the *Sindicato de Trabajadores de Standard Fruit Company* (SITRASFCO), both of which are a part of the *Confederación de Trabajadores de Honduras* (CTH), which has over 160,000 rural and industrial members. Its peasant group is the *Asociación Nacional de Campesinos de Honduras* (ANACH), with more than 160,000 participants. In recent years the CTH has been challenged by the rapidly growing *Confederación General de Trabajadores* (CGT), a Catholic church-sponsored group, whose peasant arm is the *Unión Nacional de Campesinos* (UNC), which has shown signs of becoming the Honduran counterpart of FECCAS or UTC, both of El Salvador. Big labor is therefore a major interest group that must be conciliated by each regime.

Other factors that create an atmosphere of pluralism in Honduras include the existence of a staunchly independent national university, the *Universidad Nacional Autónoma de Honduras*, which takes the "autonomy" in its title quite seriously and is probably the freest national university in the area, outside of Costa Rica. There is also a relatively independent press, with four major dailies, two for each of the traditional political parties and two for each of the major cities, Tegucigalpa and San Pedro Sula, the capital of the banana coast. These papers have never been intimidated to the extent newspapers have in Guatemala, nor do they serve simply as sounding boards for the oligarchy, as has been true in El Salvador.

Like Nicaragua, Honduras has had a traditional two-party system. These parties probably were influenced by the struggle between proclerical conservatives and progressive, anticlerical liberals, imbued with the ideas of Adam Smith and J.S. Mill, in the nineteenth century; but the actual origins of the parties are fairly recent, and today they bear little ideological resemblance to their nineteenth-century ancestors. The Liberal Party was formally constituted by President Policarpo Bonilla, who then used it to oust the conservative Ponciano Leiva from the presidency in 1893. The ousted Ponciano Leiva first began to label his conservative group the National Party, and the group received *personería jurídica* under that title in 1916.[3]

The elements of the Honduran National Party did not long remain united, as the charismatic leader Tiburcio Carías Andino split off his own Democratic National Party shortly after its birth. By 1924, however, they had reunited under Carías Andino, who stood as the party's candidate in the presidential elections of that year. Although he won a plurality of the votes, the Liberal-dominated National Assembly deprived him of his victory. The customary civil war followed until a compromise was reached. Eight years later, a relatively honest election brought Carías to power, and there he remained for many years.

In many ways, Carías Andino was an unusual Honduran. He was six feet four inches literally towering over his contemporaries. He had a broad career as soldier, landholder, and professor of mathematics. It says a good deal for his abilities that Honduras was one of the few Latin American countries not to see a serious upheaval in the early thirties, under the impact of the great depression. Instead, the imposing president shepherded his people with a combination of belt-tightening measures and public works. He also kept the confidence of the Yankee fruit companies, which was indispensable for success-ful governance. His term would have ended in 1936 but there was enough support for his continued leadership to have the constitution changed to allow the current president and vice president to remain in office until January 1943. Thus began the period of *continuismo* in Honduran politics. The legislature in 1939 once again extended the term of office, this time until January 1949, 13 years after the original end of Carías's term of office. At first popular and successful, the regime finally became mired in graft and corruption.[4] When Tiburcio Carías Andino finally stepped down, he was succeeded, through an election in the Assembly, by his hand-picked successor, Juan Manuel Gálvez, in whose final year of office the great strike of 1954 occurred.

This was an election year, and Carías sought to make a comeback as the National Party candidate; but his party split and a dissident group ran another candidate on the *Reformista* ticket. The result was that Liberal candidate Ramón Villeda Morales won a plurality, throwing the election into the Congress, which the Nationals then boycotted to prevent a decision. In the midst of the crisis, Vice President Julio Lozano Díaz took over from the ailing Gálvez, annulled the elections, and ruled as dictator. Even by Honduran standards, this was high-handed behavior; and when Lozano proceeded to rig the legislative elections of October 1956, he was overthrown by a group of young military officers.

Honduras henceforth would be plagued with the same sort of professional military domination of politics that had existed in the other three countries under discussion, since the early thirties. After 1956, it was the career soldiers, with their illusions of universal competence, who intervened time and again. This time, however, they were content to fade into the background after arranging free legislative elections for September 1957. The Liberals dom-inated the Assembly which emerged; and they chose as president, for a six-year term, Villeda Morales, as they could legally do under the current Honduran constitution.

Villeda was an astute politician who understood the power of the fruit-company unions and frequently backed them against the North American-owned companies and other large landholders. These policies led to frequent revolts against his government, the most serious of which was the military uprising of Col. Armando Velásquez Cerrato in 1959. Despite his quarrel with the fruit companies, his policies in general won the support of the United States, and John F. Kennedy lavished aid upon the Villeda government through the Alliance for Progress.[5] Emboldened by this support from abroad, Villeda decided to do something more tangible for the peasantry, who sought a larger percentage of the land, for the problem of *latifundios* owning a disproportionate share of the arable land was hardly less acute than in El Salvador.[6] He created the *Instituto Nacional Argraria* (INA) in March 1961, and put through a land-reform law in September 1962. This law originally provided for compensation in long-term bonds, but, under fruit-company pressure, this was changed to cash compensation, which greatly limited its effectiveness.

Before any land reform was out of the planning stages, it was necessary to elect a new president. Direct popular elections were scheduled for 13 October 1963 and the winner appeared to be the chief of the Liberal Party, Modesto Rodas Alvarado. If he had been elected, he would have been quite likely to try to carry through the reforms set by Villeda; but powerful landholders of the National Party, the fruit companies, and a clique of conservative officers took measures to prevent this. On 3 October a coup was successfully launched, Villeda was exiled, and the elections were canceled. John F. Kennedy, who had warmly admired Villeda, refused to recognize the new government, but in January 1964, Johnson granted recognition.

In retrospect, the coup of 1963 ranks second only to the great strike of 1954 in its importance for Honduran history, but unlike the great strike, its influence was destined to be tragic. The man who now became chief of state without benefit of election was the military leader of the movement, Col. Oswaldo López Arellano, the commander of the air force, a hard-eyed little man. His influence upon the politics of his country was extensive and, on the whole, baleful. He used the National Party as one instrument of his rule, the military as another, and, as a third, the rather loose organization called the *Mancha Brava*. This was a group of shock troops drawn from the ranks of public employees and Nationalist politicians and "authorized to attack and kill" the enemies of the new government.[7] They operated chiefly in the rural areas and were especially active in the semifeudal province of Olancho. Unlike his predecessor, López Arellano distrusted the Alliance for Progress and would accept aid from the government of Lyndon Johnson only if he could, as he said, "institutionalize it," which meant channeling the funds into the pockets of his associates.[8]

As the government was patently unconstitutional, the constitution was abolished and a new Constituent Assembly called for, to draft still another Honduran constitution. The elections, which took place on 16 February 1965, were obviously fraudulent, despite the presence of observers from the Organization of American States. Ricardo Zúñiga Augustinas, leader of the National Party, was in charge of orchestrating the election. He made sure that *Mancha Brava* thugs and compliant army men were at the polling places to insure the proper result. The Nationals then gave themselves 35 of the 64 seats in the Assembly.

Indirect presidential elections have not been uncommon in Honduran history, Ramón Villeda Morales having been chosen in that fashion in 1957, as was Juan Manuel Gálvez in 1949. It was consequently not unusual that the Constituent Assembly proceeded to give itself the power of election and then chose, to no one's surprise, López Arellano as the new president. Some liberal members of the Assembly, led by labor leader Céleo González, refused to participate in this election; but the majority went along, thus giving the election of López a certain veneer of legitimacy.

The government of López Arellano soon found itself caught up in the land-reform issue. Although Honduras, with a population of just 2 million, could not be considered overpopulated in absolute terms, this population was growing at the rate of 3.5 percent a year, and as the life expectancy of the average Honduran was only 50 years, every other person was under 15 and had to be supported. Further, the haciendas, as in El Salvador, were rapidly extending their domain, by fair means and foul, to take advantage of the sudden spurt in the profitability of cotton and cattle raising.[9] The peasantry, more militant and better organized than that of any other Central American country, responded with *tomas*, or land seizures. These seizures were backed by ANACH. They often resulted in shootouts between the squatters and the estate owners. FENAGH, the landholders' organization, became quite alarmed at this turn of events, especially as the agitation was increased to make effective use of INA and the Land Reform Act of 1962.

Under López Arellano, the economy began to sag. In May 1967, Miguel Angel Rivera, the head of the Superior Economic Planning Council, made a report that detailed the scandalous state of the nation's finances and, in particular, the lack of public investment, the corruption, and the graft. This aroused the anger of Ricardo Zúñiga, now secretary of the presidency and the real brains of the administration, who saw to it that Rivera was soon forced to resign. But sacking the bearer of bad tidings hardly solved the problems of unemployment and economic stagnation.

The deepening governmental crisis was not helped by the fraudulent municipal elections of March 1968, in which the government saw to it that the Liberals won only 35 of the 260 mayoralties being contested. Oscar Gale Varela, the secretary general of SITRATERCO and a leading Liberal, demanded new elections; but the government brushed aside all protest, whereupon Gale Varela followed Rivera in resigning from the Superior Economic Planning Council. César A. Batres, himself a member of the National Party and president of the *Asociación Nacional de Industriales*, called for a dialogue between the government and the Liberals, but it was not to be. And when the government showed its indifference to popular discontent by imposing new consumer taxes, there was a strike on the north coast, led by the CTH. The strike became general and included unions in both San Pedro Sula and the capital as well as in the agrarian sector. The government imposed a state of siege and arrested Céleo Gonzáles, the president of the *Federación Sindical de Trabajadores del Norte* (FESITRAN), the umbrella organization of the major fruit-company unions and then put Gale Varela under surveillance. On the whole, the repression was brutal and effective, including an attack on the sacred precincts of the UNAH. But despite the apparent victory of the government, there were new waves of strikes in 1969.

It is against this background of internal turmoil that the expulsions of Salvadoreans that led to the so-called Soccer War must be considered. Since the turn of the century, large numbers of Salvadoreans had migrated into the country to work on the banana plantations, and then—after the unions had closed that opportunity to them—to search for empty land where they might farm. These *campesinos* from El Salvador were resented by some Hondurans; even more resented were the small number of businessmen from that country who settled in the cities and, through their characteristic enterprise, managed to enrich themselves at the expense of Hondurans. Another resentment was against industry inside El Salvador, which, thanks to the Central American Common Market (MCCA), had built up a very favorable balance of trade with Honduras. The symbol of Salvadorean economic domination came to be the ubiquitous ADOC shoe stores, an enterprise based in El Salvador with branches in every country of the region. It was also said that Salvadoreans controlled 60 percent of the grain trade.[10]

Villeda Morales had made a halfhearted effort to expel some of the Salvadoreans, almost all of whom lacked proper entry documents, but it was only in the time of Oswaldo López Arellano that they came to be seen as a scapegoat for the obvious incompetence of the government. The *Mancha Brava*, urged on by FENAGH, which sought to divert attention from the land grabs by its members, began anti-Salvadorean activities on a large scale in 1967.

Matters came to a head with the Salvadorean seizure of a Honduran border bandid named Antonio Martínez Argueta, in May 1967. Martínez Argueta happened to be a close friend of López Arellano; and his arrest, on a raid across the border by police from El Salvador, stirred up a controversy. The situation was further heated when a Salvadorean patrol of some 40 men was captured at the Honduran border town of Nueva Ocotepeque in June. Ultimately an exchange of prisoners was worked out under pressure from Lyndon Johnson, but relations between the two Central American neighbors had been so poisoned that a further clash was almost inevitable.

As the economic situation of Honduras deteriorated in the spring of 1969, the government decided to apply fully the provisions of the Agrarian Reform Law of 1963. The director of INA at this time was Rigoberto Sandoval Corea, an able and energetic man who believed in a Honduras for the Hondurans. Encouraged by the president and Zúñiga, he began to expropriate lands upon which Salvadoreans were squatting, in May 1969. This pleased the Honduran peasants, and the CTH, ANACH, and FENAGH as well, for the only persons to suffer were foreigners. And suffer they did, with the *Departimiento de Investigaciones Nacionales* (DIN—the Honduran Secret Police), the *Mancha Brava*, and the army all using considerable cruelty, torture, rape, and even murder to expel the foreigners. The Honduran press lost no opportunity to stir up vigilantes and even the leader of the Liberal Party, Modesto Rodas Alvarado, became a leading propagandist for expulsion.

Although the victims of physical persecution may have numbered no more than a couple of hundred, this was sufficient, when combined with threatening proclamations from Rigoberto Sandoval, to create a stampede; and by the first week of July 1969, some 20,000 Salvadorean immigrants had fled back across the border from Honduras, taking with them only what they could carry on their backs. These pitiful refugees taxed the resources of their native country, already overcrowded and in economic difficulties. It was now the turn of the press in El Salvador to have an anti-Honduran field day. The fact that a series of three soccer matches in the World Cup series was being played between the two countries did not help matters, and the Honduran team was booed and almost mobbed when it visited El Salvador for the second game.

War actually broke out when El Salvador invaded Honduras on the evening of 14 July. Thanks to OAS intervention, the fighting lasted less than a week, but the Honduran army was humiliated on the ground, although the air force won some victories. Not until August did the troops from El Salvador leave the occupied territory. At first, the war brought an outpouring of patriotism, along with much anti-Salvadorean violence, which included the burning of ADOC shoe stores and other Salvadorean businesses, but it also brought in its wake further disenchantment with the government of López Arellano, whose only claim to fame was that it had, after all, distributed land to about 17,000 peasant families by 1980.[11] By 1970, the country was, to use the pun of Rafael Leiva Vivas, "*un país en honduras*"—a country in the depths.

To climb from these depths, it was decided that López Arellano would step down at the end of his term, although he would have dearly loved a new version of *continuismo*, and that a direct election for the presidency, the first since that of Carías Andino in 1932, would be held along with elections to the National Assembly. The two major parties got together and agreed that although the presidency would be actually contested, the legislative elections would be rigged so as to give equal representation to both parties in the 64-member Assembly. It was further decided that the speaker of the Assembly would be a member of the National Party while the president of the Supreme Court would be a Liberal. There was so little popular faith in the system that only 900,000 voters turned out for the March 1971 contest, which pitted Liberal Jorge Buezo Arias against Nationalist Rámon Ernesto Cruz. Cruz, backed by López, won the election.

The former strongman did not in fact relinquish power entirely. He remained as the chief of the armed forces, which gave him a virtual veto over the actions of the new government. These actions did not please López Arellano very long. The FENAGH was very strong in the National Party, and Cruz was soon persuaded to sack Rigoberto Sandoval Corea from his INA post and to adopt a go-slow policy toward land reform. Now that most of the Salvadoreans were gone (80,000 having been expelled in 1970), the contest over the land was between Hondurans and increasingly bitter. The Liberals of Modesto Rodas Alvarado also broke their pact of cooperation and began to use this peasant discontent to challenge the Cruz government. There was gross fiscal mismanagement, and the president's wife became involved in a scandal concerning the national lottery. Further, Cruz himself violated the pact with the Liberals by appointing Nationals to the Supreme Court. Not liking the drift of events, López Arellano launched a bloodless military coup on 3 December 1972, overthrowing the National Party government after a scant 20 months in office. It was the fourth coup since 1954.

One reason for the failure of the Cruz government was the poor performance of the economy. Between 1970 and 1973, the gross national product rose by only 6.2 percent in total and while exports were up 18 percent in 1972, the value of imports had risen by 37 percent, deepening the balance-of-payments crisis that had been ongoing through the sixties.[12] When López Arellano took over the second time, he began to remedy this by encouraging domestic industry and by encouraging such export crops as sugar. By the mid-seventies, Honduras was doing a good business in sugar with several of its Central American neighbors. It was also helped by aid from the United States, which decided to concentrate on aid to the very poorest Latin American countries. And despite the disastrous Hurricane Fifi, of 19 and 20 September 1974, the country began to make satisfactory economic progress.

The hurricane in fact had certain positive results, despite the fact that it killed an estimated 10,000 Hondurans. The large landholders abandoned many of the lands devastated by the storm and a few were only too happy to see them turned over to INA, now once again under Sandoval, for redistribution with compensation. This gave López an opportunity to build up a constituency of his own among the *campesinos*. In January 1975, the government issued Decree 170, a new Land Reform Act designed to distribute 600,000 hectares (about 1.5 million acres) among 120,000 families over the space of about five years. It provided a sliding scale, depending on the value of the land, for how much a single individual could hold, but in no case was this to be more than 500 hectares. The London newsletter *Latin America* hailed this as "the most significant development in a decade" and called it a "brave and bold course" for the government to take.[13]

While some landholders were anxious to part with hurricane-damaged holdings, others were not; and FENAGH, headed by Fernando Lardizábal, was prepared to resist land expropriations by force of arms. The *Consejo Hondureño de la Empresa Privada* (COHEP) also denounced land reform. The struggle was particularly vicious in Olancho, a huge and remote province in the central part of the country that is larger than the entire country of El Salvador. Local landholders there had long maintained a feudal structure, keeping private armies and using terror against the peasants, often in cooperation with local authorities. On the peasant side, the church-backed UNC was more active than ANACH. Members of the UNC boldly seized 108 haciendas in anticipation of their expropriation by INA. Thereupon, the commandant of Olancho, Maj. José Enrique Chinchilla, mounted a bloody attack upon the UNC on behalf of the landholders. He and a group of FENAGH vigilantes rounded up a bunch of UNC peasant leaders and two missionary priests, one a North Amercan and one a Colombian, who were aiding the *campesinos*. They took them to a large baking oven and gave the peasant leaders a choice of being castrated or baked alive in the oven. They all chose the latter and died horribly. The priests were given no choice and received both treatments.[14] In fairness to the government of Honduras, it should be noted that Major Chinchilla and one of his sergeants were duly tried, convicted, and imprisoned for this crime. Nevertheless, it illustrated the lengths to which some land-holders would go in order to block reform.

By the time of the Olancho atrocity, López Arellano was no longer in power. He owed his demise to a bizarre series of events involving the banana industry. In February 1974, the representatives of most of the banana-exporting countries had met and formed the *Unión de Países Exportadores de Banano*, dedicated to getting a higher return from the foreign corporations. It was agreed that each nation would substantially hike its export duties, by, in the case of Honduras, 50¢ a crate. This charge duly went into effect on 25 April 1974, in spite of protests from the fruit companies and from Washington. Despite its potential effects upon operations, the tax was hailed by SIT-RASFCO leader Napoleón Acevedo Granados as a method of increasing revenues.

United Fruit had recently been taken over by the wily Eli Black, who had changed the name of the firm to United Brands. Black now began to maneuver behind the scenes, and the government mysteriously canceled the tax on 24 August 1974. A U.S. Senate probe into the activities of multi-nationals, brought on by events in Chile, soon solved the mystery. Black was reported to have paid $1.25 million to Economcs Minister Abraham Bennaton Ramos, and smaller sums to other Honduran politicos, including President López. Black's replied by throwing himself out of his twenty-fifth-story office window in New York on 3 February 1975, leaving López Arellano holding the bag. The inevitable coup soon followed. On 31 March 1975, the senior officers of the army politely overthrew López Arellano. The man who as-sumed the presidency of the military junta, and became therefore chief of state, was Col. Juan Alberto Melgar Castro. Portly and dark complexioned, he was a man of the people, having risen from an impressed private through the ranks to colonel. Although linked to the National Party, he had opposed the frauds used in the election of March 1968, when he commanded the northern zone at San Pedro Sula. He had been, for a time, minister of justice and of the interior under López and just after the banana scandal broke, he replaced him as armed-forces commander in chief. During his period as head of state, he cultivated his popular image, walking without guards around the streets of the capital and chatting with the common people.

Although Melgar was running the government, he was not running the army. The new commander in chief, Policarpo Paz García, presided over the army's policy-making group, the *Consejo Superior de las Fuerzas Armadas* (CONSUFA), composed of 25 senior officers. CONSUFA played an important role in government decisions. It was a sign of Melgar's weakness that he was forced to give up the role of commander in chief.

Like many self-made men, Melgar had little real feeling for the land hunger of the peasants. Listening to the voice of FENAGH, he followed a go-slow policy in the implementation of Decree 170. This led to protests from the UNAH and from the Peasant Front, an umbrella group covering ANACH and the UNC along with other smaller movements, such as the *Ligas Agrarias del Sur* (based in Choluteca) and the *Ligas Agrarias de Oriente* (in El Paraíso), and comprising in total some 150,000 peasants. The front issued an ultimatum to the government in October 1975, in the wake of the Olancho massacre: implement Decree 170 at once or face a *campesino* revolt. Melgar responded by returning Sandoval Corea to INA, and Sandoval remained as its head until March 1977. He had an uphill fight. The powerful *Asociación de Ganaderos y Agricultores del Valle de Sula* (AGAS) denounced Sandoval and his superior, Labor Minister Enrique Flores Valeriano, as "sympathetic to communism." Whereupon, Sandoval responded by calling those in AGAS "enemies of social change and social justice."[15]

The focus of agrarian discontent came to be the commune of Isletas on the north coast. Originally a plantation of Standard Fruit, it had been abandoned after Hurricane Fifi, and a group of *campesinos*, rendered unemployed by the storm, had moved in, encouraged by SITRASFCO. INA aided them to establish themselves as an agricultural unit, but the attitude of the government toward these squatters was ambiguous. The American Institute for Free Labor Development (AIFLD), an inter-American agency sponsored by the AFL-CIO and backed with U.S. government funds, also took an interest in the Isletas project, but, in its murky fashion, became so involved in the intrigues of the peasant leadership that it was hard to determine whether AIFLD intended to aid or to destroy the project.[16] Dissensions among the *campesinos* over the role of INA and AIFLD led to a military intervention by the Melgar government, which invaded the commune on 12 February 1977. The National University, the bastion of the more socialist-minded members of the Liberal Party, took an active part in aiding the nine peasant leaders jailed by the government, through the university's union, SITRAUNAH (*Sindical de Trabajadores de UNAH*). This incident helped to bring about the resignation of Sandoval the following month.

Besides Sandoval's resignation, there were other signs that the government was moving to the right. In January 1977, Col. César Elvir Sierra, a reformer, was removed from his post as chief of staff of the army and replaced by Col. Mario Cárcamo Chinchilla, former defense minister, who was succeeded in that post by Col. Omar Antonio Zelaya Reyes. Flores Valeriano, long a target of FENAGH and AGAS, also was forced to resign in January as labor minister and was replaced by Alberto Discua. These changes represented a shift to a more conservative course,[17] presided over by Secretary of the Presidency César A. Batres, an aristocrat and law partner of Alberto Discua, who had the ear of Melgar Castro. Finance Minister Porfirio Zavala Sandoval was the main figure on the economic front of the government, and he, along with Batres, steered the government toward a successful economic policy. Exports increased and the image of Honduras as a perennially poverty-stricken land began to be erased.

But the military regime held politics in abeyance. The handsome National Assembly building, constructed in the seventies, had been empty since 1976 when the last Assembly was turned out of office. Elections were postponed until April 1980. There was also growing evidence that when they did come, they would only serve to legitimize the rule of Melgar Castro, whose smiling face began to appear in photos everywhere. Socially looked down upon by many officers and regarded with suspicion by National Party leader Ricardo Zúñinga, Melgar by July 1978, was beginning to feel the rumbles of discontent.

The Liberal Party had long been in disarray. Modesto Rodas Alvarado was the secretary general; but an important faction, the Popular Alliance (ALIPO), was headed by UNAH rector Jorge Arturo Reina and his brother, the distinguished jurist, Carlos Roberto Reina. Another faction was led by Jorge Buezo Arias, the party's candidate in the 1970 election. But in July 1978, the Liberal Party held a convention, cemented itself together, and made its internal workings more democratic, clearly hoping that it would have an election to contest. Two other political groups also began to emerge, the *Partido de Inovación y Unidad* (PINU), headed by businessman Miguel Andonie, and the Christian Democrats (PDCH). These new parties also hoped to participate in the future election, although the PDCH lacked *personería jurídica*.

The discontent in the country was fueled by a series of scandals among the ruling officer elite. In December 1977, the Ferraris, a man and wife implicated in the activities of the Mafia in Honduras, were kidnapped and later found murdered. Manuel Gamero, editor of *El Tiempo*, the influential Liberal daily, declared that he had tapes of conversations implicating high-ranking officers in the drug traffic and Ferrari murders. He was arrested and detained for several days in June 1978 on grounds he was suppressing evidence, but he was then released, and his evidence was not made public. There were allegations in the Liberal press as well that Lt. Col. Juan Angel Arias, the minister of the interior, had been paid off by Standard Fruit to protect their interests when he commanded the garrisons at La Ceiba, while the Honduran Interpol chief, Lt. Juan Angel Barahona charged that Paz García, a hero of the war of 1969 and now commander in chief, was linked to the Mafia and the drug traffic. It was pointed out that Colonel Paz was coowner of a hacienda with Ramón Matta, the country's reputed Mafia boss.

Perhaps the last straw was the fact that preparations for the long-delayed Assembly elections, and especially the registration of voters, seemed to be grinding to a halt. They had been put under the charge of Zavala Sandoval, who appeared to be deliberately sabotaging the process, perhaps with an eye to forcing still another postponement to further entrench Melgar in power.

But it was not to be, for on the evening of 7 August 1978, the Melgar government was overthrown in a bloodless coup. Indeed, it was not even officially referred to as a coup, but only as a "change in the government." Melgar Castro was said to have resigned; and only César Batres had the courage to announce what had really happened, for which he was forced to sever all connections with the new government. The leaders of the coup were Commander in Chief Policarpo Paz García, air force commander Lt. Col. Domingo Alvarez, and national police commander Lt. Col. Amílcar Zelaya Rodríguez; but behind them and supporting the coup were López Arellano, who managed to be out of the country for the event, as he had been in 1971, and Ricardo Zúñiga, the secretary general of the National Party. César Elvir Sierra, the deposed army chief of staff, was said to have provided the link between the soldiers and the National Party.

A three-man junta was set up, composed of the three leaders of the coup, with Paz García taking the role of chief of state and president of the junta. He defended his coup on the grounds that progress toward elections had been impeded by Zavala Sandoval and that Melgar was trying to create a permanent dictatorship, but cynics wondered if he had not acted to forestall further embarrassing revelations of his own involvement in the organized crime endemic to Honduras. In any event, thanks chiefly to César Batres, he had inherited a country on the economic upswing, a banana republic in the process of transforming itself into a diversified exporter of agricultural products, minerals, and industrial goods.

NOTES

1. William H. Durham, *Scarcity and Survival in Central America: Ecological Origins of the Soccer War* (Stanford, Calif.: Stanford University Press, 1979), p. 112.
2. J. Mayone Stycos and Cornell Capa, *Margin of Life: Population and Poverty in the Americas* (New York: Grossman, 1974), p. 9.
3. William S. Stokes, *Honduras: A Case Study in Government* (Madison: University of Wisconsin Press, 1950), pp. 44-45, 209-14.
4. Ibid., pp. 56-57; John Martz, *Central America: The Crisis and the Challenge* (Chapel Hill: University of North Carolina Press, 1959), p. 122.
5. Eddy Jiménez, *La Guerra no Fue de Fútbol* (Havana: Casa de las Americas, 1974), p. 91.
6. Durham, *Scarcity and Survival*, pp. 110-15.
7. Rafael Leiva Vivas, *Un País en Honduras* (Tegucigalpa: Emprenta Calderon, 1969), p. 12.
8. Jiménez, *La Guerra*, p. 91.

9. Stycos and Capa, *Margin of Life*, pp. 9, 115-16.

10. Marco Virgilio Carías, Daniel Slutzky, et al., *La Guerra Inutil: Analisis socioeconomico del conflicto entre Honduras y El Salvador* (San José: EDUCA, 1971), pp. 62-63.

11. Stycos and Capa, *Margin of Life*, pp. 122-23.

12. Edmundo Valades, *Los Contratos del Diablo: las concesiones bananeras en Honduras y Centroamerica* (Mexico City: Editores Asociados, 1975), pp. 50-52.

13. *Latin America*, 17 January 1975.

14. *Latin America*, 18 July 1975, 7 May 1976.

15. *Latin America*, 3 December 1976.

16. *Latin America Political Report*, 28 April 1978.

17. *Latin America Political Report*, 21 January 1977.

9

Honduras: From Coup to Election

Despite some progress, the country which Gen. Paz García took over was by no means wealthy. Its per capita income of $569.50 remained the lowest among the Central American states, thanks to a 3.7 percent annual population growth rate, although the rate of growth of the national income in 1977-78 was 12.5 percent, the highest in the region. Also highest in the region for those years was the actual growth of the gross domestic product, 7.9 percent, and the gross formation of fixed capital was an impressive 16.8 percent. One reason for the burst of prosperity was the high price of coffee, 1.4 million *quintales* of which were harvested in 1978.[1] The question was: Could the Paz government continue to move in a positive economic direction?

Also in question was the idea of returning to some sort of constitutional rule, after so many years of military dictatorship. Elections were tentatively scheduled for April 1980 and everyone wondered if Policarpo Paz would in fact go through with them. Given his reputation for dubious dealings, it was felt that there might either be no elections or that the elections to the Constituent Assembly would be arranged so that Paz himself would be chosen president.

While Melgar Castro had been closer to the Nationals than to the Liberals, he had not really been identified with any party, and this fact had been a partial cause of his downfall. Paz now introduced three members of the National Party into his cabinet. To replace Batres as secretary of the presidency in the new cabinet, he chose Gustavo Acosta Mejía, a choice that did not help the protracted negotiations with El Salvador, for he was widely regarded as a bitter enemy of that country. As his unofficial advisor, the chief of the junta chose Ricardo Zúñiga, the National Party boss, who was also close to López Arellano. Among the five ministers sacked was Col. Erick O'Conner, the minister of culture, who had been promoting Melgar for the role of elected president. Oddly enough, Porfirio Zavala Sandoval, the finance minister, who had been so criticized for his organization of the 1980 election process, was retained, as were Benjamín Villaneuva Mejía, of the economics ministry, and Roberto Palma Gálvez, the long-term foreign minister.

Col. Palma Gálvez however was not long destined to keep his job. He resigned on 6 July 1979, because of the Nicaraguan question, which was taking on increasing importance in Honduran domestic politics. Both Honduras and Costa Rica border upon troubled Nicaragua; but Costa Rica, a stable democracy, had little to fear from any Nicaraguan subversive influence. Honduras, on the contrary, with its corrupt and unstable regimes of rightist officers, offered a constant temptation to the Sandinistas. Prior to the victory of the Sandinista movement in Nicaragua, on 19 July 1979, the Honduran military had been deeply divided, with the senior officers generally supporting Somoza and the younger ones favoring the FSLN. The government was also divided on the issue, though Paz personally favored Somoza, as did the National Party. Palma Gálvez was sent at the end of June 1979 to a meeting of the Organization of American States in Washington, called to discuss the Nicaraguan crisis. There, having no clear instructions, he followed his own leanings and appeared to favor the resolution of the Andean Pact countries, demanding Somoza's resignation. But just before the vote on the resolution was taken, he received a dispatch telling him to vote with Guatemala and El Salvador, two Somoza supporters, against the resolution. He then promptly resigned, declaring that his government had put him "in a ridiculous position."[2] Eliseo Pérez Cadalso, the former ambassador to Mexico, replaced him. This served to stall once more the negotiations for resuming normal relations with El Salvador. Relations with the new Nicaraguan government soon became quite strained. Two aides of Ricardo Wheelock, the Nicaraguan ambassador, were beaten by police in Tegucigalpa; and Col. Erick O'Conner was expelled from his post in Managua. At the core of the problem were the estimated 3,000 former members of the Somoza *Guardia* who had fled to Honduras and were believed to be making mischief for Nicaragua, with the aid of the Honduran army.

Another shakeup which occurred in the same month was the replacement of the youngest and reputedly most reform-minded member of the junta, José Domingo Alvarez, by the then ambassador to Guatemala, Col. Oscar Colindres Corrales. This suggested that the Paz government might be turning still more to the right.

But the signals were unclear, for in November of that year, the government infuriated COHEP, the private-enterprise lobby, by announcing a substantial rise in taxes. The income tax was to be raised from a range of 3 to 44 percent to a range of 6 to 55 percent. Further, sales taxes, which in a peasant economy are paid chiefly by the middle and upper classes, were raised from 3 to 6 percent. COHEP leader Gustavo Alfaro derisively referred to this as the government's "Christmas present" to the Honduran people, and demanded that the government broaden credits to the private sector.

One way in which the conservatism of the government did indeed show was in its go-slow approach to land reform. Víctor Inocencio Peralta, the secretary general of the church-backed UNC, declared in October 1978 that only 15 percent of the 600,000 hectares projected under the agrarian-reform plan of 1974-78 had actually been distributed to the peasantry. Further, Paz, like Melgar before him, imprisoned a number of peasants who tried to invade estates or who presented their demands too forcefully. In September 1978, more than 400 such peasants were being held.[3] The various *campesino* organizations, including UNC and ANACH, had formed a *Frente de Unidad Nacional Campesina de Honduras* (FUNANCAMPH), which, in November of that year, called for and forced the resignation of Fabio David Salgado, the head of the INA, because of his corruption. But not all the corruption and favoritism was outside the peasant movement. A missionary priest, James Carney Handley, called for a shakeup of the leadership of ANACH, whose chief, Reyes Rodríguez Arévalo, was a friend of Paz García; and for his pains, the priest was expelled from the country in November 1979. This caused students from the National University to occupy the cathedral of Tegucigalpa in December, as a protest.[4]

Policarpo Paz García continued to deny that agrarian reform had halted or was being sabotaged by the government. Early in 1980, he declared, in a speech made in New York, that the reform had merely paused "for consolidation," going on to say, "We realize that agrarian reform is not a matter of parceling out lands to peasants but also involves technical assistance and credit." To back up this sort of talk, the government embarked upon a $20-million rural development plan for the department of Ocotepeque, hard hit by war with El Salvador, and whose population had been steadily moving away to San Pedro Sula and the north coast, where work was more plentiful. The money was to be chiefly used for agricultural education.[5]

There may well have been something in the government's contention that a period of consolidation was necessary, but the peasantry could not see it, and FUNANCAMPH launched a series of land seizures in February and March 1980. In the middle of the latter month, the leader of this *campesino* organization, Francisco Ramos, declared that 6,000 hectares had been seized and that these seizures would go on until the land-reform program was revived.[6] For the most part, the *tomas* were not marked by great violence, the leader of the junta not wanting to damage his future presidential possibilities by arousing too greatly such an important sector; but there continued to be some arrests.

It was not only the land problem that continued to give the government trouble with the masses. Labor, both urban and rural, was also on the warpath. The basic reason was the rapid rise in the cost of living, up 25 percent annually between 1975 and the beginning of 1979. March 1979 saw a large and violent strike among the textile workers in San Pedro Sula, in which three strikers were killed by the police. The government charged that professional communist agitators were trying to stir up trouble and block the promised return to constitutional rule by creating anarchy.[7] October of the same year was the most strike-prone month in some years, with a massive strike of 14,000 sugarcane workers in the middle of the harvest. The workers, belonging to the CGT, declared that their contracts were not being fulfilled. Because of its timing, the strike was successful in not merely restoring past gains, but in getting higher salary arrangements and better benefits. At the same time, in the middle of a banana-harvesting period, 6,000 workers of SITRATERCO struck United Brands, casually leaving 100,000 crates of bananas to rot on the docks. The public health workers were also out during October; and there were rumbles of a strike at the Texaco refinery, the only refinery in the country, and at Standard Fruit.[8]

The United Brands strike dragged on into the new year, and on 12 February, SITRASFCO joined in by striking Standard. The upshot was that large gains were made by labor, SITRATERCO accepting a 66 percent percent wage hike, over three years, from United Brands. Even this amount disappointed some radicals within the union who wanted an 80 percent increase.

Still another problem of the Paz government was its reputation for unbridled corruption. Corruption in Honduran politics had always been an art, but Paz and his cronies made it into a systematic science. Particularly important was the role of certain prominent officers in the narcotics trade, where they were linked to the flourishing Honduran Mafia. In addition, almost every conceivable project was milked for kickbacks and graft. Prominent officers drove a Mercedes and their wives flaunted expensive jewels. This tended to bring the army and the Nationals into disrepute.

While worker and *campesino* restiveness and changes of corruption caused concern within the government, the problem which overshadowed all others was that of preparing for the elections of 20 April 1980. The two traditional parties—the Nationals of Ricardo Zúñiga, and the Liberals under Secretary General Roberto Suazo Córdova, who had succeeded the late Modesto Rodas Alvarado and followed his ideas—were both preparing strong campaigns, although the Liberals still suffered from internal splits, particularly that between Suazo's moderate forces, known as the *Movimiento Nacional Rodista* (MNR), and the leftist *Alianza Popular*. Suazo Córdova was generally regarded as a weak leader in ill health, who had come to power almost accidentally upon the sudden death of Rodas. PINU, the middle-class, businessmen's party of Miguel Andonie, also had legal status, since December

1979, and was preparing to field candidates. But there were other groups not so fortunate. The Chrisitian Democratic Party of Honduras (PDCH)—led by its secretary general, Hernán Corrales Padilla—was debarred from participating, under the electoral law of 1 January 1978, because it received part of its funding from abroad—in particular, from the oil-rich Christian Democrats of Venezuela. This was felt by many to be a mere quibble and simply a means of cutting off from the election a party that might have made great inroads into the strength of the two traditional groups. Also debarred by the same law was the *Partido Comunista de Honduras* (PCH), on the grounds that it was a party contrary to the "democratic spirit of the Honduran people."[9] This party, now led by Secretary General Rigoberto Padilla Rush, was quite small and not likely to do well in an election, anyway. Two other small parties similarly excluded were the *Partido Revolucionario* (PR) and the *Partido Socialista* (PS).

The United States, working through Ambassador Mari-Luci Jaramillo, was very anxious for the elections to be held, and for them to be honest. To encourage these desirable results, the North Americans began to lavish aid upon Honduras, giving the military alone $500,000 and promising ten times that amount after the elections. In a statement to the U.S. Congress in September 1979, Viron Vaky of the State Department explained that Honduras would be part of the plan to "contain the Nicaraguan revolution," which caused columnist Jack Anderson to remark that Honduras was to be "our new Nicaragua."[10]

That the elections would be held appeared quite possible; that they would be honest was another question. There seemed little doubt that Policarpo Paz wanted things arranged so that the National Party would win. Then, either the Constituent Assembly would name him president, or it would postpone the choosing of a president for a direct popular election at some future date and leave the chief of state in power until that time. But there were several problems with this scenario. First, there was the U.S. embassy pressure for a clean contest. Secondly, there were the ambitions of Ricardo Zúñiga himself, who also wanted to be either chosen president by the Assembly or elected to that office. Thirdly, there were deep divisions in the army, where many officers distrusted Paz and resented his ambitions.

Within the military, there were, as has been noted in dealing with the question of Nicaraguan relations, two major factions. The conservative, anti-Sandinista group of generally senior officers was led by the chief of military intelligence, Col. Leonidas Torres Arias, a friend of Anastasio Somoza. On the other side were younger, leftist officers. Some of these were said to belong to a secret group known as the *Organización Secreta de Oficiales Subalternos* (OSOS), or "the bears" (for there is a longstanding tradition of giving animal names to such factions). These leftist officers accused the government of corruption and were convinced this would carry over into the conduct of elections. They were on close terms with the *Alianza Popular* and with the

PDCH, which had formed a *Frente Nacional Patriótica* (FNP), and was threatening to boycott the election if the legal right of the PDCH to participate was not recognized. The military leftists were so convinced that fraud was inevitable that they first joined the above mentioned parties in petitioning Paz to delay them, and, when that failed, evidently decided upon a coup as the only solution. Like the young soldiers in El Salvador, they are said to have presented their plan for a coup, in February 1980, to the U.S. ambassador. The ambassador evidently dissuaded them, encouraging them to, instead, enter into a dialogue with the influential "hard-liner," Col. Gustavo Alvarez, who commanded the northern district.[11] The best way to stave off a coup was to insure honest elections, and the embassy now redoubled its pressure in that direction, evidently with a good effect.

Another factor that might have influenced the desire to hold a relatively clean contest was the general unrest in the country. There were disturbances between troops and peasants, in January, in Comayagua; in Macuelizo, located in Santa Barbara; and in Mosquitia. In March, 100 employees on strike against Cervecería Hondureña were arrested by the military, which led to student protests at UNAH.

During the last few weeks of the electoral campaign, the two wings of the Liberal Party managed to patch up their differences, the *Alianza Popular* agreeing that it would now, after all, participate, although not all members agreed; and it was too late for ALIPO to enter candidates. Thus, 1.3 million registered voters could go to the polls to choose between the Liberals, the Nationals, and PINU, although most outside observers thought that the National Party was sure to win.[12] The extreme leftists were so certain that the elections could only damage the creditability of the government that a group of them announced, beforehand, the formation of a guerrilla movement called the *Frente Morazanista para la Liberación de Honduras* (FMLH), which was to begin operations as soon as the "electoral farce" was over.[13] The radical-leftist *Partido Revolucionario de Trabajadores Centroamericanos* (PRTC) even sought to disrupt the election itself by bombings and by the kidnapping of Texaco executive Arnold Quirós in San Pedro Sula.

Most were shocked, and many were disappointed, when the elections came off fairly cleanly and with great public enthusiasm, the people boasting that while El Salvador and Guatemala might be in turmoil, Hondurans still knew how to settle things with ballots rather than bullets. Of the registered voters, an impressive 80 percent actually voted (see Table 9.1). The proof of the relative honesty of the contest was that the Liberals gained a large plurality of the votes. The Liberals claimed that this was despite the fact that the Nationals had used the military to intimidate voters. The PN, on the other hand, charged that PL and PINU poll watchers had teamed up to throw out some 10,000 PN supporters. Early indications on 22 April showed the Liberals ahead of the Nationals by 57,000 votes, and the *New York Times* of that date announced that they were assured a six- or seven-seat majority in the

Population, Honduras, 1971 and 1980 Elections

Department	Number of Registered Voters 1971[a]	Percent Voting 1971[a]	Number of Registered Voters 1979[b]	Percent Voting 1980[b]	Percent of Estimated Population Voting 1971/1974	Percent of Estimated Population Voting 1980[c]
Atlántida	42,483	82.8	64,329	77.4	21.7	23.9
Colón	20,262	52.4	32,617	72.1	12.6	27.9
Comayagua	48,468	65.8	72,766	82.6	21.5	32.5
Copán	52,966	68.2	75,606	85.7	21.9	33.1
Cortes	98,915	66.3	183,372	82.1	16.2	27.9
Choluteca	72,124	72.9	27,211	81.6	25.1	25.2
El Paraíso	55,284	66.8	71,998	81.4	24.0	31.8
Francisco Morazán	144,683	73.4	189,631	82.6	21.5	24.6
Gracias a Dios	3,775	63.0	6,519	67.1	10.3	14.3
Intibucá	33,557	72.2	37,411	83.8	27.2	30.8
Islas de la Babia	4,475	65.4	6,324	76.2	26.3	28.7
La Paz	27,755	69.8	33,429	87.7	27.1	36.8
Lempira	59,062	65.7	58,218	84.5	27.9	29.7
Ocotepeque	23,051	63.9	28,070	85.6	26.4	39.7
Olancho	53,091	62.3	73,351	79.7	20.1	29.0
Santa Barbara	48,813	57.8	91,470	84.9	24.1	30.6
Valle	35,804	63.1	37,195	82.5	22.8	27.0
Yoro	61,096	61.6	91,939	78.5	17.7	27.5
	900,158	68.2	1,233,756	81.4	21.2	27.9

[a]Data obtained from archives/files of the Tegucigalpa office of *El Tiempo*.

[b]Data were not available for the number of registered voters for each department on the day of the election. The 1979 data are from material published by the Tribunal Nacional de Elecciones in the Tegucigalpa office of *Tiempo*. Because of charges by officials of all three registered parties, that the other parties were registering fraudulent voters, various municipal and departmental voting lists were purged so that the final registered total of voters for the 20 April 1980 election was reduced to 1,003,680.

[c]The percentage figure for 1980 voting is calculated by dividing the actual number of persons voting into the number of voters listed by the tribunal as being eligible in 1980.

Source: Neale J. Pearson, "Honduras: The Impact of the 1980 Constituent Assembly Elections," unpublished, 1981.

129

Constituent Assembly. This proved overly sanguine, as the Nationals edged a little closer, getting, in a nearly final tally, 426,622 votes (42.2 percent) to 496,787 (49.4 percent) for the Liberals, and a dismal 35,052 (3.5 percent) for PINU. Nevertheless, it was chiefly to the advantage of this last party that the electoral system worked, for PINU ended with three seats in the Assembly. As the Liberals had 35 and the Nationals 33, this meant that the tiny PINU held the balance of power in the 71-member body.[14] Ambassador Jaramillo declared herself to be very pleased at the election results. Others were less pleased, especially some in the business community, which had prospered under the stability of three successive military regimes and was concerned lest the politicos might be unable to govern effectively. Thus a massive capital flight, estimated at $60-100 million, was an immediate result of the election.[15]

As expected, the political infighting began as soon as the results of the balloting were clear. The leaders of the three legal parties, Ricardo Zúñiga, Roberto Suazo Córdova, and Miguel Andonie Fernández, met with Col. Gustavo Alvarez and other officers, representing the interests of the military, in order to divide control of the ministries in the provisional government which was now to be established. Both of the major parties wanted the key ministries of finance, economics, and public works. PINU, fearing that it would be left with the dregs, walked out of the meeting, but eventually everything was patched up—on the surface, at least—with Miguel Andonie's brother, Juan, of the PL, becoming minister of health. In the provisional cabinet, there would be nine persons selected by the Constituent Assembly. There would also be five persons appointed by the Superior Military Council and they, not the civilian appointees, would hold most of the vital posts. While military men actually held only the ministries of foreign relations and defense, under Col. César Elvir Sierra and Col. Mario Flores Theresin, respectively, their other appointments, which went to PN sympathizers, gave the army control of public works, finance, and economic planning. Thus, as César Batres commented to this writer, the army would control the ministry that collected money, the one that dispensed most of it, and all the guns. Further, since Elvir and Flores were also PN sympathizers, that party had nine seats, to five for the Liberals. An officer, Col. Manuel Enrique Suárez, was to retain the directorship of INA. The Liberal leader, Suazo Córdova, was made president of the Constituent Assembly while other posts in the legislative body were to be divided.[16] These points being settled, the former military cabinet resigned on 20 July. About the same time, the Supreme Court was also reorganized to include five PL members, three PN members, and one judge from PINU. Further, the PN domination of the election tribunal was ended when Ubodoro Arriaga Irahete replaced the irascible PN leader Virgilio Gálvez.

Before the election, the National Party had been so certain of victory that it had proposed that the legislative body itself should choose the new president, for which there was ample precedent. Afterward, however, both the Nationals and PINU began clamoring for a direct presidential election, which the Liberals had already accepted as a condition of ALIPO's participation. The Nationals also did an about-face in regard to the legal registration of both the PDCH and the PCH, parties they now wished to legalize in the interests of democratic pluralism. Lest it be thought that this was pure altruism on the part of the Nationals, they were keenly aware that both the Christian Democrats and the Communist Party were likely to draw off support from the Liberals, rather than from themselves, in a direct presidential election. The legal recognition of the PDCH came in July 1980. Since all parties now agreed on a direct presidential election, it seemed likely that the new president would be chosen in that manner, but that might take a long time to arrange, and new legislative elections would probably be deferred even longer; so the life of the Constituent Assembly might be anywhere from 18 to 36 months.[17] No one would be more pleased by a long delay than Policarpo Paz García, assuming that he could hold onto his position as chief of state.

In regard to Policarpo Paz, it seems likely that his continuance in power had been one of the conditions under which the military accepted an honest election; but the Assembly declared that he was to be provisional president, as a "gesture of good will" toward the army. This, however, raised a number of constitutional issues. As Paz was to be no longer simply the head man of a junta, but the real president of the country, would he have, like other presidents of Honduras, a veto over the actions of the Assembly? Further, would he now have to take an oath of office as president, and would it be the same oath traditionally taken by presidents, or a special one for a provisional president? The Liberals and PINU, which now seemed to discover a community of interests, declared that, by tradition, a Constituent Assembly was sovereign, and its actions could not be vetoed. This the Assembly finally agreed to, after prolonged debate, on 8 August 1980. However, the National Party leader, Nicolás Cruz Torres, still insisted that legislation would have to go to the president for his promulgation and sanction.[18]

The oath-of-office question was equally sticky. Paz García, at first, sent word to the Assembly that he wanted to take an oath of office and be sworn in as the legitimate provisional president. The Liberals and PINU then used their majority to frame an oath of office which was quite different from that for a regular president and which had various provisions the general would consider insulting, as they made him subordinate to the Assembly. The swearing-in ceremony was scheduled for 31 July, but when the appointed hour arrived, and all the dignitaries were assembled, the oath taker was nowhere to be found. A few hours later, he was located and he then promptly informed the Assembly what it could do with the oath. This represented a severe crisis involving the military, which was plainly still in control. The majority in the Assembly now reversed itself and declared that, as Paz was only provisional president, no oath of office was necessary. All this underscored the bad blood between the Liberals and the army. The Liberals blamed this on the Nationals, who had turned the army against them. But as long as the Liberals and PINU insisted, very properly, if somewhat unrealistically, on maintaining the principle of civilian supremacy, the tension would continue.

Perhaps with the intention of showing the civilian legislature that it still could run its own show, the 30-member *Consejo Militar Superior* decided on a purge, in August 1980, of the ranks of some of the most prominent army officers. Twenty-six senior military men were put on the retired list, including former heads of state López Arellano and Melgar Castro, along with Col. Roberto Palma Gálvez, the former foreign minister. Although most of these men had only nominal duties, they had been drawing full pay and participating in military decisions until this time. Most of those retired represented the more progressive wing of the officer corps, and, therefore, forces hostile to Paz García—a clear indication that Paz was consolidating his position. Further, the Constituent Assembly was not even notified of this purge until after it had taken place.[19]

That all was not well in the country was indicated by the fact that the *Fuerzas de Seguridad Publica* (FUSEP), the national police force, under the defense minister, announced on the first of May that it had seized 11 "terrorists." Among those taken was the radical leftist leader, Carlos Alvarenga. They were accused of various actions to disrupt the elections, including the bombing of a factory in San Pedro Sula, and the Quirós kidnapping. These arrests might be the military's way of warning the leftists that the return to civilian participation in the government did not necessarily mean that they would be free to agitate as they pleased. But the government appeared to have little to fear from leftist radicals in the short run, for, as one of them remarked to Alan Riding, "We're even too underdeveloped to have a revolution."[20]

The peasants might not yet be revolutionary, but they were showing increasing signs of dissatisfaction. The three major groups in FUNAN-CAMPH, the UNC, ANACH, and FECORA, began, shortly after the April election, to demand a new land-reform code to replace the outmoded statutes of the López Arellano years. Such legislation was certainly long overdue, and the achievement of a new agrarian code would go a long way toward boosting the prestige of the Assembly, while failure to do so might give an opening to the revolutionary left.

An indication of massive peasant unrest was the strike of the peasant citrus and palm cooperative in September 1980. These peasants lived on land that had presumably been redistributed, but now they declared that they were little more than "chattels of the state." The UNC and the *Federación de Cooperativistas de la Reforma Agraria* (FECORA) backed the 110,000 strikers who were demanding a raise to $2.50 a day, from the pitiful $1.50 then paid for their work on the cooperatives. The strike lasted 18 days and succeeded in forcing the desired concessions by the government, including, for 1980, a bonus of $2,000 for every *cooperativista*. There was still trouble in the presumed peasant paradise of Isletas as well, with thugs from Standard Fruit and security forces frequently invading the commune to overturn the elected peasant leadership. A labor leader told this writer that one could expect to find 200 to 300 peasant leaders in prison at any one time.

Urban workers and government employees were also showing signs of great restiveness. Twelve thousand striking teachers paraded through the streets of the capital in August 1980, demanding better wages. Such events encouraged the newly formed FMLH, which exploded several bombs in San Pedro Sula, to mar the 15 September, Independence Day, celebration. There were also a number of kidnappings of wealthy Hondurans, attributed by some to Salvadorean guerrillas seeking to raise funds.

Another perennial problem with which the government would have to deal was that of the multinational corporations. These included not only the great banana companies previously mentioned, but also mining, textile, and petroleum interests. A case in point was the dispute with the country's only oil refiner, Texaco, in the fall of 1979. Texaco not only refined this oil for itself, but also sold oil to both Shell and Exxon. In September 1979, Texaco raised the price of the fuel refined in the country, a move which the government branded as illegal. It was known that Colonel Alvarez was backing the position of the refinery, while the military left was opposing the price hikes, pointing out that, according to a survey made by UNAH, Texaco's profits were about $4 million a year on the operation. Many ministers of state were also thought to have been bribed by Texaco. A liberal distribution of bribes might have had something to do with the fact that the government reversed itself early in November and permitted the price hikes. At the same time, Policarpo Paz, angered at the oil refiners, and Colonel Alvarez began negotiations with Ageep Petroleum of Texas, for a second refinery. No sooner had the price hike been declared legal than the Texaco workers went on strike for higher wages.[21]

Rosario Mining Company, which was facing expropriation in Nicaragua, also became the subject of government ire. It was accused of illegally exporting uranium to Europe, Japan, and the United States, from its El Mochito mine in Santa Barbara. In January 1980, the government threatened the company with nationalization, but this was probably an empty threat.

The chief task facing the Constituent Assembly was that of drafting a bill of rights and a new constitution. Among provisions discussed were easier regulations for the registration of political parties, for although the PDCH had been legalized soon after the elections, the PCH, the PS, and the PR remained outside the fold. The Constituent Assembly was also said to be discussing constitutional provisions on the relationship of the army to the state. As far as the latter was concerned, it seemed likely that the military would emerge with all its *fueros* (or privileges and exemptions) intact.

The constitution would be the fifteenth in the country's history, indicating that Honduran constitutions can be expected, on the average, to last a little over a decade. Stability and continuity in the government will therefore quite likely remain major problems. Without continuity, it will be almost impossible to carry out such long-term projects as land reform. But stability in itself cannot be a goal, as the United States found in dealing with the regime of the PCN in El Salvador. The government of Honduras must be willing to act to benefit its people, in this most impoverished of all the nations on the American continents.

Since July 1979, the leaders of Honduras have felt the heat of the Nicaraguan revolution. And the success or failure of the revolution in Nicaragua might have a great deal to do with future events in Honduras. If the Nicaraguans prosper, while the traditional Honduran parties regress to their usual self-serving practices, the chances of the revolution spilling over along the lengthy border with Nicaragua are considerable. There are even certain elements in the Honduran military who would welcome a Nicaraguan solution to the problems of their country. Of course, there are other soldiers who would fight the revolution to the death.

The present problems and the past history of the country suggest that it might be foolish for the United States to be too enthusiastic in touting Honduras as a new showpiece of democracy. The army still ruled Honduras after the April 1980 election and probably would have a strong say in the government and exercise a strong inhibiting influence for some time to come, whether or not a civilian sits in Tegucigalpa's grotesque presidential palace.

NOTES

1. *Central America Reports*, 17 September, 10 December 1979.
2. *Central America Reports*, 16 July 1979.
3. *Latin America Political Report*, 1 September, 20 October 1978.
4. *This Week Central America and Panama*, 3 December 1980; *Latin America Weekly Report*, 4 January 1980.
5. *This Week Central America and Panama*, 28 January, 3 March 1980.
6. *This Week Central America and Panama*, 17 March 1980.
7. *Latin America Political Report*, 16 March 1979.
8. *Central America Update*, November 1979; *Central America Reports*, 19 November 1979.
9. Neale J. Pearson, "Honduras," *Yearbook on International Communist Affairs* (Stanford, Calif.: Hoover Institution Press, 1979), pp. 360-61.
10. *Latin America Political Report*, 14 September 1979; *Latin America Update*, March/April 1980.
11. *Latin America Weekly Report*, 14 March 1980.
12. *This Week Central America and Panama*, 11 February, 28 April 1980.
13. *This Week Central America and Panama*, 11 February 1980; *New York Times*, 10 February 1980.
14. *This Week Central America and Panama*, 28 April, 12 May 1980.
15. *Central America Update*, June 1980.
16. *This Week Central America and Panama*, 28 July 1980.
17. *Ibid.*
18. *La Tribuna* (Tegucigalpa), 11 August 1980.

19. *This Week Central America and Panama*, 11 August 1980.

20. *This Week Central America and Panama*, 5 May, 1980; *New York Times*, 8 July 1980.

21. *Latin America Weekly Report*, 9 November 1979; *Central America Reports*, 5 and 19 November 1979.

10

Honduras Analysis:
Illusions of Progress

Honduras is the Tibet of Central America. It has no Indian community, like that of Guatemala, to attract the romantic anthropologist, nor does it present for the political observer the Liliputian charms of El Salvador. Few major studies of its government and society have been done in the last 30 years. As a result, even those close to the scene, such as the officers who wander through the labyrinthian U.S. embassy, are reduced to a series of clichés, most of which are inexact and some of which are entirely off the mark.

High on the list of such clichés is the notion that there is less of a gap between rich and poor than in other Central American countries. It is claimed that the wealth, or, to be more exact, the poverty, is well distributed. But the analyses of William Durham and J. Mayone Stykos suggest that grinding poverty is the lot of most Hondurans, while others live in considerable luxury. A walk through the center of the capital, from the cathedral to the Holiday Inn, reveals shops which sell $30 shirts and $80 shoes, in sizes too small to suggest that they are for tourists. Jewelers offer even more elaborate wares, not only stones and precious metals but also crystal and porcelain. That there are blocks of such stores, in a country with the lowest per capita income of any nation on the American continents, tells us a good deal about the real gap between rich and poor. And it must be remembered that Tegucigalpa is only the dowdy big sister of the country's real capital of wealth and fashion, San Pedro Sula. The poor are equally poor as those of El Salvador, which is to say that they are about as poor as human beings can be and still survive. A peasant leader recently estimated to me that 80,000 families were entirely without land, despite two decades of lip service to land reform. Although theories to the contrary are often conveniently propounded in the lounge of the Hotel Maya, there is a fierce resentment on the part of the poor toward the rich.

This resentment is all the more ominous because Hondurans are not, as the cliché tells us, "peaceful people." They come from the same ethnic background as Salvadoreans and Nicaraguans, and the same legacy of violence. The frequency of violent overturns in Honduran politics, the rampages of the *Mancha Brava* during the 1960s, and the violence of the war with El Salvador all suggest that it would be unwise to count upon the peaceful character of the Honduran people. However, this myth continues even in high places. Paz García proudly announced to his new cabinet, "We are vaccinated against violence."[1]

It is also frequently stated that Honduras is too poor to have a revolution. This is based on the assumption that all revolutions must follow the pattern that Alexis de Tocqueville first saw in the French Revolution—they must be revolutions of rising expectations. But what was happening in 1981 in El Salvador was essentially a revolution of declining expectations—one could no longer get enough food to have even a meager existence; and this may be the source of a revolution in Honduras.

The most misleading and persistent of the clichés regarding Honduras is that the military regime is not repressive. This continues to be believed because the world's press ignores events in Honduras. No one mentions the hundreds of *campesino* leaders in jail or the beatings and disappearances. And even if these things did not go on, as Jorge Arturo Reina put it so well, the poverty of the country is itself a kind of violence perpetrated against the poor. Allowing children to die of hunger is itself a crime. It is true, however, that the military in Honduras uses the glove more frequently than the fist. In 1981 Honduras was about where El Salvador was in 1975. The path of reform is still open, but the door is rapidly closing.

THE POLITICAL SPECTRUM

Since the Nicaraguan revolution, Honduras is the only country in Central America in which the two traditional parties, here called the Liberals and the Nationals, continue to operate. The issues that once divided them are long dead, and they linger on as rather aristocratic clubs of gentlemen playing politics. The Nationals are close to the military, and occupy the extreme legal right of the political spectrum. Their leader, Ricardo Zúñiga Augustinas, is the old fox of Honduran politics, the king maker for Oswaldo López Arellano and still a power in the regime of Policarpo Paz García. Now old, but astute, he is grooming his daughter to be his successor. He candidly told me, in a recent talk, that "the armed forces exercise political power," and he was quite content with that situation.

Roberto Suazo Córdova, who leads the Liberal Party, was propelled into that role by the untimely death of Modesto Rodas Alvarado. But he rivals Hernán Corrales Padilla, the Christian Democratic leader, for the title as the most boring and pedantic speaker in Honduras. Further, his party is rent by faction. The most prominent of these factions is the *Alianza Popular* (ALIPO), whose founder was Carlos Roberto Reina, now a judge in the Inter-American Court of Human Rights in San José. Roberto, as he is known, is still the president of ALIPO, but its real leadership has passed into the hands of his brother, the secretary general of the group, Jorge Arturo Reina, the former rector of the National University. Both of the brothers are extremely intelligent and articulate, but Jorge Arturo, who is some five inches shorter than Roberto, is much more volatile and effusive. Their idea has been to transform the Liberal Party from being "liberal" in the nineteenth-century, European sense of the term to being "liberal" in the way that this term is used in the United States. There was, in 1981, extremely bad blood between Jorge Arturo Reina and Roberto Suazo. The latter told me that Jorge Arturo is a "communist" because he has been to Cuba and his children have been to Russia. This sort of vituperation is rare among Central American politicians, who usually speak well of each other even when plotting assassinations, and suggests the degree of pressure that the official leadership of the party feels from this moderately leftist group. Nevertheless, the goals of ALIPO are extremely modest, considering the magnitude of the problems which Honduras faces. Suazo Córdova, fearing ALIPO may grow in strength, has been pushing for early national electons while he still controls the machinery of his party.

As in Guatemala, the Christian Democrats, newly endowed with *personería jurídica*, occupy the center of the political spectrum. They remain small and poorly organized for want of a dynamic leader. Corrales Padilla certainly lacks the appeal of José Napoleón Duarte in El Salvador and seems bent on not rocking the boat. But there are young Turks in the party and they might transform the movement into a true opposition party. Nudging the PDCH for room in the center is PINU, the brainchild of Miguel Andonie, a wealthy business leader of Arabic descent. Although it is essentially a middle-of-the-road party, PINU had the good sense to draw a third of its candidates in the April 1980 elections from the ranks of the peasantry; and one of these, the able Julio Méndez, won election to the Constituent Assembly. PINU blamed its generally poor showing in that election on the campaign against voting conducted by the PDCH; but, such squabbles aside, the two parties might well band together, possibly bringing in ALIPO as well, in a coalition similar to that of the UNO in El Salvador during the seventies. Such a coalition might be a viable loyal opposition to the PL and the PN and give the voters a real choice in the intended presidential elections.

That no party to the left of center had even gained legal recognition, as of January 1981, says something about the boasted political freedom of Honduras. Such parties as did exist were small and poor. The *Partido Revolucionario*, despite its imposing title, was hardly revolutionary, being modeled on Social Democratic parties like that of Costa Rica. The *Partido Socialista*, however, was made up of genuine radicals and might, at some future date, present a challenge to the existing order.

Outside the regular spectrum of political parties, there were growing movements of both the left and the right. The Central American Workers' Party was busy organizing, and occasionally, as at the Independence Day celebrations in San Pedro Sula, displaying its ability to disrupt society. A Coordinating Committee of Solidarity with the People of El Salvador, linked to the FDR, had also been formed, and, because of the long border, was able to offer substantial aid to the Salvadorean guerrillas. In November 1980, 25 leftists seized the Red Cross office in Tegucigalpa and held 40 hostages, to protest the Salvadorean civil war. An attempt was also made to occupy the cathedral in San Pedro Sula.[2] Meanwhile, the rumors in Tegucigalpa was that Maj. Adolfo Díaz, of FUSEP, the national police force, was organizing a new gang of right-wing toughs into a death squad. Ominous hit lists were reportedly being prepared, with the Reina brothers high on the roll of potential targets.

SOCIAL CLASSES AND FORCES

Remaining the saving grace of Honduras is the existence of certain institutions over which the government could exercise little direct control. One of these is the very autonomous National University (UNAH), which has campuses in both major cities. Under the rectorship of Jorge Arturo Reina, the university was a haven for all sorts of views to the left of center, from that of his own ALIPO to the frankly revolutionary movements. There are also small, private universities, but these have very little impact.

The press is also a major force in Honduran life, and the papers in this country have not been intimidated into silence, like those of Guatemala, nor are they tightly controlled by the oligarchy, like most of those in El Salvador. *La Tribuna* of Tegucigalpa represents the orthodox PL view, while ALIPO has the warm support of Manuel Gamero's *Tiempo* (of San Pedro Sula). Also in the capital of the north coast is *La Prensa*, which tends to follow the PN line, as does *El Heraldo* of Tegucigalpa. There also exists the struggling and venerable *La Cronista* of Carlos Flores, the longest-lived of any Honduran paper. These papers are free in that government control is absent, and they frequently use this freedom to explore juicy political scandals, such as the previously mentioned Ferrari case. But they share a limitation in that the owners of the papers, with the exception perhaps of those who own *Tiempo*, are basically conservative and tend not to let their journalists print things which might have an adverse effect upon the present structure of society.

The unions and the peasant associations are a third major force that helps maintain a certain basis for pluralism in Honduras. The union movement of that country is unparalleled elsewhere in the region, and unusual for any nation in Latin America. There is a complex structure of hierarchies in the two main movements (see Figure 10.1). The church-backed group continues to gain ground against its larger rival and there is every evidence that the unionists, as a whole, are becoming more militant.

This trinity of institutions—the UNAH, the five national papers, and the unions—has been extremely important in maintaining a certain precarious freedom even under such dictators as López Arellano. Another organization, formerly a firm backer of the status quo, is beginning to emerge in Honduras,

Figure 10.1. The Structure of Unionism in Honduras

MOVIMIENTO SINDICAL LIBRE
CONFEDERACIÓN DE TRABAJADORES DE HONDURAS

FESITRAN (San Pedro)   ANACH   FCESITLIH (Tegucigalpa)
                            (*Campesinos*)

SITRATERCO SUTRASFCO   *Communications, banking*
(*United Brands*) (*Standard*)   *and other locals*

        other locals

FEDERACIÓN SINDICAL HONDUREÑO

SIMPROH (*Motoristas*)

Hospital workers

others

MOVIMIENTO SINDICAL DEMÓCRATA CRISTIANO
CONFEDERACIÓN GENERAL DE TRABAJADORES

FESISUR   UNIÓN NACIONAL   FESHTRAL-SPS
(Choluteca)   DE CAMPESINOS   (*food processing*)

Source: Constructed by the author.

as elsewhere in Central America, as a force for change. This is the Catholic church. There are 400 priests in the country, many of them missionaries; and they have not been immune to the influence operating on their opposite numbers elsewhere in Central America. But the archbishop of Tegucigalpa, Msgr. Héctor Enrique Santos, long thought to be the epitome of conservatism, startled the world in late December 1980, by calling on the government of Paz García to "take a step in the direction of socialism." That such a message would come from such a source indicated that all was not as well in Honduras as many observers would have liked to believe.

When the archbishop spoke of moving toward socialism, he was doubtlessly thinking of some form of social action on behalf of the peasants, who form such a large part of the Honduran people. Eighty thousand families were still landless and many others could barely manage on their acreage. Nor was the lot of those who had benefited from the land-reform program necessarily ideal, as the continued problems of Isletas and the citrus cooperatives suggested. Best off, materially, were those who worked for the great fruit companies, but there existed a longstanding antagonism between worker and manager, and labor trouble was virtually an annual event on the north coast.

The urban working class, although frequently unionized, remained very small, for Honduran manufacturing was still in its infancy and what workforce there was was largely in the building trades and service industries. While an urban middle sector existed, it was certainly poorer than that of the surrounding countries and not a very effective force politically. Indeed, the chief political attitude of those who had risen above the ranks of peasant or artisan appeared to be apathy. A bustling upper-middle sector of business and professional men was also present, inhabiting the tall office buildings that rose in Tegucigalpa, but with the exception of such men as Miguel Andonie or César Batres, it made little effort to reform the country.

In the depths of such provinces as Olancho, local colonels continued to preside over the destinies of all within their area, in an almost feudal way. So rugged and remote is most of the country that contact with the central authority was frequently interrupted and orders from above customarily ignored. Local leaders frequently took the law into their own hands and a wild-West attitude generally prevailed. But the local magnates seldom attempted to achieve anything on the national scene, and the sudden rise to national prominence of someone like Martínez Argueta, in 1967, was a mere fluke.

In a nation so diffuse and amorphous, it was hardly surprising that the military played a preponderant role. First called to the political scene by the Liberals, it had ended by allying itself to the PN and had imposed three successive military rulers on the country, the third of whom still functioned in 1981 as the provisional president. The machinery of military rule was provided by the Superior Military Council, a secret group said to comprise most of the senior garrison commanders, the chiefs of staff of the army and air force, and other highly placed officers. The army, however, has never been without its divisions and factions. The recent purge which retired Melgar Castro, López Arellano, and so many other senior officers indicated that Policarpo Paz García still feared their influence. Leftist officers are not unknown, especially in the junior ranks, where impatience with slowness of promotion often leads to radicalism. The shadowy OSOS, which surfaced in 1980, might have had little influence; but its manifesto, demanding reforms through society, clearly showed that not all within the armed services were blind to the real situation of the country.

The military has not generally operated in Honduras in the same terrorist manner as in Guatemala, but there were occasional abuses. However, as in the case of the barbarous Olancho murders of 1975, the army could point with pride to the fact that it had stepped in and punished the culprits. It should be pointed out, on the other hand, that the general amnesty which followed the election of the Constituent Assembly was given, at the insistence of the military, to free Major Padilla and the others responsible for the Olancho crimes, and the major had in fact served less than two years of his sentence. The army thus looked after its own.

Factors Making for Stability

In no other country covered in this study is the articulation of opinion so open, through the press, the schools, and the unions. Even in the time of greatest repression, this had led politically aware Hondurans to believe that they had some input in the decision-making process. The government is able to receive a large amount of feedback and input, and sometimes, as in the land-reform program of 1967 to 1975, it has acted upon popular demands. The two-party system of the past has been very useful in this regard. By joining one or the other of the two traditional parties, a citizen can be assured of a certain amount of influence, perhaps a job, and, certainly, immunities from petty legal restraints, when that party is in power. The two parties have long existed even on the village level. Despite the aristocratic image of the National Party, it is not unusual to find simple peasants who are proud to call themselves members and who can boast of a long history of family connections with that party. In recent years, with the country run by a military-and-National-Party alliance, the government has still had to practice the sort of conflict resolution typical of more democratic regimes. It never cut itself off entirely from the powerful unions and had to square their demands with those of the armed forces, the PL, COHEP, and other business and agricultural groups.

Destabilizing Factors

It may be, however, that the public has become increasingly disillusioned with the activities of the two traditional parties. This cannot be seen in the

April 1980 elections, which had a surprisingly high turnout, and in which all but some 3 percent of the voters voted for the PN or the PL. But the message of the voters, many observers believe, was not an endorsement of either party, but rather a clear demand for a return to civilian government. It could also be pointed out that PINU was new and poorly organized and other parties were not allowed to participate.

The increasing labor violence of 1980 was an indication that many felt the government was no longer listening to their inputs, nor satisfying their demands. Perhaps without the presence of a revolutionary regime on one border and a strong Marxist guerrilla movement on the other, the extreme left might have had a hard time organizing in Honduras, but those conditions did exist at the beginning of the eighties and inevitably led to the establishment of similar movements in Honduras.

ECONOMIC FACTORS

Outside of the persistent problem of corruption, most of the complaints of Hondurans centered upon the economy. For several years during the mid-seventies, the economy seemed to be making genuine advances, although, thanks to the soaring birth rate, this did not translate into a real gain in per capita income. But by 1981, there was spiraling inflation—well over 20 percent a year—a falling real per capita income, and a lack of any government plan to deal with such problems as exchange controls or monetary policy. The government, in June of 1980, had announced that it was working with the International Monetary Fund to establish a rigid monetary policy and that it would control inflation through tight credit and wage controls.[3] But these latter items proved politically unpalatable and had not been seriously applied by the end of the year.

The budget of the government for 1980 was $568.4 million and that for 1981 was to be $650 million, but this was labeled by the finance minister, Valentín Mendoza, an "austerity budget," which he promised to balance without new taxes. The GDP had risen 6.9 percent in 1979 and 6 percent in 1980, which were encouraging figures but the growth of the population also had to be taken into account. The foreign debt also remained extremely burdensome, representing 35.8 percent of the GDP (compared to a general average of 27 percent of all Latin American countries).[4] Capital flight was also placing a burden upon the nation's economy. Thanks to fears of left-wing guerrilla activity spreading into the country, $50 million fled the country in 1980.[5]

A number of measures have been taken to improve the economic picture. As coffee had replaced bananas in the role of the leading export crop, the health of that industry was all important (see Table 10.1). Therefore, the Banco Hondureño de Café was founded in 1980 by the government, its capital partially raised by a new tax of 50¢ a bag on coffee exports, and in part by the

TABLE 10.1. Honduran Coffee Export Values

Year	Value of Exports of Coffee	Percent of Total Export Value
1976	$ 48,500,000	18
1977	169,000,000	33
1978	212,000,000	35
1979	196,500,000	no data

Source: *This Week Central America and Panama*, 2 June 1980.

Coffee Institute of Honduras (IHCAFE), a growers' association. The purpose of the bank was to make loans more abundant to growers at the very time that the government was concentrating on making loans generally harder to get. The government's tight money policy also seemed to be contradicted by several other ambitious economic projects. One of the great untapped resources of the country is the vast pine forest of Olancho. Olancho Forest Enterprises Corporation (CORFINO), a joint government and private organization, was set up in the late seventies to exploit this resource; it obtained a loan of $8.6 million from the U.S. Export-Import Bank to help erect a $17.3-million sawmill. This sawmill, and a pulp mill also projected, would be close enough to the Atlantic coast for the forest products to be brought out of the country by ship. For this purpose, the little port of Castillo was being developed. Another Atlantic coast project involved extensive offshore oil exploration, small pockets having been discovered in the 1940s. For this purpose, the World Bank lent $3 million in 1980.[6]

Perhaps the most unpromising of all the government's projects was the scheme to double the volume of tourist business. Outside of the gleaming sand beaches of Roatán and the north coast, Honduras has few attractions for the tourist. Copán, its only notable ruin, while of interest, has only been partially restored. Until recently it was accessible only by air, but in 1981 a paved road was being pushed through to replace the red clay track that wound through 60 kilometers of jungle from the main highway. As part of the tourist-development enterprise, a gigantic Sheraton Hotel was being rushed to completion in Tegucigalpa, though one would think that with four downtown, high-rise hotels, the capital, hardly a tourist mecca, was probably overstocked already.

As part of its plan to make Honduras a bastion of democracy and stability in Central America, the United States was hovering anxiously over the economy and making sure that international lending agencies would do their share. The effort might well pay off, for the economy was by no means hopeless. A great deal depended upon the success of the Olancho project and upon the price the world was willing to pay for coffee, bananas, and sugar.

FOREIGN AFFAIRS

Situated, with its two long borders, between El Salvador and Nicaragua, Honduras appeared to be in the jaws of a giant nutcracker. If El Salvador were to fall to rebel forces, Honduras's position would be precarious indeed, from the standpoint of its current government. Perhaps this was why the government rushed, after years of delay, to sign a peace accord with El Salvador, on 30 October 1980. This was hailed by the negotiator, former President Bustamante of Peru, as "a gesture of reconciliation and an example of peace in the world." It is quite possible that the United States exerted heavy pressure on Honduras, particularly promising large amounts of military hardware, to insure the signing of this treaty. The treaty had another military consequence, in that it allowed Honduras to rejoin CONDECA, the regional defense organization from which it had been absent for 11 years.[7] Even before that, however, Honduras had been working closely with the Salvadorean army against the rebels. There was a little-publicized "summit meeting" on 1 May in Guatemala, with Romeo Lucas, Policarpo Paz, José Napoleón Duarte, and Jaime Abdul Gutiérrez all in attendance. The main concern was the Salvadorean-Honduran frontier, though possibly there was talk that an eventual invasion of Nicaragua itself would occur from Honduras.[8]

Honduran relations with Nicaragua, another dropout from CONDECA, remained icy. As early as December 1979, Honduran foreign minister Pérez Cadalso had declared that "the Honduran government is preoccupied by the eventual emergence of a socialist government in Nicaragua, because we don't want that type of regime in our neighborhood."[9] Diplomatic hassles and expulsions soon became the rule, but the most serious problem concerned the several thousand ex-*Guardia* members and other Somozistas residing in Honduras. These led frequent raids across the border into Nicaragua, killing Sandinista soldiers and often bringing back quantities of cattle. Tomás Borge estimated that there were 39 such incursions in October and November 1980. This led to military maneuvers on both sides and a Nicaraguan army helicopter was forced down in Honduras near Duyure in mid-November. However, Honduran Ambassador Roberto Suazo reassured the Nicaraguans that "we will never allow our territory to be used as a base for aggression against your country."[10] Nevertheless, in January 1981, José Francisco Cardenal, head of the anti-Sandinista armed group, the *Unión Democrática Nicaraguense* (UDN), announced that his group was continuing forays from Honduras into the department of Jinotega.[11]

U.S. FOREIGN POLICY AND HONDURAS

In a very real sense, there are no options for U.S. policy in Honduras, unless complete abandonment of the country might be called an option. The

North Americans had little choice but to pursue a policy of aid, both economic and military, in an effort to nurse the country toward democracy. The hope would be that the forthcoming national elections would indeed take place; that the army would permit the transition to civilian rule and stay in its barracks; and that the new government would undertake sweeping reforms designed to head off revolutionary violence. The foregoing discussion might suggest that while all these things are possible, they are by no means certain. Unless the United States can nurture such a transformation, Honduras will probably confront more disorder and violent pressures for change.

NOTES

1. *This Week Central America and Panama*, 1 September 1980.
2. *This Week Central America and Panama*, 24 November 1980.
3. *Latin America Region Report, Central America and Mexico*, 6 June 1980.
4. Ibid.
5. *This Week Central America and Panama*, 20 October 1980.
6. *This Week Central America and Panama*, 23 June and 4 August 1980.
7. *Update Latin America*, November/December 1980.
8. *Central America Update*, October 1980.
9. *Central America Reports*, 10 December 1979.
10. *This Week Central America and Panama*, 17 November 1980.
11. *This Week Central America and Panama*, 26 January 1981.

PART IV
NICARAGUA

11

Nicaragua: The Somoza Era

Nicaragua is the largest of the Central American republics, and in terms of agricultural and mineral wealth, potentially the most prosperous. Besides mining gold, it produces coffee, bananas, cotton, lumber, cacao, and cattle. Nicaragua runs largely north-south between Costa Rica and Honduras and is cut by several ranges of volcanic peaks, but the dominant geographic features of the country are the two large lakes, Nicaragua and Managua. Lake Nicaragua, the larger of the two, is a deep, island-dotted body of water near the Costa Rican border that has long been seen by engineers as a potential new site for a canal across the isthmus. Farther west, the capital city is built upon the south shore of the lake of the same name. Although Lake Managua may look handsome from the windows of the Intercontinental Hotel, it is in fact shallow and dead, a cesspool for the cities and villages along its shore.

The racial composition of Nicaragua is very like that of Honduras, with mestizos being dominant, although there are a large number of blacks and mulattos in the province of Zelaya, which makes up Nicaragua's share of the almost inaccessible Mosquito coast. Like Honduras, the country is under-populated. For its 50,000 square miles, it had only 2,373,000 persons in 1975, giving it a density of only 43 persons per square mile, as compared to Honduras's 71.[1] There is every natural reason why the people of Nicaragua should be prosperous, and indeed the per capita income was higher in the seventies than that of any of the other countries under discussion in this work, but it was very badly distributed. Most of the urban and rural poor actually lived on the verge of starvation. Half the children died by the age of five, with gastrointestinal diseases accounting for 90 percent of these deaths. This was also the leading cause of death overall, killing almost a quarter of all Nicaraguans. The second leading cause of death was the category of homicide and manslaughter, for Nicaragua, along with El Salvador, claims one of the highest murder rates in the world.[2]

Politically, Nicaragua has also been very much like Honduras in having two traditional parties which grew out of the church-state issues of the nineteenth century. They are named, appropriately enough, the Liberals and the Conservatives. Neither of these titles should be taken in the modern sense, and, as clericalism ceased to be a major issue in the twentieth century, the two parties came simply to represent rival factions within the landed oligarchy. A Liberal *caudillo* dominated the country around the turn of the century: the unscrupulous José Santos Zelaya, who ruled for 16 years, from his successful revolt in 1893 to his ouster by North American intervention in 1909. Zelaya had run a cruel and graft-ridden administration at home and a belligerent foreign policy abroad, and brought the country into bankruptcy. As a result, the new Conservative leadership allowed the United States to take over the collection of its revenues and to use them to pay off the New York banks to which the country was deeply indebted. In 1912, the Liberals attempted to end this humiliating arrangement, and overthrow President Adolfo Díaz, but a force of U.S. Marines arrived to preserve the Conservative rule and the debt collection process. The marines stayed until 1925, visible evidence of U.S. control.

Alfonso Díaz had once been installed as president before the marines departed, but he soon found a rival government being formed under Liberal leader Juan Bautista Sacasa. Fearing a Liberal victory, the United States returned in 1927 with a large contingent of marines who soon brought an end to the fighting and supervised an election, which ironically brought into power the Liberal José Maria Moncada. But one Liberal *caudillo* refused to lay down his arms, declaring that Moncada was still nothing but a puppet of the United States. This was Augusto César Sandino, the illegitimate son of a small landholder, and a leader closely identified with the peasant masses. Considering the history of the movement that bears his name, it is well to remember that Sandino was a nationalist with vague reformist leanings, by no means a socialist, and still less a communist. He kicked out of his forces Agustín Farabundo Martí, the martyr of the 1932 uprising in El Salvador, precisely because Martí was a communist. Whatever else he was, Sandino was a competent guerrilla warrior who led the U.S. Marines on a merry chase through the tangled backcountry. Unable to catch him, they at last persuaded him to lay down his arms when a more genuine Liberal, Juan B. Sacasa, won the presidency in an honest election in 1933.

Sandino remained suspicious of U.S. involvement, even though the marines went home, and even more suspicious of the men around Sacasa—in particular, Anastasio Somoza García, Sacasa's nephew, the *jefe director* of the

Guardia Nacional. The body which Somoza headed had been created in 1927, in the presidency of Adolfo Díaz, by officers of the U.S. Marine Corps, and was modeled after a similar organization in the Dominican Republic, also a Marine Corps creation. It was envisioned as a constabulary, that is to say, a force combining the roles of an army and a police force, and not as a force operating independently of the army, like the Salvadorean *Guardia*. Though it was at first officered by Conservatives, the coming to power of the Liberals in Nicaragua necessitated a change in *Guardia* leadership, and the U.S. minister, Matthew Hanna, personally picked Somoza, a Liberal, as the new chief in 1932.

Sandino's suspicions of the *Guardia* and its chief were reciprocated. Somoza and his officers believed Sandino had considerably more armed men than the 100 allowed him in the peace pact and that he was stockpiling arms for a new campaign. Sacasa sought to mediate between the two Liberal chiefs and, for this purpose, invited Sandino out of the mountains to meet with him in February 1934. Sandino proved difficult, demanding the disbanding of the *Guardia*; but an accord appeared to have been patched up. On 21 February the president held a farewell dinner at his palace for the departing Sandino, but as the latter left, he and two of his followers were arrested by officers loyal to Somoza, driven to the airfield, and shot. Somoza at first expressed innocence, but later took full responsibility for this bloody deed.[3]

Sacasa was henceforth under the domination of Somoza, who now clearly intended to succeed to the presidency. To prevent this, Sacasa's wife and some supporters planned to attack him in his fortress of La Loma, which dominates Managua; but they were deterred by the U.S. minister, Arthur Bliss Lane, who did not want Nicaragua destabilized. Somoza, in addition to the backing of the *Guardia*, had a fascist-type paramilitary force known as the Blue Shirts who began to exercise political muscle. With such powers of intimidation, Somoza had no trouble being elected as the candidate of the Liberals in the December 1935 balloting. He had disbanded his *Camisas Azules* just before the election, but when he was installed as president, he took care to combine the post of *jefe director* of the *Guardia* with the presidency.

Anastasio Somoza was a typical liberal dictator of the period, similar to Ubico, Martínez, or to Rafael Trujillo in the Dominican Republic. His economic attitudes were "neopositivist," with the state encouraging the individual entrepreneur to exploit the wealth of the country and its labor as well. He shared with other liberals the dislike of the church, and his presidency saw it shorn of the last vestiges of its former wealth. Typical, too, of his age was his warm admiration for Hitler and Mussolini, with whom he liked to be compared until he at last discovered the benefits of cooperation with the United States.[4]

In his joint role as president and director of the National Guard, he controlled the entire military strength of the country, and many other services as well, for the *Guardia* comprised not only the sole military and police establishments, but also the customs service, without whose permission no one could enter or leave the country, the postal service, telegraph and radio networks, the licensing of weapons, and even the sanitation department.[5] It was hardly an exaggeration to say that the *Guardia* was official Nicaragua.

With this kind of support, it is easy to understand why Somoza felt that he could extend his term of office, officially only four years, indefinitely. To this end, he called a new Constituent Assembly in 1939, which obligingly wrote a constitution that provided a six-year term for the president, with no reelection (a provision which was not to apply to the present incumbent). The Constituent Assembly then itself chose Anastasio Somoza García as president for an eight-year term, to run from 1939 to 1947. During these years of stable power, Somoza did an about-face in regard to his former fascist leanings, becoming the great and good friend of his good neighbor, Franklin D. Roosevelt, who in turn professed to see many democratic and progressive qualities in General Somoza. As a token of this friendship, a North American major was sent to establish an *Academia Militar*, the old *Escuela Politécnica* now being defunct. From then on, the academy turned out its yearly cadre of officers for the *Guardia*, most of them taking their senior year at the School of the Americas, the U.S. military training center in Panama.

But Roosevelt died before Somoza could have himself reelected president in 1947 and Harry Truman wanted Somoza to step aside. At the time, Somoza balked, but in the end he allowed Leonardo Argüello to run on the Liberal ticket, and in February 1947, he declared him the winner of a very fraudulent election. Somoza, while stepping down as president, did not give up his role as *jefe director*. He simply retired from the presidential palace to the new palace of La Curva that he had built upon the fortress of La Loma. Argüello, however, had some quaint notion that he was really president and he demanded that Somoza resign as *jefe* and go into exile. In a twinkling, he was overthrown in May 1947 and a Somoza relative, Benjamín Lacayo Sacasa, installed in his place. Lacayo then gave way to Víctor Román y Reyes in September. This occasioned a revolt by one of the perennial troublemakers, the Conservative Gen. Emiliano Chamorro, but it failed and Chamorro was exiled, only to be allowed back for the 1950 election, in which he was allowed to run against Anastasio Somoza; and, of course, he lost.[6]

Shortly before the next election was to be held, Somoza was shot and mortally wounded by an idealistic poet, Rigoberto López Pérez, who was immediately cut down by Somoza's guards. General Eisenhower's personal physician, who was flown to the Panama hospital where the dictator lay dying, was not able to save Somoza; but he left his legacy. He had accumulated, through graft and shady deals, an estimated $100-$150 million in money and land in a country where the per capita income then stood at less then $300. He had also entrenched his relatives in power. Luis Somoza Debayle, the elder legitimate son, was first designate, or roughly vice president. The younger son, Anastasio Somoza Debayle (West Point, class of 1946), had been given the

National Guard as his graduation present and upon the death of his father, assumed the rank of *jefe director*, aided by his half brother, the illegitimate Major José Somoza. The Somozas, backed by U.S. Ambassador Thomas Whelan, soon consolidated their rule and arrested Emiliano Chamorro and young Pedro Joaquín Chamorro Cardenal, publisher of the Conservative daily, *La Prensa*. The election plans went ahead, with Luis as the candidate against a puppet of the newly created Conservative National Party.

Luis and Anastasio Somoza Debayle shared with their father a tendency toward corpulence, libertinism, and rapacity, but neither of them had his administrative ability. Luis was particularly easygoing, which accounted for the relative mildness of his presidential years. His relaxation of repression did not, however, exempt him from revolts. Pedro Joaquín Chamorro led an unsuccessful one in 1959 and was exiled. Luis Somoza, following the dictates of the constitution, actually retired from the presidency in 1963, making René Schick, a Liberal puppet of the Somozas, his successor. Schick died in office on 3 August 1966, and was succeeded by another tame Liberal, Lorenzo Guerrero, who finished the term of office in January 1967.

In August 1966, the Liberal National Party nominated Anastasio Somoza Debayle as its candidate. This required a change in the constitution, for Luis, who preferred to see the family in the background, had amended it to prohibit the election of close relatives of the president. This also meant that Anastasio had to step down as *jefe director*, which he did, but he continued to live in La Curva and to be the real power in the *Guardia*. The opposition Conservatives, a breakaway Liberal Party faction known as the Independent Liberals, and the Christian Democrats formed a *Unión Nacional Opositora* and ran the Conservative leader Dr. Fernando Agüero, previously defeated by Argüello in 1947. The election was attended by much violence, and Pedro Joaquín Chamorro staged a massive demonstration on 22 January involving some 40,000 to 60,000. Forty demonstrators were shot by the *Guardia*, Chamarro was imprisoned once more, and Anastasio Somoza Debayle was elected as planned. A few months later, Luis suddenly died, leaving all the power concentrated in the hands of his younger brother.[7]

But a cloud had already appeared on the horizon. In 1959, despairing of overturning the Somozas by any legal means, a group of students had formed the *Frente de Liberación Nacional* to try force of arms. In 1961, this had become the *Frente Sandinista de Liberación Nacional* (FSLN), under the leadership of Carlos Fonseca Amador. The FSLN tried terrorism and occasional guerrilla attacks through the 1960s, but with very little result. In June 1969, they suffered a major setback in Managua when several of their leaders in the capital, including Julio César Buitrago, were killed in a shootout with the *Guardia*. An even worse blow was the September 1969 arrest, on bank-robbery charges in Costa Rica, of Fonseca himself. His release was only obtained when the Sandinistas hijacked a Costa Rican airliner and exchanged the hostages for him in October 1970. By that time, the FSLN appeared to have been virtually eliminated as a threat.[8] But the Sandinistas, despite many failures, always came back.

In the meantime, Anastasio Somoza the younger, known as Tacho, like his father, strove to consolidate his power. Also like his father, he filled many important positions with his relatives. Noel Pallais Debayle, his cousin, headed the National Development Bank (*Institución Nacional de Desarrollo*). His brother-in-law, Guillermo Sevilla Sacasa, was the virtually permanent ambassador to the United States. Meanwhile, Ramiro Sacasa was minister of education, and uncle Manuel Debayle headed the national electric company. Tacho's wife Hope headed the social security program. Even *Novedades*, the Liberal newspaper which backed the Somoza dynasty, was run by a cousin, Luis Pallais, while José Somoza remained a powerful figure in the *Guardia*.

By 1970 the family owned more than half the agricultural production of the country and vast amounts of its industry, including the agricultural firm of *Agrotécnica S.A.*, the Nicaraguan cigar-making firm, the television network *Televisión de Nicaragua, S.A.*, the Mamenic steamship lines, the *Banco de Centroamérica*, and a half interest in the Intercontinental Hotel, as well as considerable stock in the Lanica Airline. The total wealth of Anastasio Somoza Debayle was put at $500 million.[9]

Somoza had also welcomed North American investment, and firms from the United States picked up many crumbs left by the rapacious Somozas. U.S.-owned firms included *Empacadora Nicaragüense* (Alberti Foods), Booth of Nicaragua and Nicamar (Booth Fisheries), Industrias Geminas (General Mills), the Banco de América, Química Borden, Rosario Mining Company of Nicaragua (ASARCO), and Lanica (Hughes Tool Company).[10] This last came in 1971, with the arrival of the millionaire recluse, Howard Hughes, in Nicaragua. He rented the entire top floor of the Hotel Intercontinental (now rented by the Soviet embassy) and proceeded to get on good terms with the Somozas. Part of the good terms was to bail out the financially troubled national airline by buying a controlling interest in it. Hughes probably planned to make Managua his home; but after the earthquake of 23 December 1972, he appeared to find Nicaragua a bit too shaky and left.

Despite its apparent economic and political stranglehold on the country, the Somoza regime was none too stable, either. In 1970 there were rumors of an impending coup by elements of the *Guardia*, but as in the cases of Matthew Hanna, Arthur Bliss Lane, and Thomas Whelan, a North American diplomat came to the rescue. This was Ambassador Turner B. Shelton, surely the most sycophantic U.S. ambassador ever to serve in Nicaragua. During his long tenure (1970-75), he became Somoza's closest crony. The dictator, it might be noted, generally preferred North Americans to his fellow countrymen, and it was maliciously (though falsely) rumored that his Spanish was so bad after his long residence in the United States that he could really only express himself in

English. Shelton arranged a triumphal trip to the United States to convince Nicaraguans that God was still on Somoza's side; Somoza met privately with President Richard Nixon.

Since the then constitution prohibited reelection, it appeared to be time once more to rewrite the constitution to keep Somoza in office beyond 1972. For this purpose, he met in early 1971 with the leader of the Conservative Party and a former presidential candidate, Fernando Agüero. Agüero, in what may have been a serious miscalculation, agreed to the dissolution of Congress and the setting up of a junta which would then call still another Constituent Assembly. Plainly, the new constitution would be designed to engineer Somoza's return as president, so Agüero was selling out his party and his principles; but the bait was that Agüero himself would be the chief man on the three-member junta. Although the Conservatives went along with their leader's decision, the Independent Liberals of Ramiro Sacasa and the Christian Democrats firmly opposed the scheme. However, in May 1972, the junta came into being. Supporting the position of the Christian Democrats, the new archbishop of Managua, Miguel Obando y Bravo, boycotted the transfer-of-power ceremonies, and a joint pastoral letter of the Nicaraguan bishops called for "a completely new order."[11] It was the opening salvo of a major war between the church and the Nicaraguan state.

Relations between church and state were further embittered by the behavior of the government following the great earthquake of December 1972. Two days before Christmas, the entire center of the city of Managua was reduced to rubble. Unlike the Guatemalan quake of 1976, this was an extremely localized, though very powerful, quake. Some 10,000 Managuans were killed and almost all the businesses were wiped out. Amid the rubble, only Somoza's Intercontinental remained standing. The behavior of the Somozas and the *Guardia* in the months that followed was disgraceful. Large amounts of foreign aid, much of it from the United States, came in, only to disappear into the hoards of the *Guardia* officers and the civilian politicos. Scenes have been described to this writer in which National Guard officers actually threatened to kill Red Cross officials if they did not hand over the medicines and food. The result was tragic: The center of Managua remained a vast ruin, never rebuilt under the Somozas. Indeed, only in the time of the Sandinistas has even the rubble been removed. Somoza preferred to leave the center that way because he and his cronies had bought up large parcels of land on the perimeter of the city. There they located new housing and shops after the quake, making a vast fortune from the disaster.[12]

Msgr. Obando y Bravo lost no time in denouncing the behavior of Somoza and the *Guardia*, but Somoza's only response was to blame everything on the supposedly ruling junta, from which he now removed the gullible Fernando Agüero. The Constituent Assembly then got down to business and worked out a document which permitted Somoza to run again in 1974.

However, it did provide that no member of the military could be a candidate, which meant that Somoza was forced to abandon the post of *jefe director*. He simply styled himself *jefe supremo*, and remained in actual charge.

But the foundations of the regime, shaky since 1970, now began to crumble in earnest. Somoza himself grew excessively fat and lethargic, his weight eventually climbing to 300 pounds. Worse still, his companion, Turner Shelton, was recalled to the United States, thanks to reports of his conduct in Jack Anderson's column and to reports sent, via the dissent channel, from the embassy itself by Political Affairs Officer James Cheek (later deputy assistant secretary of state for Central America). Shelton was replaced by James Theberge. As things deteriorated, Somoza's family and friends jockeyed for position. One faction formed around Gen. Reinaldo Pérez Vega, the head of the *Guardia*; another, around Col. José Somoza; and still another, around young Anastasio Somoza, "Tachito," who was a West Point dropout and a captain in the National Guard. Another rival for eventual power was Dinora Sampson, Somoza's smashing-looking mistress who had inserted her people everywhere.[13]

The FSLN, presumed dead since 1970, began to revive as the economy worsened. The wealthy businessman José Castillo Quant held a Christmas time farewell party for Turner Shelton on 27 December 1974, inviting all the potentates of the dynasty; but shortly after the guest of honor departed, the Sandinistas, under Eduardo Contreras Escobar, rushed in and seized 40 of the guests, including the mayor of Managua, the ambassador to the United States, Guillermo Sevilla Sacasa, and Noel Pallais Debayle. These persons were then held as hostages until the Sandinistas, through the mediation of the archbishop, received $5 million, 15 political prisoners, and a flight to Havana. The sudden Sandinista revival caused Somoza to declare a state of siege, which lasted through all of 1975. The Managua raid was followed by stepped-up activity by the FSLN throughout the remote provinces, especially in Zelaya, using techniques learned in Cuba to win the peasantry.

The National Guard, although having a paper strength of some 7,000 men, was not really well prepared to deal with such matters. More than half its personnel were engaged in police and other nonmilitary duties and no more than 1,000 men were really combat-ready troops. Nevertheless, the *Guardia* made up for its deficiencies by extreme brutality, wiping out whole villages suspected of harboring Sandinistas. Faced with such tactics, the handful of guerrillas made little headway. Then, in November 1976, the FSLN was dealt two stunning blows. On 7 November, Eduardo Contreras Escobar was killed in a Managua shootout with the *Guardia*. The very next day, the *Guardia* ambushed and killed Secretary General Carlos Fonseca Amador and his Mexican lieutenant, Julio Tirado López, in the Cordillera Isabelia in northern Nicaragua. This led the influential publication *Latin America* to declare the Sandinistas "virtually eliminated" as a threat.[14] The Sandinistas continued to make occasional forays throughout 1977, but Penny Lernoux saw these as nothing but "a tiny hit-and-run campaign designed primarily to attract international publicity," and declared that the FSLN was no threat to Somoza.[15]

One problem of the FSLN was that it was riddled with factionalism. In 1975 a quarrel developed between those who favored a long, drawn-out guerrilla war of attrition (the *Guerra Prolongada Popular*—GPP), and those who favored a sudden, mass insurrection in the cities (the proletarian tendency). A group led by Víctor Manuel Tirado López, brother of the fallen Julio, and the brothers Daniel and Humberto Ortega tried to mediate between the other two tendencies and ended up by forming their own, appropriately called the *terceristas*, which had the reputation of being more moderate than the others and of being linked to the progressive business community in Managua.[16]

With the FSLN counted out, the fortunes of Somoza appeared to revive. With Dinora's aid, he went on a diet and trimmed off 100 pounds while cutting down the fifth of vodka a day he had been consuming. Early in January 1978, he reshuffled his cabinet to make it more effective, naming Julio Quintana as foreign minister and making Guillermo Noguera minister of defense. But on the tenth of the month, his henchmen committed an act of folly that went a long way toward bringing down the regime. It involved Pedro Joaquín Chamorro Cardenal, the son of parents from two of the most powerful of the old Conservative families. As publisher of the respected newspaper *La Prensa*, he was a perpetual thorn in the side of the government, for Somoza allowed a certain amount of freedom of the press. Several times in the past, Chamorro had engaged in armed insurrection against the Somozas, but each time, he had been pardoned and allowed to return to Managua. The Somozas, however, hated him, and none with a more bitter fury than Tachito, the heir apparent. The immediate cause of the anger was a series of *La Prensa* articles about Plasmaferesis, the Somoza-owned commercial blood-plasma operation through which Somoza sold the blood of his people to the United States. Several cars filled with *Guardia*, surrounded the vehicle of Pedro Joaquín Chamorro as he drove along a street in the rubble-strewn old center of Managua. They forced him to the curb and shot him point-blank.[17]

At the time, an effort was made to blame the murder on Pedro Ramos, president of Plasmaferesis, but many suspected a more direct Somoza connection with it. Thirty thousand persons followed Chamorro's body to the grave, and widespread rioting broke out. Many factions, previously at odds, now combined for a general strike under the leadership of the *Unión Democrática de Liberación* (UDEL). These included the *Consejo Superior de la Empresa Privada* (COSEP), representing business and manufacturing, and the *Confederación General de Trabajo Independiente* (CGTI) and the *Central de Trabajadores de Nicaragua* (CTN), two powerful unions. The purpose of the strike was to force Somoza's resignation, which was also called for by René Sandino Arguelo, now head of the Conservative Party. The general strike, after considerable violence and *Guardia* repression, petered out in the first week of February 1978, but the forces it had unleashed continued to work.

What had happened was that the Somozas had now broken the unwritten rules by which the political game had always been played in Nicaragua. Under these rules, it was perfectly permissible for the *Guardia* to enter remote villages and rape, plunder, and kill at will. It was also permitted to jail and torture Sandinistas and other outlaw opponents of the regime, and the tortures in Somoza's jails were up to the best Guatemalan standards. But within the magic circle of old families, Liberal or Conservative, a certain toleration was allowed. At a cocktail party or a meeting of COSEP, one could and did speak freely by criticizing the dynasty, while *La Prensa*, with the largest circulation of any daily, was permitted to run exposés, such as the one about Plasmaferesis. But if Pedro Joaquín Chamorro could be killed, then everyone was in danger, and the Somozas would have to go. This became the thinking of the Nicaraguan elite. A knowledgeable observer has even suggested, perhaps ironically, that Somoza finally fell because he had never been a thoroughgoing-enough dictator and had not stifled the opposition of the press, the church, and the business community.

But Somoza was not about to go, vowing to stay on until 1981, when he would, in his own words, "hand over the presidency to the Republic and the leadership of the *Guardia* and go home like any other Liberal."[18] Speculation on a successor centered on Tachito or brother José.

The murder of Chamorro and the subsequent general strike served to revive the morale of the Sandinistas, who launched in July a series of attacks against the *Guardia* in Jinotepe, then in Masaya and San Marcos. Heavy fighting was also reported along the Costa Rican border, the chief route of FSLN infiltration into the country. On 20 July came the most brazen attack so far, when a lone Sandinista checked into an Intercontinental room facing La Loma, and fired two rockets toward the newly completed bunker that Somoza had dug into the fortress. Plainly, the three factions had settled enough of their differences to be an effective opposition. Angered by the ineffectiveness of the National Guard, Somoza sacked 35 officers, including Alesio Gutiérrez, the chief of the Managua police detachment. But more was to come. At noon on 22 August, 25 Sandinistas disguised in *Guardia* uniforms seized the National Palace, where the legislature was in session, and rounded up 70 hostages including Interior Minister José Antonio Mora and Luis Pallais. The leader of the guerrillas, Edén Pastora, then negotiated, through Monsignor Obando, the release of more than 60 political prisoners and a ransom of half a million dollars. After 48 hours of tense negotiations, the guerrillas, the released prisoners, and the money, along with Luis Pallais and Somoza's nephew, José Somoza Abrego, were flown to Panama.[19] It was a master stroke, crippling the prestige of the Somozas. Even more important, one of the released prisoners was the implacable Tomás Borge Martínez, who had been imprisoned and tortured for over a year, in an effort to turn him into a human vegetable. He became the nemesis of the Somoza family and the driving force in the efforts of his GPP tendency, the prolonged-popular-war faction. In the wake of these events, there was an attempted coup by some officers of the *Guardia*, 35 of whom were arrested.

In September, Carter's troubleshooter, William Jorden, visited the country and conducted talks with Somoza and with the opposition. This opposition had coalesced, after the general strike, into the FAO (*Frente Amplio de Oposición*), composed of 16 organizations, including 3 labor unions, 4 factions of the Conservative Party, 2 socialist parties, the Independent Liberal Party, *Los Doce* (or The Twelve), and a new political party, the MDN. *Los Doce* was a group of prominent political figures, mostly in exile, under the leadership of Maryknoll priest Miguel D'Escoto and businessman Sergio Ramírez Mercado. The MDN (*Movimiento Democrática Nicaraguense*) had been created by industrialist Alfonso Robelo Callejas, a leader of COSEP and organizer of the general strike of January and February. Robelo, young and articulate, was considered the spokesman of the FAO and distrusted the Marxist Sandinistas. Jorden tried to arrive at some compromise between the FAO and Somoza, but failed, for the FAO insisted that Somoza must go and that the *Guardia* must be disbanded, along with the puppet congress. In November, William Bowdler, of the State Department, came down on a similar mission, along with officials from Guatemala and the Dominican Republic, but again there was no compromise between the demands of the opposition and the determination of Somoza to finish his term.

As the talks dragged on, the civil war began in earnest. On 10 September the Sandinistas temporarily abandoned hit-and-run warfare and seized the northern city of Estelí. The *Guardia*, with superior firepower, reduced the city to rubble in retaking it by the end of the month. But heavy fighting also broke out in León, where only the *cuartel* remained in government hands until a relief force drove out the Sandinistas. Masaya was, like Estelí, destroyed in a bitter siege. In addition to combat, there was a series of specific and general strikes, beginning in August, that effectively crippled the economy.

The opposition front began to fall apart in the fall when a power struggle developed between Alfonso Robelo and the more timid Adolfo Calero Portocarrero, the head of Coca Cola Bottling and a Somoza in-law, who had recently been released from political prison. Calero, who hoped to win the favor of the United States and become the next president, suggested a plebiscite be held to determine the will of the Nicaraguan people. Seeing the FAO beginning to compromise, Sergio Ramírez and *Los Doce* withdrew, followed by Rodolfo Herrera, the Independent Liberal leader. Noticing the crack in the opposition front, Somoza cleverly took advantage of it in mid-December by announcing that he would go along with the FAO requests for an end of censorship, an amnesty for political prisoners, and an end of the state of siege. The Calero faction hailed this, but Robelo and the MDN refused to see this as any real victory. From that time on, the FAO began to be left behind as more radical coalitions were formed. Washington still appeared to pin its hopes on the FAO and urged Somoza to go along with the plebiscite plan of Calero, but in mid-January the dictator categorically rejected the plan and instead announced his intention to double the size of the *Guardia* to some 15,000.

To replace the moribund FAO, 20 political and union groups formed the *Movimiento Pueblo Unido* (MPU). MPU then joined *Los Doce* to form the *Frente Patriótico Nacional* (FPN), which had links to the FSLN. About the same time, Tomás Borge, in exile, announced that the three tendencies had settled their differences and were creating a nine-member directorate consisting of himself, Henry Ruiz, and Ballardo Arce Castano of the GPP; Carlos Núñez, Luis Carrion Cruz, and Jaime Wheelock Román of the Proletarian tendency; and *terceristas* Daniel and Humberto Ortega Saavedra and Víctor Manuel Tirado López. Except for Borge, who was in his fifties, none were over 40.

In the midst of all this confusion of parties and coalitions, the United States seemed unable to develop a coherent policy. As late as June 1978, President Carter had written Somoza, praising him for the improvement in human rights in Nicaragua, at a time when persons were regularly disappearing and being tortured to death in Somoza's jails. But in the fall, Carter saw to it that the International Monetary Fund held up a loan of $65.7 million that Somoza desperately needed, in an effort to get the Nicaraguan president to agree to the plebiscite proposal.[20] With the rejection of this idea on 15 January, the United States, in early February, cut off all aid, though much that was in the pipeline continued to get through, and, oddly enough, the IMF finally delivered half of the loan money in June, just in time for Somoza to take it into exile. The U.S. ambassador, Mauricio Solaún, a Cuban-born scholar who was not a professional diplomat, was confused by the political situation, disturbed by the violence, and forced to carry out an unrealistic policy. He left in March, with Frank Tucker taking over as *chargé*. Not until 7 June did the able and dynamic Lawrence Pezzullo arrive to assume the ambassadorship. Further, despite whatever signals were being sent by the Executive Branch, Somoza had powerful friends in Congress, including John Murphy of New York, a West Point classmate. Delegations of conservative congressmen from the United States continued to make fact-finding tours of the embattled country, and to find that Somoza was our only hope against a communist takeover.

In April, the GPP tendency launched another offensive in the Estelí region, seizing the city and again being driven out in heavy fighting during Easter week. The center of fighting then shifted southward to León and the Costa Rican border, where the Sandinistas, enjoying the support of the governments of both Costa Rica and Panama, operated with impunity. The FSLN announced the start of a final offensive on 20 May, and captured Jinotega the same day, but again, the firepower of the *Guardia*, which had modern automatic rifles, tanks, armored cars, combat aircraft, and gunships, proved to be too great; and on 24 May the Sandinistas were driven out. A similar operation took place at Masaya, southeast of the capital, with the same results.

Somoza, retreating into his bunker, appeared prepared for a war to the death. Alfonso Robelo and several other leaders of both the FAO and the MPU were thrown into prison. Right-wing death squads on the Guatemalan pattern operated freely, and, in a particularly brutal incident, Conservative leader Alfonso González, and his son and nephew, both 12 years old, were gunned down at their Managua home by the *Guardia*, along with the household servants. His wife, Constancia Chamorro de González, fled to the Mexican embassy. The televised murder of ABC newsman William Stewart in June also hurt Somoza's cause.

Although the Sandinistas lost most of their battles, they were in fact winning the war. The brutality of the government was forcing many who, like Robelo, had once vowed never to cooperate with them, into their camp. Help from abroad was coming not only from Costa Rica and Panama, but also from the Andean Pact countries of Venezuela, Colombia, Peru, Ecuador, and Bolivia, as well as from Mexico. Somoza indeed enjoyed the backing of the southern-cone dictatorships and of his fellow Central American conservative regimes, but this backing was not very substantial. With the arrival of Ambassador Pezzullo, even the United States appeared to have turned against him.

Early in June, the Sandinistas began to infiltrate into Managua, and on 8 June they launched their offensive in the capital, seizing barrios both east and west of the central zone. The government was taken by surprise in the suddenness of the onslaught. But Somoza, crouched in his bunker, ordered a counterattack; tanks and cars turned their guns upon the city, along with artillery; planes bombed and strafed, and even helicopters were loaded with 500-pound bombs which were rolled out the doors and into the houses and factories below. Despite all this firepower, the assault on the capital came close to succeeding. Only a lack of ammunition prevented the storming of La Loma itself. As it was, the *Guardia* regained control of the western barrios in a week, but the eastern sections of Managua remained in the hands of the Sandinistas until 27 June, when they conducted an orderly retreat under cover of darkness, some 12 miles to Masaya, which then became their headquarters.

The devastation of June 1979 finished what the earthquake had spared. Driving along the Carretera del Norte, early in July 1979, this writer was reminded of photos of the destruction of Hiroshima. Ruined factories with twisted girders, burnt-out machinery, and parts of vehicles lay everywhere. Only a few businesses appeared to have escaped destruction and these were watched over by cold-eyed *Guardia*. These, I was told, were spared because Somoza owned an interest in them.

The retreat to Masaya had been in fact only a tactical withdrawal. From there, the Sandinistas fanned out to surround the capital, pinning the *Guardia* against Lake Managua. The encirclement was completed with the fall of Jinotepe, on 5 July. The only way in or out of the capital then was by Las Mercedes Airport, some six miles east of the city. The Sandinistas could have taken it at will, but they allowed it to remain in government hands, perhaps as a means of escape for Somoza and his cronies so that another assault and pitched battle might be avoided. Fighting continued to rage in other areas of the country. Near the Costa Rican border, Edén Pastora was locked in combat with the *Guardia*, under the redoubtable Maj. José Emilio Salazar, while Estelí was still being contested in the northwest.

Confident now of victory, the Sandinista directorate named a government in exile, consisting of a five-member junta. Two members of the junta were non-Marxists: Alfonso Robelo and Violeta Barrios de Chamorro, widow of the martyred Pedro Joaquín; but the other three were drawn from the Sandinista leadership: Sergio Ramírez, a recent convert to the FSLN, the Marxist intellectual Daniel Ortega Saavedra; and Moises Hassan. The United States did not approve of the Marxist majority on the new junta, and William Bowdler was dispatched to try to persuade the FSLN to broaden the base of the junta. Even such North American liberals as Edward Kennedy were calling for "any measure to prevent the installation of a Marxist regime in Nicaragua."[21] But the response was that by including the MDN leader and a prominent Conservative, the Sandinistas had already bent over backward to create a representative body. They pointed out that the persons suggested by the United States—Aldolfo Calero, Gen. Julio Gutiérrez of the *Guardia*, Emilio Alvarez (Conservative), Ernesto Fernández (a Liberal friend of Somoza), Mariano Fiallos, another Liberal, and Conservative Jaime Chamorro of *La Prensa*—would give the old order a dominant voice and be simply "*Somocismo* without Somoza."

While Bowdler tried to bargain with the Sandinistas, Pezzullo was intent on effecting Somoza's departure. In this he had a firm ally in Archbishop Obando y Bravo, who was doing everything possible to discredit the regime and persuade the United States to accept the inevitable FSLN victory. So active was the archbishop that Somoza was rumored to have made a vow that if he were forced to flee, his last act would be to shoot "Comandante Miguelito," as he styled the archbishop. The story in Managua about Pezzullo was that one of Somoza's subordinates noticed how the chief always returned rattled from a conference with the new ambassador and asked another functionary about it. The latter said, "You know how Somoza talks to you? Well, that's how Pezzullo talks to Somoza." In the end, this jawboning had the desired effect and a new assault on the capital was avoided. On the night of Monday, 16 July 1979, Somoza agreed to go into exile in Florida with his entire entourage, including Dinora and Tachito. He would leave behind, as interim president, Francisco Urcuyo, the president of the lower house, to turn over power to the victorious Sandinistas. He then drove to the airport early on the morning of Tuesday, 17 July, and left Nicaragua forever.

For days before his actual departure, the handwriting had been on the wall. Bands of demoralized *Guardia* roamed the streets of the capital, mostly very young boys and old reservists, shooting at random and terrorizing the populace. In the Intercontinental, where the members of Congress were kept, distraught women wept, men held futile political discussions, and street urchins wandered about selling bottles of pilfered wine and spirits in a scene reminiscent of the fall of Saigon. The airport, whenever a random plane was going to fly out, became a scene of panic, well-dressed families standing in long queues and haggling desperately with ticket clerks. Plainly, a whole world was ending.

Then, to add the ultimate touch of confusion, just after Somoza left, Urcuyo had the strange notion that he could manage to stay on until the expiration of Somoza's term in 1981. It is quite possible that Somoza himself, as a last malicious gesture, had inspired this, but no sooner was it communicated to Pezzullo than a furious flurry of messages rushed back and forth between Managua and Washington. Having failed to convince the Sandinistas to broaden the junta, the United States had at last decided to cut its losses and go along with the inevitable triumph of the FSLN. Urcuyo's announcement threw everything out of joint. From Washington, a high official of the State Department is said to have put through a call to Somoza in Florida, warning him that if Urcuyo stayed on, he would be immediately deported. Reluctantly, perhaps, Somoza sent out the necessary word, and the new president resigned, having been "king for 36 hours," as was said on Salvadorean radio. As he left on the nineteenth, the Sandinista government arrived.

NOTES

1. Ralph Lee Woodward, Jr., *Central America: A Nation Divided* (New York: Oxford University Press, 1976), p. 323.

2. Richard Millett, *Guardians of the Dynasty: A History of the U.S.-Created Guardia Nacional de Nicaragua and the Somoza Family* (Maryknoll, N.Y.: Orbis Books, 1977), pp. 9, 253. Guatemala and Honduras also have high murder rates.

3. For a complete account of Sandino's life and death, see Neill Macauley, *The Sandino Affair* (Chicago: Quadrangle Books, 1967).

4. Woodward, *Central America*, pp. 171-74, 220.

5. Millett, *Guardians*, p. 190.

6. Ibid., pp. 196-211.

7. Ibid., pp. 222-28.

8. Ibid., p. 233.

9. "Nicaragua de las armas al poder: La Familia Somoza," *Cuadernos de Amauta* (Lima) 1, no. 1 (August 1979):15; "No Me Voy," *The Economist*, 2 September 1978, pp. 66-67.

10. "Nicaragua de las armas al poder: La Presencia Imperialista," *Cuadernos de Amauta* 1, no. 1 (August 1979):9.

11. Millett, *Guardians*, pp. 235-36.

12. *Latin America Regional Report: Central America*, 6 June 1980.

13. *Latin America*, 26 November 1976.

14. Ibid.

15. Penny Lernoux, "The Somozas of Nicaragua," *The Nation*, 23 July 1978, pp. 72-77.

16. *Latin America Political Report*, 29 September 1978.

17. *This Week Central America and Panama*, 28 January 1980.
18. *Latin America Political Report*, 3 March 1978.
19. *Latin America Political Report*, 28 July, 18 August 1978.
20. *Latin America Political Report*, 8 December 1978.
21. *Latin America Political Report*, 22 June 1979.

12

Nicaragua:
The Red and the Black

At last, the red and black flag of the FSLN flew alongside the national ensign over the city of Managua. To many who viewed the new government with suspicion, the colors suggested the red of socialism and the black of anarchy, but actually the flag was modeled upon the old battle flag of Sandino himself, which had included a white skull and a crossed rifle and machete on the black background.

The Sandinistas had won, but the cost had been tremendous. No exact casualty statistics were kept by either side, but estimates of the dead ranged from 40,000 to 50,000. Even accepting the lowest figure, this represented a higher casualty rate than that in the U.S. Civil War. Another 100,000 had been wounded, and lay, often without proper medical attention, in makeshift hospitals about the country; 40,000 children had been orphaned and 8,000 tons of emergency food relief were needed every day to prevent famine.[1] The economic costs were equally staggering, the best estimate of war damage being $1.3 billion, with the nation debt, which the Sandinistas promised to repay, standing at $1.6 billion.[2]

The official government which would preside over the national reconstruction was the five-member junta, which had on it two non-Sandinistas. The ministers of state were to be responsible to this junta. But the real body of the country was the nine-member directorate of the FSLN, which gave its orders through the Sandinista majority on the junta. This directorate had three members from each of the tendencies. From the *terceristas* came the Ortega brothers and the Mexican Víctor Manuel Tirado López. The prolonged-popular-war faction provided the redoubtable Tomás Borge; the only survivor of the original Sandinista leadership, Henry Ruiz; and Ballardo Arce Castano. The proletarians included were Carlos Núñez; Luis Carrion Cruz, the son of a prominent banker; and Jaime Wheelock Román, the ideologue of the movement. Daniel Ortega, the one directorate member who also sat on the junta, acted as the messenger boy between the two groups.

Being on the directorate did not necessarily disqualify one for also being in the cabinet, and, in fact, two ministers in the first government were directorate members: Tomás Borge was minister of the interior, controlling the police and the prisons, while Jaime Wheelock held the crucial post of minister of agriculture. Besides these two, the most prominent figure in the cabinet was the Maryknoll priest, Miguel D'Escoto, who had been the leader of *Los Doce* and was regarded as virtually a sixth member of the junta.[3] Also from *Los Doce* was Carlos Tunnerman, the minister of education. Two important figures in the economic reconstruction were Arturo Cruz, president of the Central Bank, and the minister for internal development, Alfredo César, both of whom were prominent bankers and regarded as moderate. Two choices among the ministers were very curious ones: that of an ex-National Guard colonel, Bernardino Larios, to be minister of defense, and that of a Trappist monk, Ernesto Cardenal, to be minister of culture, thus making Nicaragua probably the only country in the world with Catholic priests in the cabinet. Larios, who had fled Nicaragua after making an attempted coup in November 1978, was replaced in December 1979 by a directorate member, Humberto Ortega; and at the same time, Henry Ruiz replaced Roberto Mayorga as minister of planning. The cabinet was obviously chosen with an eye to conciliating various interest groups and calming fears that Nicaragua might be moving toward a rigid Marxist state.

Within the army structure, even before he was named defense minister, Humberto Ortega held the post of commander in chief, with Luis Carrion Cruz designated as second in command and Tomás Borge as third in command. Designating Borge only third in the military structure was indeed seen as an attempt to downplay his role in the government, for if anyone had seemed likely to emerge as the *caudillo* of *Sandinismo*, it was Borge, a diminutive, rigidly Marxist fighter with snow-white hair, whose wife had been murdered by the *Guardia* in 1979. He was not only the most prominent member of the directorate, but also, at 50, its patriarch, for none of the directors, except Tirado, had even reached 40.

One of the most immediately vexing questions to affect the new government was that of the ex-*Guardia* members and other Somocistas. In July 1979, as garrison after garrison surrendered, there had been a number of summary executions, and even some instances of the massacre of large numbers of prisoners, such as that of Col. Julio Fonseca Talavera and his men at Puerto Cabezas.[4] In the entire country, perhaps 500 to 1,000 persons had met their end in that manner; but this was not condoned by the new government, which rapidly asserted its authority and ended the killings. This left the government with 7,000 or 8,000 political prisoners, many of whom sweltered in the steamy barracks atop La Loma, which the Sandinistas had rechristened El Chipote. Public sentiment against these prisoners, who included about 3,000 ex-*Guardia* members ran very high, and this, as Tomás Borge told me, made it impossible to free them even if he had wanted to. Some local FSLN garrisons even refused, for a time, to turn over their prisoners for fear that they would be released. On 8 January 1980, the garrison of Boaco virtually mutinied over the demand of Edén Pastora that its prisoners be surrendered. The local commandant accused Pastora (of all people) of being "bourgeois," but at last gave in.

Trials of the political prisoners finally began in January 1980, under the public prosecutor, Nora Astorga. Astorga had a reputation as a very tough Sandinista. It was she who had lured the *Guardia* leader, Gen. Reinaldo Pérez Vega, to his death by pretending to seduce him. After a preliminary screening, about 800 prisoners were released, but of those tried, almost all were convicted of some sort of war crimes even if their only real offense had been to join the *Guardia*. Coordinator of Tribunals Mario Majia Alvarez commented, "We are not judging people whose innocence can be presumed," as if there were any other kind. "At the same time," he added, "we are not going to be a machine for producing guilty verdicts. Anyone whose case cannot be proved will be set free."[5] With such agonizing slowness did the business proceed that by July 1980, only some 200 had actually been tried. Most of those convicted were found guilty under a delinquency law passed ex post facto by the new government, which made mere membership in the *Guardia* an offense.

Arrests continued after the installation of the new government. So great was the fear of subversives that the local *Comités de Defensa Sandinista*, of which more will be said later, were encouraged to act as *orejas*—ears of the government—and denounce enemies of the revolution. Often, as Borge himself admitted, these denunciations were frivolous or malicious, but one went to jail just the same. The saying was: "Two and a half million people can put you in jail, but only one man, Tomás Borge, can get you out." Indeed, Borge and his deputy, Hugo Torres, who actually ran the prison system, seemed to have built a powerful machine for potential repression. Nonetheless, Borge himself was regarded by his colleagues as a humane man. Miguel D'Escoto tells the story that Borge had met, in the prisons, one of those who had tortured him under the Somoza regime, and immediately released him, "thus returning good for evil," said Father D'Escoto. On one occasion, I went with Borge to El Chipote and saw him release, without ceremony, a man for whom the U.S. embassy had interceded. "I think you are guilty," he said, "but get your things and get out of Nicaragua in 24 hours." The question was not whether Borge used his powers wisely or not; the question was whether any man should exercise such powers, without some kind of public scrutiny.

In addition to the imprisonment of persons, there were many confiscations. Immediately, all the property of the Somoza family and its supporters was declared forfeited, but the question was where to draw the line as to who was a *Somocista*. As in the case of arrests, there were many private vengeances, and some instances of lower-level Sandinista officials profiting personally. To do the government justice, as soon as it became aware of the situation, in late November 1979, it suspended its decree on expropriation.[6]

If the political problems of the new government were difficult enough, the immediate economic problems seemed almost insurmountable. Only the firm conviction that Nicaragua was basically wealthy, and would never be, as one official put it, "a basket case like El Salvador," gave the Sandinistas the courage to declare that they would repay the national debt and maintain their economic links to the Western world. To do this, they needed immediate influxes of cash. The World Bank came through with part of this money, touting it as part of the "first set of emergency loans" to Nicaragua, but in reality, the $35.9-million loan was simply a revamped version of the loan originally promised to Somoza. The impression of government officials in Managua was that the World Bank was "really quite cool" toward the new regime. The bank, however, promised that $51 million more in loans would be forthcoming. The Inter-American Development Bank also extended $88.5 million in loans and gave almost $2 million in grants.[7] The socialist countries also promised to give limited amounts of aid; even Vietnam's Premier Pham Van Dong arrived in September to pledge moral support. More concretely, Castro's Cuba contributed a number of boats to restore the depleted fishing fleet, thus reviving a major export industry. Cuba also offered immediate shipments of food and other supplies, no doubt from the Soviet Union, and promised doctors and teachers for the reconstruction effort.

But the role of the United States remained critical. The Carter administration soon allocated $8.8 million in emergency aid; but a much larger package of $75 million, all but $5 million of which would be in loans, was proposed to the U.S. Congress. For many reasons, there were endless and unfortunate delays, until the Nicaraguans began to feel that the money was being politically held over their heads. Only in September 1980, when President Carter assured Congress that the Nicaraguan government was not aiding in the Salvadorean civil war, was the money finally freed up. About 60 percent of this loan, Arturo Cruz told me, was marked for the private sector, and Alfonso Robelo declared that it was absolutely necessary to have the aid if the private sector was to survive and a "pluralistic" Nicaragua was to develop. About 40 percent of the money was to go into the purchase of equipment from a list of countries approved by the United States. In the natural course of things, Alfredo César predicted in our conversation, $30 million of the loan would return to the lending country in the form of purchases. The U.S. loan also had a strong symbolic value, suggesting that the North Americans had not abandoned Nicaragua to the Eastern-bloc countries, and this made its yearlong delay all the more painful. In urging this aid before Congress, Deputy Secretary of State Warren Christopher commented, "I am sure that if we walk away, we will almost assure what we don't want, a Communist or Cuban regime."[8]

But while loans might keep Nicaragua afloat, they would, in the long run, compound the foreign-debt-payments problem, which was perhaps the most vexing economic problem of all. The Sandinista government had agreed to pay all the international obligations incurred under the previous government, but it knew well that many of the more recent loans had been for no purpose other than to fatten the bank accounts of Somoza and his cronies. The total sum of this debt, $1.6 billion, was equal to an entire year's GNP and to three years' exports; $700 million was owed to private banks, the rest to governments or to international agencies. Deciding to tackle the debt to private banks first, the Nicaraguan government, through New York banker Richard Weinert, negotiated, through the summer of 1980, on a formula for repayment. The government finally agreed to pay all the debts, even those they felt were phony, at a commercial rate of interest, while the banks agreed to recapitalize the back interest due and to scale down and stabilize the commercial rate, stretching out the payments so that debt servicing would be minimal until after 1985, when it would gradually begin to increase, with the whole of the Somoza debt being paid off by 1990. This agreement would probably be duplicated in dealing with nonbank lenders.[9]

Even this minimal servicing of the debt might be more than Nicaragua could handle, for the GNP had dropped from $1.75 billion in 1977 to $1.3 billion in 1979 and an expected $1.6 billion in 1980. This was coupled with an inflation rate of 60 percent for 1979. This forced the government to collect taxes at what Alfonso Robelo characterized to me as "the highest rate in our history." Of the expected government expenditures of $390 million for 1980, $90 million was expected to come from these higher taxes.[10] Such a relatively high rate of public expenditure, in relation to the economy as a whole, was indicative of the fact that the public sector was playing a much larger role in the economy than had been the case under Somoza. In the time of the dictator, public expenditure had been very low, accounting for no more than 15 percent of GNP in 1977. The new government planned for the public sector's share to be about 41 percent of the total in 1980, which is about the same as it is in Mexico and Brazil. Most of the public sector's share would be in services rather than goods, but, thanks to the various confiscations, 36 percent of industrial production was expected to be from state farms and factories in 1980.[11]

The above figures suggest that Nicaragua was confronting its problems in a fashion not too different from that of any other Western nation with a similar situation. There was little of a revolutionary nature in paying debts or in raising taxes, but Sergio Ramírez, the leading figure on the junta, cautioned: "We have to solve the economic crisis, but do so in political terms. . . . It is easy to make immediate demands on the revolution without seeing the long-term revolutionary project."[12] However, a number of measures were taken to immediately benefit the poor. Rents of $50 to $100 a month were cut, in late 1979, by 40 percent, with a 50 percent reduction given in rents of less than $50. This was, of course, a blow to middle-class landlords, although Arturo Cruz, then president of the Central Bank, promised that their own mortgages would be restructured for their benefit. Massive housing projects were also launched, in part because so much needed to be rebuilt after the war, and in part as a means of putting people back to work and lowering the 40 percent unemployment rate.

There was evidence, by the middle of 1980, that the economic policies of the government were beginning to pay off, although there was much mismanagement due to lack of experience. The country's economic viability ultimately would have to rest on its balance of payments, and, to the distress of the government, a trade deficit of $190 million was forecast for 1980.[13]

In the rebuilding of the economy, the role of the private sector remained vital, but there was a built-in suspicion between the avowedly socialist government and private enterprise. Businessmen were worried about the wave of expropriations that followed the revolution, and which continued, off and on, thereafter. They were also worried about the increasing demands of the *Central Sandinista de Trabajadores* (CST), the Sandinista labor movement, which was seeking a share in the management of many firms. In addition, in view of the state's increasing activity in manufacturing and in the building industry, private business was concerned about direct competition from the public sector. Prior to the success of the revolution, the chief spokesman for the concerns of business had been Alfonso Robelo, the young cooking-oil millionaire; but when he assumed his seat upon the junta, he was seen increasingly as a radical by the more conservative members of the business community. José Francisco Cardenal then became a leading figure among the anti-Somoza businessmen, but, to everyone's surprise, Cardenal left the country in the spring of 1980, denouncing the revolution as communist. Some business leaders ascribed this about-face to personal business reversals Cardenal had suffered. In mid-1980, perhaps the most important business leader in Nicaragua was Enrique Dreyfus, the president of COSEP, who continued to try to work out a *modus vivendi* between the private sector and the government.

The growth of the public sector was particularly evident in mining and in agriculture. In regard to the former, the holdings of NORANA—a Canadian firm—ASARCO, and Rosario Mining Company, of New York, were all seized and operated by the government after Robelo accused the mines of trying to smuggle gold out of Nicaragua. Land reform was under the *Instituto Nacional de Reforma Agraria* (INRA), which had quickly seized about a quarter of the nation's arable land from the Somoza family and its supporters, following the Sandinista victory. Jaime Wheelock, who, as minister of agriculture and agrarian reform, administered the program, aimed at maintaining these estates as production units, rather than breaking them into individual plots where the peasants might raise what they pleased. By mid-September 1979, Wheelock had already settled 45,000 peasants on the government lands, chiefly in cooperatives. The government controlled 200 coffee *fincas*—producing 12 percent of the total national crop—half the sugar lands, one-third of the rice lands, and one-fourth of the cotton lands. The question remained, however, whether the inexperienced government could run these land effectively and raise production, which was down, from 1978 to 1979, by about 50 percent in corn and beans and 36 percent in rice.[14] The economic record of cooperatives in Latin America has not been good, but the FSLN remained optimistic about its venture.

While the government favored the production cooperative as the basic agricultural unit, it also saw the need to aid the small, independent farmer. Service cooperatives were formed so that such farmers could sell their produce and buy their supplies and equipment together. In addition PROCAMPO, a small-farmer assistance program with 40 offices throughout the country, arranged loans and gave advice to the farmers. For rental lands, the renter was protected by a maximum of $10 per *manzana* (1.7 acres) in yearly rent. The large estates also continued to exist, especially in the cotton and sugar lands, but their existence was an uneasy one, with no one ever sure when the government might decide that the time for expropriation might come.

To take an entire nation, devastated by a prolonged civil war, and transform its economy was a task of such magnitude that it could not possibly be accomplished without resort to new forms of social organization. The Sandinistas therefore created the Organizations of the Masses, which owed their origin both to the example of the Cuban revolution and to the spontaneous responses of the people during the period of the fighting. Many outside observers viewed these organizations with alarm, one State Department official suggesting that they were the reason Nicaragua stood "a 75 percent chance of becoming a dreary, communist dictatorship." However, non-Sandinista political leaders, with whom I spoke more than a year after the revolution, seemed to regard them as benign institutions.[15]

The mass organizations were political instruments of the FSLN, reporting to the directorate. The most prominent of them was the association of *Comités de Defensa Sandinista* (CDS), which had grown out of the *Comités de Defensa Civil*, established in the cities and villages of Nicaragua during the civil war in order to aid the Sandinista armed forces, by acting as an intelligence network; by providing food, shelter, and medicine; and by repairing war damage as it occurred. After the end of the hostilities, the CDSs emerged on a national level with branches in almost every department, and the departments were organized on a hierarchical basis, the lowest unit of which was the block committee. This was not much different from the organizations that had emerged in Cuba following the revolution. In an interview with the

Sandinista paper *Barricada* (31 December 1979), the secretary general of the CDSs, Patricia Orozco, outlined some of the ways in which the CDSs were aiding in the reconstruction of the country. She pointed out that through "volunteer work," the CDSs had been very active in cleaning up the damage of the war. Further, the CDSs were active in aiding those left destitute by the revolution or who had been wounded in the struggle. On a more political level, the CDSs promoted "political fraternity," and enforced the government's price-control measures, especially in the open-air markets. The committees also worked to control vices, by monitoring the hours and sales of liquor stores and taverns and reporting prostitutes.

Other roles of the CDSs proved more controversial. One of these was the granting of *constancias*, permissions which were required to be signed by the head of the block committee before one could get a visa or take out any sort of license. The requirement in regard to visas, which was originally designed to prevent Somoza collaborators from slipping out of the country, especially smacked of totalitarianism and was abandoned early in 1980. The question of the *constancias* was linked to the more general one of the role of the CDSs in hunting down Somocistas and other subversives. The government, late in 1979, put out a directive urging the CDSs to report on the activities of counter-revolutionaries and to testify against them before the *Tribunas Populares*; but this was greatly resented, even among those who favored the revolution, as smacking of *Somocismo*.[16] Though there were denunciations—and, indeed, some irresponsible ones—on the whole, the Nicaraguans refused to play what they considered a despicable role.

One of the greatest triumphs of the CDSs was in working with the massive literacy campaign conducted by Father Fernando Cardenal, a cousin of cabinet member Ernesto Cardenal, in the spring and summer of 1980; the goal was to reduce illiteracy from 54 percent to practically zero. The CDSs, along with other mass organizations, provided teachers, facilities, housing for teachers from other parts of the country, and school supplies for this program which Carlos Carrion declared had reduced the illiteracy rate to 12 percent by August 1980.[17] Another praiseworthy effort of the block committees was in the establishment of housing-material banks, where local persons seeking better housing could receive, through low-cost loans, lumber, bricks, cement, and other materials for house building.[18] On the whole, it was the consensus of most Nicaraguans that the CDSs flourished in working-class neighborhoods, but were, on the whole, treated as a joke in more affluent neighborhoods, which had, of course, less need of their services.

Second in importance among the mass organizations was the Sandinista labor union—the *Central Sandinista de Trabajadores*, whose head, Iván García, estimated, at the close of 1979, that there were 100,000 members in its 360 syndicates.[19] This group competed for membership with the Christian Democrats' *Central de Trabajadores de Nicaragua* (CTN) and the *Confederación Unida de Sindicatos* (CUS), the ORIT affiliate, backed by AIFLD, as well as with other independent unions. The CST also started as a clandestine movement in 1977 and was legalized when Somoza fell. As a mass organization, the CST held political seminars for its members, to indoctrinate them in Sandinista ideology—a vague combination of nationalism and Marxism—and to acquaint them with the slogan of the organization, *Pueblo, Ejército, Unidad, Garantía de la Victoria.* Not only was solidarity with the people's Sandinista army stressed, but also, solidarity with the *Asociación de Trabajadores del Campo* (ATC), whose harvests were sometimes aided by CST volunteers. For longer-range political indoctrination, workers were sent to Cuba and to the Soviet Union.[20] Ironically enough, the one activity that the CST seemed least capable of doing was that of functioning as a legitimate labor union seeking wages and benefits for its workers through negotiations and strikes. The CST was in fact under orders to keep wage demands down and to keep productivity up.

This gave the CST a built-in disadvantage in attracting workers away from other unions, many of whom annoyed the government with their tactics. When 2,000 factory workers in Managua struck in early March 1980, under the banner of the radical Marxist *Central de Acción Unidad Sindical* (CAUS), the government was outraged at their demands for a 100 percent wage increase, and Ballardo Arce declared that these communists were in league with the CIA.[21] The solution to the problem of competing organizations would be to do away with all rivals, by law, and to make the CST the only labor organization—an idea much applauded within the organization, because, as organizer Denis Meléndez put it, "organized labor was the vanguard of the FSLN." One area in which this has been achieved is in the field of journalism, where all practicing journalists in any medium had to join the CST affiliate, the *Unión de Periodistas Nicaragüenses* (UPN). Two radio journalists, running a small, ultraleft station, were expelled from the UPN and forced to close their operation in February 1980, after being denounced for "counter-revolutionary reporting."[22] In general, other unions, especially the CTN, have more than managed to hold their own.

But one other area in which the CST has managed to maintain a monopoly has been in the organization of teachers on every level from the university to the primary school. These are served by a CST affiliate, the *Asociación Nacional de Educadores Nicaragüenses* (ANDEN), boasting some 9,000 members. ANDEN suffers from the ambiguities common to Sandinista unions. While one might expect it to be working in an adversary role to that of the minister of education (like the AFT in the United States), the opposite was in fact the case. Its director, Bruno Gallardo, declared: "There cannot exist contradictions with the ministry of education now that education ought to serve the needs of the masses."[23] The organization served chiefly to keep the teachers in line, both in terms of their economic demands, and their ideology, which it closely monitored.

The ATC has also developed significantly since the success of the revolution, having 1,184 base organizations by December 1979; 392 of these were on production cooperatives, with a total of 13,202 ATC members, the rest being on haciendas or small farms. The total membership at the end of 1979 was about 57,674, and this later grew to over 80,000. Like the other Sandinista mass organizations, the ATC functioned in a variety of roles. As a peasant movement, it worked for better conditions for laborers on private farms, while it helped to organize small farmers into seller and buyer cooperatives. It also provided the formal structure for the members of the production cooperatives, and of course functioned as a source of indoctrination, through its rural schools of political formation. Further, it was through the ATC that 10,000 nonrural workers were mobilized voluntarily for the coffee harvest of 1979. As a rural workers' union, the ATC often caused displeasure among owners of large farms, by demanding a share in management. It also ran into strong competition from the farm workers' unions sponsored by the CTN. Although sponsored by the government, the ATC did not hesitate to defend its members against government bureaucrats.

Considering the fact that Sandinismo has always been a youth movement, and that children as young as 12 often fought in the battles of the civil war, it is hardly surprising that the mass organizations contain a youth movement, the *Juventud Sandinista, 19 de Julio* (JS-19), formed out of the revolutionary group known as the *Juventud Revolucionaria Nicaragüense*, which flourished in the period of armed struggle. Designed as an organization of secondary school students, JS-19's chief purpose was indoctrination and, as its director, Sergio Martinez, put it, "unconditional support of the FSLN."[24] The JS-19 provided many of the hands necessary for the coffee harvest and other such projects and played a large part in the literacy campaign.

For the very young, there was the *Asociación de Niños Sandinistas* (ANS), which specialized in indoctrination through hagiolatry, with pilgrimages to the birthplaces of Sandino and Carlos Fonseca Amador being common exercises. This organization ran into a great deal of suspicion from parents, who accused it of deliberately weakening the family bonds and teaching Marxism; but the ANS did a great deal of good in broadening the horizons of many lower-class children. It also aided the *Asociación de Mujeres Nicaraguenses, Luisa Amanda Espinosa* (AMNLAE) in its campaign to provide milk for deprived children.

AMNLAE itself appeared to be the most successful and dynamic of the Sandinista organizations. Like the others, it grew out of the experiences of the war, when Nicaraguan women formed committees to protest against the frequent disappearances. During the civil war period, women not only made up a large part of the Sandinista fighting force (though not the 50 percent sometimes claimed), but also fulfilled more traditional roles as nurses and suppliers of provisions and shelter. AMNLAE grew out of the new self-consciousness created by those experiences. Among its primary tasks were the holding of seminars and discussion groups to combat the old domestic slavery of women, which had seldom been more entrenched than in the Nicaragua of

Somoza. In addition, the organization established a commission to rewrite the law code in regard to such things as marriage, divorce, and property rights. Originally an organization of the urban middle class, AMNLAE made heroic efforts to reach out to the peasant women and even to propagandize on the distant Atlantic coast.

Another organization in postrevolutionary Nicaragua was the *Militia Popular Sandinista* (MPS), founded in February 1980 as an adjunct to the Sandinista Popular Army, the regular armed forces of the country. The militia was placed under the command of Edén Pastora, the number-two man in the military, and soon had thousands of volunteers drilling in town squares all over the country. Less a fighting force than a means of keeping up the revolutionary spirit, the MPS nonetheless emphasized the continuing fear of armed counterrevolutionary attack by the Somocistas in Honduras or perhaps by Nicaragua's three northern neighbors.

The very existence of the mass organizations conjured up in the minds of many, both inside and outside the country, an Orwellian nightmare of thought control and constant surveillance. A phrase in the literacy-campaign text read, "The block committees are vigilant day and night."[25] But the realities after over a year of revolutionary government appeared far less sinister. When asked about this aspect of Nicaraguan life, Nicaraguans declared over and over, "Nicaraguans are not Cubans." While it would be dangerous to put too much confidence in a national character, it did indeed seem that the Nicaraguans took none of these groups, even the MPS, all that seriously.

The issue of personal liberty is, however, a very real one, and nowhere better illustrated than in the fragile freedom of the press that prevailed after the revolution. After Somoza fell, *La Prensa*, whose plant had been burned by the dictator, resumed publication under the Chamorro family; junta member Violeta Barrios de Chamorro served as publisher, with her son, Pedro Joaquín, and Xavier Chamorro Cardenal, his uncle, as editors. The Sandinistas themselves launched a new daily, *Barricada*, which soon earned a reputation for revolutionary militancy. The extreme Trotskyist-Marxist left also launched a paper, *El Pueblo*, edited by Melvin Wallace. This last paper soon found itself in trouble with the government; Tomás Borge himself warned it that it must "serve the needs of the revolution" and not criticize the FSLN for being too conservative. When the paper failed to heed these warnings, it was first temporarily suspended and then shut down altogether, in February 1980. Melvin Wallace was jailed along with two of his staff, until July 1980, for "stories against the revolutionary process and the interests of the people."[26]

La Prensa, the venerable newspaper of one of the revolution's most famous martyrs, seldom attacked the government directly; and it even obliged it by running such stories as one by Philip Agee, charging CIA penetration in the country (2 January 1980). But the Nicaraguan abstention in the UN vote to condemn the Soviet Union for its invasion of Afghanistan brought a stinging editorial from Pedro Joaquín Chamorro Barrios, who asked, "If Sandino had been born in Afghanistan, on whose side would he be fighting?"[27] About two months later, the board of directors, led by Violeta and her son Pedro Joaquin, ousted Xavier Chamorro as editor, for his being too subservient to the government line. But Xavier Chamorro would not leave so tamely. The newspaper's staff, belonging to a CTS affiliate, went on strike on 21 April, demanding that Xavier be reinstated. The publishers, backed by COSEP, refused these demands and the workers had a sitdown strike in the plant. All this was thoroughly embarassing to the government, which already had a monopoly on television broadcasting and had shut down one of the opposition radio stations. After almost a month, a settlement was reached, by which the workers agreed to a monetary compensaton, and some three-quarters of them joined with Xavier Chamorro in founding a new paper, *La Nueva Diario*. *La Prensa* itself resumed publication on 26 May, but in late August, Humberto Ortega announced, on behalf of the directorate, that there was to be no political campaigning in the press and that neither shortages nor security matters, such as disturbances, could be mentioned in the press.[28] This did not bode well for continued freedom of the press. In 1981, *La Prensa* was briefly suspended on several occasions.

Although some viewed the question of bourgeois elections, along with freedom of the press, as a mere formality of Western democracy, the question of elections played a large part in the editorials of *La Prensa* and in the thinking of many Nicaraguans. When I spoke to junta member Alfonso Robelo in January 1980, he was postulating that local elections would be held in a year or two, with elections for a National Constituent Assembly occurring in three years and presidential elections in four years or so. But these hopes proved overly optimistic; the tipoff for this was the decision of the directorate that the role of the Council of State—to be chosen in May—would be changed from a legislative to a consultative one, and that its membership would be increased to include many more members of the organizations of the masses, while only one member of Robelo's MDN would be included. Robelo, along with most non-Sandinista political leaders, had already acquiesced to a delay in the appointment of this body, but the changes in its composition, along with the new limitations in its role, caused him considerable concern. He was also disturbed that many on the directorate did not seem to share his enthusiasm for early elections and he was anxious to get busy on the organization of the MDN. This insistence of Robelo on a role for his own and other parties caused *Barricada* to warn against "democratism," and to caution, "Liberal bourgeois liberty must never be confused with popular liberty, which represents the interests of the people."[29] Given these differences with the FSLN, there was little surprise shown when Robelo announced his resignation from the junta in mid-April 1980, declaring that he wished to devote full time to his party. His resignation was soon followed by that of Violeta Barrios de Chamorro, who was in ill health and upset over the controversies at *La Prensa*.

To replace the resigning members of the junta, the directorate once more chose two persons who were not members of the FSLN—Arturo Cruz, the president of the Central Bank, and a supreme court judge, Rafael Córdoba Rivas. Both of these men had strong anti-Somocistas credentials. Cruz, a leftist, had been a member of *Los Doce*, while Córdoba Rivas had been imprisoned 17 times under the Somoza regime. Cruz was succeeded in the presidency of the Central Bank by Alfredo Alainz, while Lourdes Bolanos was elevated to the Supreme Court.

Robelo, now off the junta, not only worked to strengthen his own party, but began to form a coalition of non-Marxist-Leninist parties. These included the *Partido Social Demócrata* (PSD) of Wilfredo Montalván, a mildly leftist group linked to the European Social Democrats; the Christian Democratic *Partido Cristiano Social* (PCS); and the *Partido Conservador Demócrata* (PCD), under Coca Cola head Adolfo Calero. Together with the MDN, these three formed the *Frente Amplio de Oposición* (FAO), to which the two major non-Sandinista unions, the CTN and the CUS, also adhered. The weakness of the coalition lay in its diversity. While Robelo and Montalván represented the progressive left, Calero, although he had suffered much under the regime of his in-law, General Somoza, was essentially a man of the old order. For his efforts, Robelo received stinging criticism from his former associates in the government; Tomás Borge likened him to Hitler and declared that the Somoza forces were using him.[30]

To counter the FAO, the Sandinistas formed a progovernment front of their own, the *Frente Revolucionario*, comprising the FSLN, the *Partido Liberal Independiente* (PLI), a remnant of the anti-Somoza Liberals; the *Partido Socialista Nicaraguense* (PSN), a communist, pro-Soviet group; and the *Partido Popular Cristiano Social* (PPCS), a militant Marxist splinter group from the PCS. All these parties held positions in the government. The ultraradical and anti-Soviet Communist Party was not a part of this group.

The 43-member Council of State was to meet in May, but there was great dissatisfaction among the opposition groups as to its composition and its functions. Rather than being elected, it was to have delegates appointed by various governmental and nongovernmental groups. A large bloc of members was to come from the organizations of the masses, and a bloc of six from COSEP. All the recognized political parties, including the opposition, were also to be represented, but the largest percentage of total delegates would be from groups supporting the FSLN. Further, although it had originally been envisioned as a legislative body, and perhaps one which would create a constitution and hold elections, it had been reduced to merely advisory status, giving it no more power than the junta, which was also mere window dressing for the directorate. At first, Enrique Dreyfus refused to let COSEP take the seats allotted to it, and the FAO parties also showed a disinclination to serve, but Robelo realized that it would be better not to give the impression of totally disavowing the government and thus had the MDN representative, Alvaro Jerez, take his seat. At Robelo's urging, COSEP and the other groups also entered the council. The object, as Robelo put it, was to "criticize errors and abuses of the revolutionary leaders."[31] Ballardo Arce, who had been elected to the presidency of the Council of State, soon resigned and was replaced by Carlos Núñez. Arce evidently wanted to devote full time to the political committee of the FSLN, which with Jaime Wheelock and Humberto Ortega, had formed to keep watch on the ideological purity of the movement.

While much of the criticism from the opposition groups centered on domestic problems, the erratic and often bellicose foreign policy of the Sandinista government was also a cause for concern in Nicaragua. Not only did tensions with Honduras continue, but Nicaragua seemed determined to alienate many of those countries which had supported the FSLN against Somoza. A dispute with Colombia, over the San Andres and Providencia Islands, caused the latter to recall its ambassador in February 1980; it accused the Nicaraguans of "breaking the most elemental principles of law" in denouncing the 1928 treaty that has regulated the status of the islands.[32] The relations of the Nicaraguan government with another strong supporter from the war period, Panama, also began to cool. The Panamanians had sent military advisors to help train the new Sandinista army, but these were withdrawn following disputes between the Panamanians and Cuban advisors, who had begun to arrive in large numbers.[33]

The government stirred up trouble for itself by adopting a pro-Soviet line in regard to the world beyond the Americas. Not only did the Nicaraguan representative to the United Nations abstain on the Afghanistan question, but Nicaragua steadfastly maintained relations with Taiwan, thus making it impossible to exchange ambassadors with China. To embarrass the government, Alvaro Jerez of the MDN rose in the Council of State and proposed the recognition of Red China and the breaking of relations with Taiwan. The proposal was defeated, but the irony of Nicaragua refusing to recognize the world's largest socialist country was not lost on the public.

The public, in fact, soon appeared to have had enough of the Soviets, who crowded the Intercontinental Hotel and proved difficult guests, and of their much more numerus Cuban associates. These latter became known as *gusanos*—worms, because of their burrowing into the Nicaraguan government. Though generally well behaved, the Cuban military advisors, the 2,000 teachers, and 800 medical personnel sent to aid in the reconstruction sometimes got themselves into trouble by mocking Christian customs, such as Christmas and saints' days.[34] Nothing could have created more resentment among the deeply religious Nicaraguan people. Cuban jokes abounded, such as the ubiquitous one in which a newly arrived Cuban announced in wonder, "You Nicaraguans eat the way we did 20 years ago!" Fidel Castro's visit to the 19 July 1980 anniversary celebration was a huge success all the same, for the Cuban leader had enough sense to praise his hosts and to declare, "I am here to learn from you."

Two groups on the platform appeared disconcerted by the 19 July celebration—the North American delegation, led by James Cheek, which quietly walked out before the playing of the new Nicaraguan national anthem labeling Yankee imperialism "the enemy of humanity"; and the church, whose chief representative, Msgr. Obando y Bravo, was not even invited to speak. This was in marked contrast to the New Year's Day celebration for 1980, when Archbishop Obando had joined the top Sandinista commanders in reviewing the troops and heard Borge deliver a sermon praising the church and declaring that Christian virtue and Sandinista ideals were the same.[35] The basic attitude of the church, as the bishop of Estelí characterized it to me, remained "positive but critical," but there was evidence that the church was beginning to disassociate itself from the revolutionary process. One such bit of evidence was a public denunciation by the archbishop in February of the anti-Christian attacks of the Cubans; and a second was the pastoral letter of the Nicaraguan bishops, in May 1980, telling priests to leave the government or risk being reduced to lay status. Most refused, including the irrepressible foreign minister, Miguel D'Escoto. The future of church-state relations remained cloudy. However, the church ardently backed government decrees forbidding the use of Santa Claus and other commercial exploitation of Christmas, under penalty of imprisonment.

The election situation also remained cloudy. When he was in the government, Robelo had counted on elections in a reasonably short time; but these hopes were dashed by Humberto Ortega, speaking for the directorate, in late August 1980. He announced that there would be no elections of any variety until 1985 and no campaigning or propaganda by parties until 1984. Even for 1985, the type of elections Ortega had in mind remained mysterious. He declared that these elections would be to "improve the revolutionary power," and stated, "These will not be elections to decide who is in power, because the people hold power, through their vanguard, the *Frente Sandinista*."[36] This was just another way of saying what one often heard from members of the FSLN: that the people had in effect voted in the civil war. To which the obvious rejoinder was, "Are you going to hold a civil war every five years?" Or, as Pedro Joaquín Chamorro Barrios commented, "For how long is a vanguard elected?"

Those who thought that the Council of State could function smoothly as a governing body reckoned without the deeply growing tensions in the country. These tensions were made worse by antigovernment border incursions and by the murder of seven volunteers, during the literacy campaign, presumably by Somocistas. Tomás Borge told a Sandinista rally that Robelo was morally responsible for these murders and heard the crowd answer with chants of "Robelo to the firing squad."[37]

In mid-November, Robelo had planned a rally of the MDN at Nandiame, 66 kilometers south of Managua; and some 60,000 were expected to attend, making an impressive antigovernment show of force. When asked, Arturo Cruz, then on the junta, declared that his group would have no objections; but 48 hours prior to the rally, Borge informed Robelo that the rally would be a violation of Decree 513, which put off all political activity until 1984. When the MDN leader objected, Comandante Borge replied, "We have the arms, we have the power and we're not going to let it go. The revolution is irreversible."[38] On 16 November, a group of young people from JS-19 sacked the MDN headquarters in Managua, with no hindrance from the police. This was followed by attacks upon other opposition-party headquarters.

A worse crisis erupted the next day. Jorge Salazar, president of the agricultural producers' association and acting president of COSEP, stopped at a gas station, which was evidently also a police checkpoint. A political associate of his, Ernesto Moncada, also drove up. As the two men got out of their cars, someone fired a shot. Several policemen rushed to the scene and shot Salazar dead. No one denied that Salazar was unarmed, though some claimed that Moncada had fired the first shot.

Tomás Borge, who was in charge of the nation's police, declared that the shooting was "accidental," though he also declared that Salazar had given $50,000 to National Guard elements seeking to overthrow the state. Salazar's brother, Alejandro, and Leonardo Somarriba, the vice president of the Chamber of Commerce, were then arrested, and they allegedly confessed that they, along with the late Jorge Salazar, had indeed been plotting the overthrow of the government. They were convicted in December. In the meantime, on 20 November 1980, Borge staged a huge rally involving about 100,000 supporters in Managua, to denounce counterrevolutionaries.

For the opposition members of the Council of State, this was the final straw. Alvaro Jerez led the opposition parties and COSEP members, 11 in all, in an exit from the council; and they presented their resignations.[39] The Salazars probably had been plotting to overthrow the government, possibly in league with José Francisco Cardenal, that inveterate plotter who had so often tried to overthrow Somoza; but it also seems true that Jorge Salazar was set up and deliberately murdered, though Borge might have known nothing of this. Certainly, the mood of the country was one in which plots and counterplots were regularly reported, and Lenin Cerna, the chief of police, was said to be running a secret prison, where torture was not uncommon. The existence of such a prison was confirmed by José Esteban González, head of the private Permanent Commission on Human Rights in Nicaragua, in an interview in early January 1981. Shortly after, González was arrested by Borge, and although he was soon released, due to international pressure, his organization, long a foe of Somoza, was largely suppressed. In particular, a group of former Somocistas called the *Fuerzas Armadas Democráticas* (FAD) was blamed for guerrilla attacks in the northwest of the country and for subversion everywhere.

One area, in particular, where the government professed to see the hand of the FAD was the Bluefields area of the Atlantic coast. Some 200,000 Nicaraguans who live scattered throughout that region have long remained outside the national life. They are an amalgam of Indians (generally known as the Mosquito Indians, though there are several tribes), English settlers of an earlier era, and English-speaking blacks from the islands of the Caribbean. The dominant language of the region is English, though Indian dialects are also spoken. Left alone by the Somozas, the people of this region continued their own patterns of society, which included strong tribal cohesiveness, and a communal farming pattern with no private ownership. As these people were in fact indigenous socialists, it might have been imagined that they would rapidly fall into line with the revolution. In fact, they were resentful and suspicious of the Spanish-speaking foreigners who came to conduct a literacy campaign; to found CDS organizations, which the natives felt they did not need; and to change their cooperative pattern of agriculture into something more formally socialistic.

In late September, there was an uprising in the Bluefields area, in which over 5,000 English-speaking residents took part. Attempts were made to squelch the reporting of this and the government threatened to use the anti-subversion laws with full vigor.[40] The rebellion, led by Norman Campbell, soon took on a separatist tone. "We native people have farmed our lands communally for generations," he declared.[41] The FAD was said to have been behind this protest, but in reality the problem was a cultural rather than a political one. The introduction of English-speaking functionaries at the end of 1980 appeared to have quieted resentment for a time.

Despite many concerns over the political future of the country, two things about the first two years that the Sandinistas were in power were impressive. One of these was the immense amount of work that had been done in restoring the devastated country. Perhaps the most appropriate symbol of this was the huge park being built in what was once downtown Managua, before the earthquake of 1972. The late dictator had left that section a ruin, to profit from rebuilding elsewhere.[42] The new government cleared the rubble away and began to construct a garden spot, including a monument at the spot where Pedro Joaquín Chamorro was killed and even a memorial to Bill Stewart, the newsman whose death helped convince the world that Somoza must go. But while the new park was a symbol, the greatest work was being done in rural areas, with a will and an enthusiasm which suggested that the revolution retained its popularity.

The second impressive thing was the way in which the directorate managed to present an appearance of harmony and solidarity. Rumor had it that there were private disputes, and even bitter feelings between such men as Jaime Wheelock and his rival ideologue, Tomás Borge. But whatever happened in the confines of closed meetings, the public facade of unanimity was maintained in this collective leadership. This unity of purpose more than made up for the inexperience and occasional ineptitude of the government.

NOTES

1. *Nicaragua and Central America Report*, December 1979.
2. *New York Times*, 8 July 1980.
3. *Miami Herald*, 16 July 1979.
4. *This Week Central America and Panama*, 26 November 1979.
5. *New York Times*, 3 March 1980.
6. *Latin America Political Report*, 30 November 1979.
7. *Central America Reports*, 24 September 1979; *Latin America Weekly Report*, 23 November 1979.
8. *Central America Update*, October 1979.
9. Remarks of Richard Weinert, Yale Workshop on Central America, New Haven, 13 September 1980.
10. *Latin America Weekly Report*, 21 December 1979.
11. *This Week Central America and Panama*, 3 March 1980.
12. *New York Times*, 31 January 1980.
13. *Latin America Regional Report*, 11 July 1980.
14. *Central America Update*, November 1979.
15. Comments of Alvaro Jerez of the MDN and Adolfo Calero Portacarrero of the PCD.
16. *Boston Globe*, 21 July 1980.
17. *This Week Central America and Panama*, 11 August 1980.
18. *Latin America Regional Report*, 6 July 1980.
19. *Barricada* (Managua), 31 December 1979.
20. Ibid.
21. *This Week Central America and Panama*, 10 March 1980.
22. *This Week Central America and Panama*, 11 February 1980.
23. *Barricada*, 31 December 1979.
24. Ibid.
25. *This Week Central America and Panama*, 3 March 1980.
26. *This Week Central America and Panama*, 18 February 1980.
27. *La Prensa* (Managua), 20 January 1980.
28. *This Week Central America and Panama*, 5-12 March, 1 September 1980; *Latin America Regional Report*, 6 July 1980.
29. *This Week Central America and Panama*, 24 March 1980.
30. *This Week Central America and Panama*, 2 June 1980.
31. *This Week Central America and Panama*, 16 June 1980.
32. *This Week Central America and Panama*, 11 February 1980.
33. *Latin America Weekly Report*, 21 December 1979.
34. *National Catholic Reporter*, 22 February 1980.
35. *New York Times*, 8 February 1980.
36. *This Week Central America and Panama*, 1 September 1980.
37. *This Week Central America and Panama*, 2 June 1980.
38. *This Week Central America and Panama*, 17 November 1980.
39. *Latin America Regional Report, Central America and Mexico*, 28 November 1980.
40. *Latin America Regional Report*, 19 September 1980.
41. *Boston Globe*, 7 August 1980.
42. Anastasio Somoza Debayle was killed by assassins in Paraguay in September 1980.

13

Nicaragua Analysis:
The Paradoxical Revolution

It is extremely difficult to view the Nicaraguan revolution with anything approaching objectivity. So much depends upon the attitude of the observer toward bourgeois democracy, toward socialism, toward dictatorship, and toward underdeveloped countries. Many visitors to Nicaragua find the climate of the revolution exhilarating; others are struck by the drabness of life and the grim puritanism of the revolution's leaders. One wishes for the pen of an Alexis de Tocqueville, to see through the contradictions to the heart of the matter. But perhaps even that distinguished political philosopher would have trouble grasping a situation so new and fluid.

THE POLITICAL SPECTRUM

In discussing the politics of Nicaragua, it would be well to keep in mind that what has been set up is a dual system, not entirely dissimilar to that common in Eastern Europe, in which the party and state often have overlapping functions. Although there is a junta—now reduced to three members, Daniel Ortega, Sergio Ramírez, and Rafael Córdoba Rivas—which is the official executive body of the state, and a Council of State, which is much like a legislature, real control is exercised by the nine-member directorate of the FSLN, a party organization. Here, however, much of the similarity ends, for no dominant secretary general of the FSLN exercises dictatorial control. Indeed, there is very little party organization at all, for the three tendencies maintained, as of this writing, their separate identities. Further, as noted above, the dominant party has made itself part of the Revolutionary Front, which contains remnants of the old Liberal Party, the communist PSN and the Christian radical PPCS. These groups are represented on the Council of State.

The opposition, known as the FAO, also embraces a wide spectrum of parties. One, the PCD is considerably to the right of center, while the other three, Robelo's own MDN, the PSD and the PCS, might be styled reformist. The FAO struggled hard through 1980 to maintain its position as the loyal opposition to the government; but the government seemed ambiguous about wanting, or trusting, such an opposition. Some of this suspicion was probably justified, for evidently such figures as the late Jorge Salazar were less than completely loyal to the regime. But the Salazar case itself probably meant the end of the loyal-opposition phase, for his death was deeply resented in COSEP and the FAO.

To make sense of the situation, it is necessary to remember that Nicaragua was emerging from a civil war, was beset by enemies, and had great economic problems. Arturo Cruz remarked, "There is a situation of emergency in this country, consequently a government of emergency as well."[1] The question that would have to be answered is: How long does the emergency go on, and what sort of structure is to emerge when it ends? His son, Arturo Cruz the younger—a diplomat in Washington, pointed out to me that it was five years from the American Revolution to our first presidential election, but anyone with a rudimentary recollection of American history can recognize that as a complete red herring. It is understandable, then, that such a person as Alfonso Robelo would see the present state of affairs, as he told me, as a "period of military consolidation," in which the FSLN would build an impressive military machine (40,000 in arms and a 100,000-member militia) for the purpose of converting itself into a permanent dictatorship. If such were indeed the case, it is quite possible that eventually, all political expression might be absorbed into the FSLN or persecuted out of existence. As long as such figures as Robelo and Adolfo Calero could move about the country and air their political opinions, an open political debate would remain; if they could not, then the intentions of the dominant party would be clear.

SOCIAL CLASSES AND FORCES

Nicaragua, prior to the revolution, had the same range of social classes as the other republics under discussion here, and it would be tedious to go into their composition. Suffice it to say that, after the coming to power of the Sandinistas, the peasantry and organized labor both enjoyed a renewed sense of their own power and importance. The war against Somoza was popular with perhaps 90 percent of the populace, so much so that the label "civil war" is often denied by Nicaraguans on the grounds that no one not immediately connected with Somoza backed his government. However, certain groups among these proletarian elements felt distinctly unhappy about many of the facets of life in the early eighties. One peasant group profoundly alienated was the ethnic minority living along the Atlantic coast. As previously explained, these non-Spanish-speaking people regarded the government as an alien imposition. The non-Sandinista unions were also disgruntled, and this included the 65,000 member CTN,[2] linked to the PCS and definitely a force to be reckoned with.

The upper business sector, the very wealthy who had been companions of the Somozas, had largely gone; but the middle business sector, represented by COSEP, remained. Three days before Somoza fell, I sat at the long table at COSEP headquarters, with its members, as they talked about their plans following the fall of Somoza and their hopes for the future. Encouraged by José Francisco Cardenal, they had sketched out the bright promise of a "pluralistic" Nicaragua. Now these hopes have been dashed and, as one of the keenest observers of the postrevolutionary situation confessed, there is no place for these businessmen in the scheme of the new Nicaragua. This state of affairs has been viewed with some bitterness by the business community. Sergio Ramírez and others said that middle-class persons only belatedly supported the revolution, but the truth was that they supported it early on, and often at the risk of their lives. As Alfonso Robelo recently commented, "We were the anchor of the opposition to Somoza, without which the Sandinistas would not have had their victories."

In late 1980, the chief voice of the middle class was the newspaper *La Prensa*, which could hardly be called a latecomer to the opposition against Somoza; but this voice was saddled with all sorts of restrictions. Decrees 511 and 512 prohibited any discussion of prices and inflation, clashes between government forces and the opposition, strikes, and protest movements. According to Pedro Joaquín Chamorro Barrios, during negotiations over banana prices conducted with Standard Fruit in San Francisco in December 1980 and January 1981, the press was sent a warning letter telling it not to print anything on the subject, and then another warning, not to print the first warning letter. The above mentioned decrees provided for fines and imprisonment for violations by editors. *La Prensa*, never without resources, countered by printing on its front page, for several days, a large photograph of a monkey eating a banana, a vivid reminder, to all its readers, of the news which they knew could not be printed. Of the other newspapers, perhaps the less said, the better, for *Barricada* was busy trying to turn itself into a banana-republic version of *Pravda*, while *El Nuevo Diario* was hardly less sycophantic. That all three were edited by members of the same family was perhaps the ultimate irony.

One important group which enjoyed an ambivalent relationship with the government was the Catholic church. The church, like COSEP and *La Prensa*, had played a very large role in the overthrow of Somoza. As pointed out earlier, Msgr. Miguel Obando y Bravo was the very soul of the opposition; and the religious orders, particularly the Capuchins, were not far behind. Further, there were, at the end of 1980, no less than four priests holding cabinet-level posts in the government (D'Escoto, the two fathers Cardenal, and Edgardo Parrales, the minister of social welfare). In the pastoral letter of November 1979, the bishops of Nicaragua had appeared basically favorable to the revolution, and even to socialism, as they understood it. Having proposed several obviously false definitions of socialism, they had gone on to declare: "If socialism signifies, as it should, the pre-eminence of the interests of the majority of the Nicaraguan people and a model of national economic planning, solidarity and progressive participation, we have no objections to it."[3] Following the total lack of response to the call for priests to get out of government—since there were qualified lay personnel to replace them—the bishops adopted a harder line. Their pastoral letter issued in October 1980 reflected increasing fears of Marxist dictatorship and denounced the "materialism" of the Sandinista philosophy. It went on to charge the priests who remained members of the government with a scandalous disregard of the teachings of Pope John Paul II—which could hardly be denied—and warned of the dangers of a totalitarian state.[4] Everyone knew that this represented the thinking of the majority of the bishops, with Rubén López being perhaps the outstanding dissident; and that it represented, above all, the feelings of the powerful archbishop of Managua himself, the man who had done so much to bring down Somoza. With that message, the church had become a formidable antagonist of the state once more.

This pointed up deep divisions within the Nicaraguan church. Monsignor Obando was no Cardinal Casariego, mired in the theology of the nineteenth century. He was a pragmatic and progressive churchman, and this made his harsh condemnation of the regime all the more telling. However, this did not mean that the archbishop and his church would cease to work with the government. Such verbal fireworks were designed to express concern over some government policies and to castigate anew such men as Miguel D'Escoto. The vast majority of the priests and religious who remained in the government, on the other hand, should not be thought of as Marxist radicals. They saw their role as one of keeping the Sandinista movement Christian and, at the same time, of supplying skills which were largely lacking in lay society.

Factors Making for Stability

Not even the enemies of the current government could deny that it continued to have, at the beginning of 1981, a broad group of constituencies which could articulate their demands and who were, on the whole, satisfied with the allocation of values determined by the regime. One reason for this support was the burst of national patriotism occasioned by a sanguinary civil war against an unpopular regime, and the ability of the Sandinistas, to take upon themselves, perhaps unfairly, the mantle of leadership in that struggle. Thus the war created a disciplined military structure that could be put to partisan ends by the FSLN and a general good will toward the party. Almost everyone wanted the new regime to succeed, particularly as Uncle Sam did not seem pleased with it. This general good will may have faded somewhat, but it was by no means dead in 1981.

As noted earlier, the Sandinistas—following, to a certain extent, the Cuban model—set up, after their victory, a series of interlocking Organizations of the Masses. Among these, the CDSs provide a source of stability and support at the most basic grass-roots level, and help cement together other diverse groups, such as the Sandinista union (CST), the peasant movement (ATC), the youth movement (JS-19), and the women's movement (AMN-LAE). Since no rival comprehensive structure existed among the opposition, the Organizations of the Masses played a vital role in maintaining the regime. It was through these organizations that the government received most of its inputs and feedback on its decisions. They represented a broad and dynamic source of support, and continued to play that role a year and a half after the revolution.

The government's main programs, such as land reform, the literacy campaign, confiscation of Somocista estates and factories, and housing construction, all met with broad popular approval, though other measures, such as control of the sugar supply, met with grumbling. The government of the FSLN was doing a great deal that was genuinely wanted, and which had been necessary for some time. This, too, provided a substantial base of support.

The powerful military establishment, being developed with Cuban and perhaps Soviet assistance, also was likely to provide stability for the regime. The often-mentioned figure of 50,000 for the regular Sandinista armed forces sounded too high, in a country of less than 2.5 million persons. Such an army would be larger than those of Guatemala, El Salvador, and Honduras combined. But the growth of military power has indeed been substantial. When the military factor is added to the others mentioned above, it becomes plain that the idea that the Sandinista government might magically go away is absurd. Barring a major economic catastrophe there was sufficient support to keep the FSLN in power for some time to come.

Destabilizing Factors

This did not mean that there was no discontent or no danger. Despite the existence of small radical-left groups, such as the Trotskyites, there appeared to be little threat from that quarter; but there was substantial danger of both subversion and military action by forces to the right. These forces were, however, rendered relatively harmless by their disunity and disorganization. If there were such a thing as a formal leader of the exile community, it would have to be the former vice president, and provisional president for 36 hours, Francisco Urcuyo Maleaño, residing in Guatemala at the end of 1980. He proclaimed that he had founded a government in exile, but the Guatemalan government forbade him to launch any activities there, under penalty of deportation. The government in exile would therefore probably set up shop in some other country, possibly Bolivia. Urcuyo himself had little reputation as a leader and it was difficult to see how he could expect to manage his group from such a distant place as Bolivia. The other major contender for leadership, since the death of Anastasio Somoza Debayle, by assassination on 17 September 1980, in Paraguay, has been his son, Anastasio Somoza Portocarrero, a resident of Miami. The extensive Florida exile community appeared to look to him for leadership, but "El Chiguin"—the kid, as Tachito is often called—showed little of the drive of his two illustrious ancestors.

More important than ghostly governments in exile were the armed movements. One of these was made up entirely of old Somocistas, chiefly former National Guard members, and was headed by Oscar Armando Larios (whose brother, now serving a seven-year sentence for treason, was the first defense minister of the Sandinista government). Larios's group, the *Fuerzas Armadas Democráticas*, is powerful in Honduras and well armed. It often teams with an organization known as the Popular Anti-Communist Militia, which is also an organization of former Somocistas. Then there is the organization headed by José Francisco Cardenal, whom I remember as a warm supporter of the Sandinistas in the last days before the fall of the dynasty. Cardenal, in fact, had first teamed with his cousin, Pedro Joaquín Chamorro Cardenal, to try to topple the Somozas in 1959. So prominent was he that he became vice president of the Council of State in May 1980, only to leave the country soon after, denouncing the regime as "communist." His *Unión Democrática Nicaraguense* is composed mostly of disillusioned supporters of the revolution, such as Edmundo Chamorro, who made the famous rocket attack on La Loma, from the Intercontinental Hotel in 1978, and Comandante Fabian, an ex-FSLN guerrilla leader who now operates, with a band, from Honduras.[5] Men of this sort can hardly be dismissed as radical rightists, and their opposition has a propaganda effect far beyond their armed strength. As pointed out above, the Sandinista government had sufficient strength to weather all the attacks and sabotaging by these groups at the beginning of 1981. The danger was that they might persuade Honduras and Guatemala to launch an attack along with them, possibly supported covertly by the United States. While this scenario seemed unlikely, it was regarded with great seriousness in Nicaragua. Another source of potential opposition was formed in July 1981, when MPS chief Edén Pastora and Vice Minister of the Interior José Valdivia suddenly quit their posts and left Nicaragua. Rumor had it that they had quarreled with Borge and Humberto Ortega over Cuban and Soviet influence in the country.

ECONOMIC FACTORS

Nicaragua was definitely poorer after the revolution than it had been before. The fall in per capita income, which had reached nearly $1,000 in 1978, had been severe. In August 1980, an economist "close to the government," was said to have painted a most gloomy picture. Worker efficiency was down from prerevolutionary norms, as was production. Discipline among the workforce was almost nonexistent, with a widespread belief that no one need work after the revolution. State-run enterprise had been ill managed and had created many unnecessary items. The government, claimed the same economist, was not even able to spend much of the money it had managed, with such difficulty, to borrow. Inflation was also a problem: Officially estimated at 22 percent for 1980, the real rate was probably closer to 35 percent.[6]

COSEP, which, by the end of 1980, had little reason to flatter the government, put out its own figures, which showed the Nicaraguan economy falling "far short" of the goals announced by the government at the beginning of the year. Industrial activity, the COSEP report stated, was only 65 percent of what had been anticipated and agriculture also lagged. The trade deficit was estimated to be over $200 million, and even the government admitted that it would be $176 million.[7] Not all was bleak on the economic scene, however. The aim of the government was to counter food shortages by buying food abroad and selling it cheaply, while, at the same time, ending the foreign exchange shortage through the exports of such products as coffee, cotton, and sugar, which would therefore have to remain in scant supply at home. The government could point to the fact that while the GDP had been down 25 percent in 1979, it had surged back about 15 percent in 1980, though still below 1978 levels.

Some sectors of the economy were doing well, such as textiles and the construction industry.[8] To aid the textile recovery, more cotton was to be sown in 1981—121,400 hectares, as opposed to 45,200 hectares for 1980. This increased acreage would yield between 310,000 and 430,00 bales, an impressive amount but still below that for the Somoza years, when Nicaragua had raised 500,000 bales a year.[9] Massive new construction projects were being launched, especially in Managua, where some *barrios* were to be entirely rebuilt.[10]

The banking activities of the country had been in good hands since the revolution, first under Arturo Cruz, and then under Alfredo Alainz, head of the Central Bank. Foreign exchange reserves had stood at just 48 million córdobas (or 3 million dollars) when the Somoza government fell, but by June 1980, Alainz could declare that he had a reserve which included $119 million. There were also 44,000 ounces of gold on hand. He had the agricultural sector to thank for this, especially coffee, plus the fact that 26,000 ounces of gold were coming annually from the nationalized mining industry.[11] The successful renegotiation of the debt to foreign bankers, described in the previous chapter, had given the world increasing confidence that Nicaragua was sound financially.

Manpower was a major problem. Not only were there problems of absenteeism and low productivity, but there was still 30 percent unemployment at the end of 1980. Obviously, many of those without work were also without skills, or failed to join the right unions. Yet when it came time to harvest the coffee, the lack of field hands severely restricted production. Somehow, labor had to be managed more efficiently than the Sandinistas had succeeded in doing so far.

Coffee production was up to over 1 million bags (or some 50,000 tons), a 10 percent increase over the harvest of 1979. Much of this coffee went to the United States, Holland, and Spain, the traditional purchasers. But contracts were also negotiated with the USSR, Bulgaria, Czechoslovakia, East Germany, and Yugoslavia; the USSR alone agreed to purchase 1,000 tons, and the total order came to about five times that amount.[12] If coffee production could be raised to prewar levels, there was evidence that it could find a buyer in Eastern Europe, regardless of world price levels, much in the same manner as Cuban sugar over the last 20 years.

To keep the economy moving required massive influxes of credit. Only a part of this could come from the Eastern-bloc countries. Cuba, for instance, could lend only $5 million to Nicaragua. Most of the money had to come from the Western world, and to get this money, Nicaragua had to remain a member of the world banking community. But, as Jaime Wheelock declared in a recent interview, "We can use the money of the imperialists to construct socialism."[13] This was precisely what the government appeared to be doing. At the end of 1980, Nicaraguan Reconstruction Fund Director Haroldo Montealegre declared that favorable terms for loans of $668 million had been negotiated, with an average of seven years of grace, 32 years to pay, and only 3.8 percent interest. These were soft loans, and the director added that these loans "have no parallel in any country in Latin America."[14]

The $75-million package from the United States, which had finally begun to flow into Nicaragua in September 1980, represented a similar soft loan, with $5 million being an outright grant and the rest being repaid over a 40-year period at 2 to 3 percent. But the loan package had carried the stipulation that it could not be authorized by the president unless he affirmed that Nicaragua was not aiding subversion abroad; and that it could be recalled at any time, with immediate payment made in full, including interest, if the United States determined that Nicaragua was indeed engaging in subversion abroad. Carter had made the required affirmation in September 1980; but the new president, as one of his first acts in office, suspended the undisbursed portion of the loan, only to find that all but $15 million had already left the United States, something of an efficiency record for bureaucratic Washington. The suspension might have been only temporary, and it was not the same as a recall; but what would happen if the United States were to go all the way and demand repayment at once? In Managua there was little doubt on that point. I heard from junta member Arturo Cruz that this would be "economic aggression," and from Miguel D'Escoto that the government would certainly default. However, as Moises Hassan put it, "We would maintain our economic pluralism, despite the United States." That meant that Nicaragua would continue to seek loans in the West as well as in the communist world, and would use those loans to bolster the private as well as the public sector. This did not entirely ring true. One of the conditions of the North American package was that 60 percent was to go to the private sector, but COSEP had begun to complain bitterly that none of the money was going to private enterprise at all; and that, along with renewed charges that Nicaragua was dabbling in the El Salvador war, led to the suspension. If Nicaragua continued to deny funds to the private sector, it would find credit sources in the West drying up.

The uncertainties concerning the resumption of U.S. aid made the economy increasingly fragile in 1981. There were genuine fears of national bankruptcy. Nevertheless, the government announced a record budget of $879 million, even though it had to admit that only some 80 percent could be covered by expected revenues.

FOREIGN AFFAIRS

Not only was Nicaragua at loggerheads with Honduras, El Salvador, and Guatemala, but the government's ability to alienate former friends appeared to be little short of miraculous. The falling out with Venezuela was probably unavoidable, as the latter was backing the opposite side in the Salvadorean conflict, while the issue with Panama had to do with the fact that Nicaragua preferred the tutelage of Fidel Castro to that of the late Omar Torrijos. But the quarrel with Colombia, over some virtually worthless islands in the Caribbean, was a comic opera, especially as Nicaragua lacked the naval muscle to make good its claim. Even stranger were the events surrounding Costa Rica's bid for a seat on the UN Security Council. Nicaragua had originally backed Cuba for this seat, but when the bid failed, and Costa Rica sought the seat, Nicaragua, instead of backing the country that had done most to bring the Sandinistas to power, announced its own candidacy. Nicaragua not only did not get the seat, but did get considerable hard feeling. All this helped to lower the credit of the government among nonaligned countries, as had the early decision to abstain on the condemnation of the Soviet invasion of Afghanistan.

By the end of 1981, evidence had begun to pile up, showing that, despite indignant denials by Managua, the government was indeed up to its neck in aid to the Salvadorean guerrillas; nor was this surprising, considering Nicaraguan interests in the region. But what was remarkable was the naive assumption that no one would notice or do anything about it. Late in January 1981, a second arms-carrying aircraft was shot down over El Salvador. This one was piloted by a flyer for Lanica, the defunct Nicaraguan airline. The arms had probably come from Costa Rica—where there was a flourishing trade, as the earlier incident demonstrated—and been transferred to Nicaragua and then across the Gulf of Fonseca to El Salvador.[15] The steady air traffic, plus the persistent landings of boats along the Salvadorean coast, could hardly have gone unnoticed by the Nicaraguan government.

As relations worsened on the American continent, Nicaragua appeared to be turning more and more toward contacts with Cuba and the Soviet bloc. This trend was not yet irreversible in early 1981, but it was becoming pronounced. If the United States and Nicaragua did not manage to patch up their quarrel over the loan and the Salvadorean civil war, it was quite likely that Nicaragua would continue turning toward Havana.

Options for U.S. Foreign Policy toward Nicaragua

Ambassador Lawrence Pezzullo may have terrified Anastasio Somoza, but he was the soul of patience and tact with the Sandinistas during the period of the Carter presidency. This was probably because the policy he pursued on behalf of the State Department was aimed at avoiding a total rupture with the Sandinistas and at steering them along a middle course between communism and capitalism. Out of this came a delicate concern, and perhaps overconcern, about COSEP and the FAO as elements maintaining pluralism within the framework of a socialist state. The pursuit of this policy was still open to the Reagan administration, but there were certain factors, beyond the control of the United States, that made it more difficult to pursue. These included the increasing international involvement in the Salvadorean civil war, and an increasing alienation from the government of those forces which tended to promote pluralism, including not only the business sector and the opposition parties, but also a large segment of the church, the nongovernment unions, and *La Prensa.*

The keystone of the Pezzullo approach, if I understand it correctly, was the North American loan package. If the suspension of the loan became permanent, or if a recall were instituted, the United States would still have the option of maintaining diplomatic relations and a formal correctness toward the government of the FSLN. This might continue even though the two countries were backing opposite sides in El Salvador and elsewhere. While this maintenance of relations might not appeal to those who favor logic and the straightforward pursuit of rational aims, it must be pointed out that diplomacy is often an irrational business in which polite fictions, well known to be false, are sometimes maintained as a convenience. In this case the convenience would be the possibility of continued dialogue and eventual détente.

Another approach would be to write off Nicaragua entirely, as already being a satellite of Cuba and a thrall of the Soviet Union. There would be a certain satisfying sense of finality in that, similar to that which government officials must have felt when the rupture with Cuba was completed. At least we would know where we stood. But where we stood would not be a very good place to be. Nicaragua would still be right where it always was, and would be implacably hostile to the United States. Only a more successful Bay of Pigs—an unlikely event, to say the least—could possibly rediscover Nicaragua. The threat of such a rupture might, however, be useful for bargaining purposes, although it is likely that many of the more radical members of the Nicaraguan government would probably welcome a break as much as would the most veteran cold warrior in Washington. A Nicaragua totally unrestrained by any dealings with the United States might indeed be a threat to the stability of the region, through aid to guerrilla movements in neighboring countries. For this reason, the decision of the Reagan administration to terminate aid to Nicaragua, in March 1981, was probably not in the best interests of either country.

Thus, short of wholehearted support of every aspect of the Nicaraguan revolution, hardly a viable option in the 1981 climate of Washington opinion, the United States could either aid and hope, while pretending not to notice the flow of arms of El Salvador; or it could withdraw all aid and then either maintain a formal relationship or erase Nicaragua from the official maps in Washington. All of these paths were perilous and none was likely to resolve the conflicts with Nicaragua in the immediate future.

NOTES

1. *This Week Central America and Panama*, 2 June 1980.
2. *Latin America Regional Report, Central America and Mexico*, 28 November 1980.
3. *Carta Pastoral del Episcopado Nicaraguense* (Managua, 1979), p. 8.
4. *This Week Central America and Panama*, 3 November 1980.
5. *This Week Central America and Panama*, 26 January 1981.
6. *Boston Globe*, 21 July 1980; *Latin America Regional Report, Central America and Mexico*, 11 July 1980.
7. *This Week Central America and Panama*, 8 December 1980.
8. *Latin America Regional Report, Central America and Mexico*, 11 July 1980.
9. *This Week Central America and Panama*, 30 June 1980.
10. *Latin America Regional Report, Central America and Mexico*, 6 June 1980.
11. *This Week Central America and Panama*, 23 June 1980.
12. *This Week Central America and Panama*, 9 June and 11 August 1980.
13. Clifford Krauss, "Sandinismo after the Fall," *The Nation*, 1 March 1980, p. 235.
14. *This Week Central America and Panama*, 22 December 1980.
15. *This Week Central America and Panama*, 2 February 1981.

Conclusions:
Arms and the Land

I will now assess the role of the various forces at work in the politics of these four countries and inquire into the prospects for each of these nations. This will include no specific predictions, for in regard to the volcanic politics of Central America, making predictions is very risky and often embarrassing.

FACTORS INVOLVED IN POLITICS

This study has suggested that the most important relationship in Central America is between man and the land. Politics is basically a struggle to secure for various interest groups a share, if not a monopoly, of the land's resources. For a very long time, an entrenched, though gradually evolving, oligarchy had the lion's share of this wealth. This oligarchy, in time, became commercial and industrial as well as agricultural, but the land remained the basis of its wealth, and few native businessmen failed to have a hacienda to which they could retreat from the strains of commerce. Concentrations of land were very great in Guatemala, El Salvador, and Nicaragua, under the Somozas, and only slightly less so in Honduras, despite popular belief to the contrary. For generations, this system was accepted, the peasant recognizing the *patrón* as the natural leader, and the system was even ratified by the church as being part of the will of God. The 1932 revolt in El Salvador was a dramatic indication that such a state of affairs would not endure forever. If that was seen as a mere aberration, the Guatemalan revolution of 1945-54 left no doubt that real changes in the old relationships were taking place.

The oligarchy responded to this challenge, for the most part, by digging in and becoming more adamantly opposed to land reform and other "communist plots" than before. Only in Honduras has there been a degree of flexibility which has, at least through mid-1981, spared it the appalling bloodbaths of its neighbors. The landholders also recognized a definite weakness in their position when they tried to deal with such overwhelming masses by using physical force and repression. Logically, they turned to the newly professionalized military and implored the soldiers to save their estates for them and for their heirs.

The soldiers, however, would exact their price. Political power became concentrated in their hands and the proud landholder had to receive the military upstart as a temporary social equal. The military, controlling the government, lavished money upon itself for every conceivable purpose except paying the poor, conscripted peasants who served in the ranks. Its pride in professionalism grew and stepped outside the bounds of mere military tactics and strategy to include the murkier realms of higher finance, jurisprudence, and business management. Thus, what has been referred to as "the illusion of military omnicompetence" grew, the soldier actually feeling a sort of contempt for the mere civilian expert. If there were any doubt about the right of the officer class to rule, such doubts could be removed with the rumble of a few tanks through the streets of the capital. Power grew out of the barrel of a gun.

The military's role as protector of the established order made it the natural antagonist of the masses, who came to regard the soldier as the enemy and, indeed, the very source of their woes, whether they were poor peasants evicted from their lands by soldiers or unionists whose strike was crushed with guns. This antagonism accounts for the ferocity of such massacres as those in Panzós in Guatemala and Aguilares in El Salvador. It can hardly be a surprise, then, that the left-wing leaders who emerged in the seventies saw as the key problem the elimination of the traditional military. This was the primary issue, the resolution of which would automatically lead to the resolution of such questions as those of land reform and economic progress for the workers. The leaders of the land-reform program in El Salvador, with whom I spoke in the summer of 1980, were distinctly puzzled as to why the Popular Forces still opposed them when they were doing such work for the peasantry. The answer was that this land reform was the army's land reform, not the people's, and to the minds of the leaders of the militant leftist movement, breaking the political power of the military forces took precedence over all other considerations and was, in fact, the sine qua non, without which no genuine reform was possible.

How to return the soldiers to their barracks and to make them passive witnesses to internal politics, as they are in the United States and, to a certain extent, Mexico, was a difficult question. Guatemala, remained, as of mid-1981, firmly in the grip of the generals and of General Lucas, who had denounced U.S. policy following the recall of Frank Ortiz, and seemed to be burning his bridges behind him as he moved into a confrontation with the left. Meanwhile, in El Salvador, events were also moving in the direction of greater military control. On 1 September, Decree 10 shifted most of the moderate officers, supporters of Majano, out of positions of power and into attaché jobs abroad. The three civilian members of the junta objected, and Colonels Gutiérrez and García promised that in proposed subsequent transfers, they would first consult the junta. But, of course, the damage was done; the hard-line officers were now firmly in control. It appeared that, as the oligarchy fled in increasing numbers to Miami, the military in El Salvador was gaining the economic power it had previously lacked by taking over abandoned estates and businesses.

Similarly, in the new cabinet of Honduras, under provisional President Paz García, the military was given control of five spots, of which two actually went to officers—defense and foreign affairs, to Col. Mario Flores Theresion and Col. César Elvir Sierra, respectively; and the rest were given in turn to their conservative allies. Even if the soldiers do eventually return to the barracks in Honduras, they will be ready to march at a moment's notice should the government fail to follow their orders. Therefore, it is hardly surprising that many Central Americans see, as the only cure for militarism, the sort of radical surgery which was performed in Nicaragua, though this in turn has produced a new revolutionary army.

The peasantry remains the major opponent of the military. It is hardly possible to imagine the lot of Central American peasants if one has not been among them; if one has not seen the hopeless villages where half the children die by the age of five, and where the water is contaminated. Suddenly, in the mid-seventies, the peasants of Guatemala and, to a larger extent, El Salvador, found their voice and articulated their misery in protests which often led to savage repression. In El Salvador they became much better organized than in Guatemala, or even than in Honduras, despite its long tradition of popular organizations. In Guatemala they have increasingly joined the guerrilla movement, as they did in Nicaragua during the last stages of the civil war.

On their side, and not really a separate caste, are the unionized urban workers. To be a union member in Guatemala or El Salvador is a suicidal undertaking; disappearance, torture, and death are frequent. That leaders still emerge suggest the depths of the desperation of these workers, who find the possibility of death little worse than the conditions under which they live and labor.

Increasingly, the church has given its powerful influence to the peasants and workers. Though there remain some conservative churchmen, the overwhelming majority of the Catholic clergy express sympathy for the plight of the peasants and urban workers, and hostility toward the military, whose work they have often seen firsthand. The role of the church in the Nicaraguan revolution was absolutely vital to its success. Even in Honduras, where the church was debilitated by the long period of Liberal, anticlerical rule, it has begun to be an effective leader for the peasants and workers.

Thus, there has been an increasing polarization of the political forces in Central America over the last decade. On one side are the military and the conservative property owners and industrialists; on the other, the vast majority of the people and much of the church. Outside of Nicaragua, only in Honduras has an absolute polarization been avoided. This statement might be objected to as an oversimplification of complex realities, and indeed it is not hard to cite individual instances in El Salvador and Guatemala where this polarization has not taken place, but the general rule remains. This by no means insures that revolutionary forces are likely to win in either of those two countries in the short run, but it does probably mean that in the long run, any government which wishes to survive must somehow solve this problem of polarization or accept total identification with one pole or the other.

This polarization makes life very hard on the Western-style political parties. As this study has pointed out, two of the four states had long-term traditional parties dating back to the clerical-anticlerical split of the nineteenth century. In Nicaragua these parties have become almost totally irrelevant to the present political situation, the remnants of the anti-Somoza Liberals clinging to the coattails of the Sandinista government, whereas the remnants of the Conservatives, under the anachronistic Adolfo Calero, have thrown in their lot with Robelo's opposition coalition. In Honduras, the traditional parties give such a brave semblance of life that one almost imagines them divided by real issues and concerns, but the only real separating factor is the extent of their relationship to the army. Guatemala and El Salvador have not had such long-term parties in recent memory, but have instead been plagued by "official parties" representing military factions and civilian cliques.

Fifteen or 20 years ago, hope seemed to lie in the development of new middle-class parties responsible to social pressures and flexible enough, as the traditional parties were not, to change with the times. While the United States, for a time mistakenly viewed the Social Democratic parties, such as the MNR in El Salvador, as communist inspired, the State Department extended its friendship to the various Christian Democratic groups that arose. Often there was little ideological difference between Social Democrat and Christian Democrat. Both groups represented the articulate middle class, the university educated, the upwardly mobile. In many cases the leaders spoke English fairly well, had been to the United States or to Europe, and were more cosmopolitan than even the traditional elites. In short, the members of the moderate middle groups, whether inspired by the encyclicals of the Popes or the policies of the parliamentary socialists of Western Europe, were the Central Americans most like North Americans. They were therefore seized upon eventually as a third force, lying between revolutionary change and the collapsing old order. But, except in Honduras, where the PDCH and PINU have begun to make a stir, it appears that their opportunity has passed, at least for a while, and perhaps forever. In Nicaragua, the MDN and the PCS appeared to have little chance of coming to power, and still less after the pronouncement by the Sandinistas that elections of any sort would be postponed unti 1985. In El Salvador, by the end of 1980, the military ruled, with a group of the PDC allowed to form a front of civilian government. In Guatemala, the Christian Democrats and the moderate left parties have been terrorized almost out of existence. These parties are, then, a frail reed for the policy of the United States to cling to in the current crisis.

This leads to the assessment of the role of still another major factor in the internal politics of the Central American states—the U.S. embassy. Whether for good or for ill, the colossus of the North can greatly influence even an unfriendly Central American government, thanks to its wealth, its military power, and its proximity. Even the enemies of the Yankees agree that they have a strategic interest in a region which separates North and South America and which sits close to the Panama Canal and to the Mexican oil fields. The role of the ambassador is of necessity a complex one requiring a high degree of skill and tact, and an ability to interpret the often-confused messages wafted down from the State Department and the National Security Council. A U.S. ambassador must deal with everything from the Byzantine intrigues of the Guatemalan court to the revolutionary bumptiousness of the Sandinistas. Much of the ambassador's dealings must be in signals, a kind of diplomatic semaphore in which gestures convey either approval or disapproval of a government's policy. The allocation of $75 million for Nicaragua's revolutionary government was one signal that the United States was willing to support the new government in Nicaragua, while preaching containment of the Nicaraguan revolution in areas outside Nicaragua. The failure of the money to arrive until a year later, after Nicaragua coincidentally had come to terms with the foreign banks that were its creditors, was quite a different signal, and one even more unwelcome to Robelo and his movement than to the FSLN. The suspension of aid in 1981 was a clear warning. Similarly, the decision to supply military aid, of a nonlethal variety, to be sure, to the Salvadorean military in early 1980 was interpreted by it as a gesture of support for an antiguerrilla policy and, oddly, appeared to have weakened the hand of Colonel Majano and those who might have come to terms with the left. The abrupt recall of Frank Ortiz in Guatemala, an ambassador who had felt the interests of his country best served by staying in friendly contact with the Lucas government, was a clear signal of displeasure with that government's abysmal human rights record. In 1980, Honduras, attempting to create a semblance of liberal democracy, was the recipient of much largess from the United States. This resulted in surprisingly honest elections for the Constituent Assembly; but it did not appear to be sufficient to convince the military to forego a major role in the new government.

The personality of the ambassador makes a difference. Ambassadors played a critical role in the rise and maintenance of the Somoza dynasty, through the period of Turner B. Shelton. Another ambassador, Lawrence Pezzullo, played a large role in Somoza's removal. The sending of such top-drawer professionals as Robert White and John Binns to ambassadorships in El Salvador and Honduras, respectively, during 1980, was an indication of growing U.S. concern with the region and its problems.

PROBLEMS AND PROSPECTS FOR EACH COUNTRY

The basic problems of Guatemala are a longstanding inequality in the distribution of land and other wealth and the difficulty of integrating the Indian community into the national life. These basic problems have been greatly compounded by the absolute domination achieved over the last quarter of a century by the Guatemalan military. Whereas in other countries, the military men have been able to share the wealth with the older oligarchy, in Guatemala they increasingly gained the lion's share. But, to maintain this situation, they have found it necessary to resort to a terrorism which has become self-perpetuating since the period in the late sixties when Col. Arana Osorio, as military governor, decimated the population of Zacapa.

By 1980, almost all forces who opposed the military domination, outside of the guerrilla movements, had been subdued. The prestigious San Carlos University was destroyed, for all practical purposes. The teachers were afraid to teach, since some 90 of them had been killed since the first of the year; and the students were afraid to attend class because of the random machine-gunnings of crowds on the campus. Opposition political parties, such as the Christian Democrats, had been forced to virtually disband under the reign of terror permitted and encouraged by the government. Of the true state of affairs, the public could learn little, for the press had long been intimidated into silence. In Guatemalan papers only the funnies were worth reading.

The basic struggle has been over the resources of the country, and these resources have suddenly increased, with the discovery of large oil deposits and some nickel in the Transversal. But the discovery of this new wealth, perhaps capable of lifting Guatemala out of the status of an underdeveloped nation, has resulted only in a savage and greedy struggle among entrenched elements of power for control of these resources. The poor have been dispossessed from their lands, uprooted to create the "mattresses of the general"—the vast estates that have sprung up in this once trackless region. If Guatemala could bring an end, or at least moderation, to its political violence and if it could enact social reforms and achieve political democracy, the future of the country might be bright. But to do these things, it would be necessary to dismantle the existing ruling structure of the army, which stands behind every president and limits government activities to those things which benefit the military and its civilian cronies. The guerrilla forces, as of 1981, were far too weak to take on the military machine, and there was no guarantee that the guerrillas, if successful, would have any real answers to the problems of Guatemala.

While Guatemala might face a bright future, could it but put its house in order, El Salvador, even though it might put its house in order, would find that the foundations themselves were in ruins and the roof about to collapse. The social and economic problems of El Salvador are beyond the solution of the wisest and most able rulers. While anthropologists continue to argue as to whether the country is overpopulated in absolute terms and Central Americans denounce population control as a Yankee plot to reduce their numbers, the population of El Salvador has simply mushroomed to the point where starvation must be the lot of many and malnutrition the lot of all but the privileged few. With the soil overtaxed, little is left to distribute. There is no oil, nor gold, nor silver, nor nickel; there is only coffee, whose production cannot be extended from the hillsides where it currently grows. The ultimate solution might be to export a large part of the Salvadorean population to such under-populated lands as Nicaragua, where, especially since the ravages of the recent civil war, the work to be done far exceeds the available hands. This might be hard to arrange, however, and Salvadoreans have bitter memories of the attempted migration to Honduras that brought about expulsion and the war of 1969.

Certainly, the efforts of the junta during 1980 were not sufficient to solve the problem. The first phase of the land reform was moderately successful, despite much confusion and considerable injustice, but the more ambitious land-to-the-tiller program, in which renters would simply be given title to the land they had rented, turned into chaos. Meanwhile, the guerrilla war raged on, at a much higher level of activity than in Guatemala. Although racked with dissension and defeated in almost every encounter, the forces of the left continued to predict eventual success, and no one who remembers how many times the Sandinista movement in Nicaragua was written off as dead can say that they might not yet succeed, if not in 1980 or 1981, at some time in the future. In 1981, plans for election were going forward, but it would be hard to imagine that any elections, given the political climate of the country, could really change the dominant role of the military.

How far the April 1980 elections in Honduras actually changed the situation in that country was also debatable. A Constituent Assembly came into being, and the Liberals, along with the PINU, would have a major say in the drafting of the new constitution, which would probably contain some safeguards against military control. But constitutions in Honduras have been notoriously short-lived and have had little effect upon the realities of power. In the meantime, the military, teamed with the National Party, managed to keep the presidency and most of the significant cabinet offices. If the military in Honduras displays the glove more often than the fist, it ruled just as surely as in Guatemala or El Salvador.

What sets Honduran politics apart is rather the multiplicity of other interests which also must be conciliated. The labor movement has enjoyed a quarter of a century of strong organization and political clout. The peasantry can also make its voice heard through its organizations. The press has been traditionally free, vociferous, and often sarcastic about national politics, while the National University has proudly resisted any efforts to curtail its independence. Rather than trying to stifle these forces through repression, on the Guatemalan model, the military has generally chosen to work with them, to listen to their problems and complaints, and to retain a certain flexibility of response. But all this might change. Honduras had a population growth rate of 3.7 percent in 1979 and was rapidly overtaking El Salvador in numbers of inhabitants. Its territory is, of course, much greater, but only slightly more of the land is really suitable for agriculture, and while Honduras has some mineral resources, these have not shown any signs of becoming dominant sources of wealth. Thus, as the competition for increasingly scarce resources grows, it may force the military into a more repressive role.

The persistent theme running through this study, as far as the three countries mentioned above have been concerned, has been the struggle for the control of the land and its resources and the role which the military has played in that struggle. This theme was also dominant in Nicaragua during the decades of Somoza's rule, but the events of 1979 wiped out the conventional military force and put into power a revolutionary government committed to safeguarding the country against a right-wing military revival. If any more evidence of the fear and hatred of the old military was needed, it was given by the arrest, in September 1980, of Col. Bernardino Larios, the ex-National Guard officer who had been the first defense minister in the Sandinista government, on charges that he had plotted to kill all nine members of the directorate. Whether a new Marxist military machine might not come to dominate society remained to be seen.

The Sandinistas have also sought to deal with the problem of competition for the land and resources of Nicaragua by declaring that they rule as a revolutionary vanguard on behalf of the people. From now on, thanks to land reform and to a voice in management for workers, the people were to have the resources of the country. But politically speaking, there is no such entity as the people; there are only individuals and interest groups. If some win, then others are likely to lose out. Recognition of this is the reason for the wariness of the private sector, which felt that if a choice had to be made, the revolutionary government would favor state enterprise over private business. This same recognition also accounted for the persistent demands of Robelo, and the other opposition leaders, for a return to bourgeois democracy, for only in the electoral process could diverse interest groups, including the private sector, make their voices heard.

A year after the revolution, Nicaragua was in the process of rebuilding, and was channeling its energy toward the creation of a new society. Exactly what forms it would take remained to be seen, but that much had been accomplished was difficult to deny. The Sandinista system functioned and was distributing benefits to a wider range of the citizenry than in the days of the Somozas, despite grave economic problems.

During recent years, when there has been so much turmoil in Central America, it has been fashionable in the North American press to trot out such headlines as "Central America in Crisis," or "El Salvador on the Brink," or perhaps "Guatemala at the Crossroads." The editors do not seem to realize that Central America has always been in a crisis, if by a crisis one means a desperate situation which requires immediate action. But the immediate action has seldom been taken. Many millions of their citizens have been condemned to misery and despair because the persistent crisis was never dealt with. There have been many times when some major incident seemed about to turn one or more of these nations toward a new course: The 1932 revolt in El Salvador and the decade of revolution in Guatemala are examples which come to mind. Now, aftershocks of the Nicaraguan revolution will probably be felt for some time to come.

The people of Central America were never blessed with anything like the natural resources of the United States and, partly as a consequence, they never had the leisure to develop the political talents of North Americans. They have often found bullets a substitute for ballots and have turned to military men for stability. Now, the military of one country has been swept away and the military of two others maintain but a precarious hold. However, it is too soon to say if this marks the beginning of a new era in Central America, or simply another stage of its perennial crisis.

This study has been an attempt to acquaint the reader with Central American politics; but to really understand the politics of the region, the reader would have to go there, not simply to chat with political leaders, educators, and journalists, but to smell the acrid odor of the diesel buses, the tang of rancid cooking oil, the scent of decomposition along the lanes of small villages. One would have to see the sights, especially the sight of the stony-eyed soldiers in olive drab, riding about the streets of the capital cities, machine guns at the ready. One would have to hear the terrifying whirr of an angry mob, and the dull thud of distant explosions. Only then could one understand the agonies which are either that of a new society trying to be born or the death throes of a civilization in decomposition.

_____Appendix

List of Abbreviations
for Organizations

GENERAL

AIFLD	American Institute for Free Labor Development (AFL-CIO)
CONDECA	Consejo Defensivo Centroamericano, Central American Defense Council
ILO	International Labor Organization
MCCA	Mercado Común Centroamericano, Central American Common Market
OAS	Organization of American States (in Spanish, OEA)
ODECA	Organización de Estados Centroamericanos, Organization of Central American States
ORIT	Organización Regional Interamericana de Trabajadores, Inter-American Regional Organization of Workers

GUATEMALA

AEU	Asociación de Estudiantes Universitarios, Association of University Students
AGUAPA	Asociación Guatemalteca de Productores de Algodón, Guatemalan Association of Cotton Producers
ANACAFE	Asociación Nacional del Café, National Coffee Association

CACIF   Consejo de Agricultores, Comerciantes, Industriales y Financieros, Council of Growers, Business Men, Industrialists and Financiers

CADEG   Comando Anticomunista de Guatemala, Guatemalan Anti-Communist Commando

CAN   Central Auténtico Nacional, Authentic National Center (a political party)

CAO   Central Aranista Organizada, Organized Center for Arana (later CAN)

CGTG   Confederación General de Trabajadores Guatemaltecos, General Confederation of Guatemalan Workers (abolished 1954)

CNT   Central Nacional de Trabajadores, National Workers' Center (a union)

CNUS   Comité Nacional de Unidad Sindical, National Committee of Union Solidarity

CRN   Comité de Reconstrucción Nacional, National Reconstruction Committee (formed after 1976 earthquake)

CTF   Confederación de Trabajadores Federados, Federated Workers Confederation

DCG   Democrácia Cristiana Guatemalteca, Guatemalan Christian Democracy (the Christian Democratic Party)

EGP   Ejército Guerrillero del Pobres, Guerrilla Army of the Poor

FAR   Fuerzas Armadas Rebeldes, Rebel Armed Forces (a guerrilla movement)

FASGUA   Federación Autónoma Sindical de Guatemala, Autonomous Union Federation of Guatemala

FPP   Frente de Participación Popular, Front for Popular Participation (a political party)

FRENU   Frente Nacional de Unidad, National Unity Front

FUR   Frente Unido de la Revolución, United Revolutionary Front

INTA   Instituto Nacional de Transformación Agraria, National Institute for Agrarian Transformation

MANO   Movimiento Anticomunista Nacional Organizado, National Organized Anti-Communist Movement (also Mano Blanca—White Hand)

MLN   Movimiento de Liberación Nacional, National Liberation Movement

MR-13   Movimiento Revolucionario del 13 de Noviembre, Revolutionary Movement of 13 November (a guerrilla movement)

NOA   Nueva Organización Anticomunista, New Anti-Communist Organization

OPRA	Organización del Pueblo en Armas, Organization of the People in Arms
PAR	Partido de Acción Revolucionaria, Party of Revolutionary Action (Arevalo's party)
PGT	Partido Guatemalteco de Trabajadores, Guatemalan Workers Party (the Communist party)
PID	Partido Institucional Democrática, Institutional Democratic Party
PR	Partido Revolucionario, Revolutionary Party
PRA	Partido Revolucionario Auténtico, Authentic Revolutionary Party
PSD	Partido Socialista Democrático, Social Democratic Party
URD	Unión Revolucionaria Democrática, Revolutionary Democratic Union (later FUR)

EL SALVADOR

ANDES	Asociación Nacional de Educadores Salvadoreño, National Association of Salvadorean Educators
ANEP	Asociación Nacional de Empresa Privada, National Association of Private Enterprise
BPR	Bloque Popular Revolucionario, Popular Revolutionary Bloc
CRM	Coordinadora Revolucionaria de las Masas, Revolutionary Coordination of the Masses
ERP	Ejército Revolucionario del Pueblo, People's Revolutionary Army
FAPU	Frente de Acción Popular Unida, United Popular Action Front
FARN	Fuerzas Armadas de Resistencia Nacional, Armed Forces of National Resistance
FARO	Frente Agraria Región Oriental, Eastern Region Agrarian Front
FDN	Frente Democrático Nacionalista, National Democratic Front (a right-wing body)
FDR	Frente Democrático Revolucionario, Democratic Revolutionary Front
FECCAS	Federación Cristiana de Campesinos Salvadoreños, Salvadorean Christian Peasants Federation
FENASTRAS	Federación Nacional Sindical de Trabajadores Salvadoreños, National Union Federation of Salvadorean Workers

FMLN	Frente Farabundo Martí de Liberacion Nacional, Farabundo Martí National Liberation Front
FPL	Fuerzas Populares de Liberación, Popular Forces of Liberation
FUSS	Federación Unida de Sindicatos Salvadoreños, United Federation of Salvadorean Unions
ISTA	Instituto Salvadoreño de Transformación Agraria, Salvadorean Institute for Agrarian Transformation
LP-28	Ligas Populares, 28 de Febrero, Popular Leagues of 28 February
MNR	Movimiento Nacional Revolucionario, National Revolutionary Movement (a Social Democratic party)
ORDEN	Organización Democrática Nacionalista, National Democratic Organization
PCES	Partido Comunista de El Salvador, Communist Party of El Salvador
PCN	Partido de Conciliación Nacional, Party of National Conciliation
PDC	Partido Demócrata Cristiano, Christian Democratic Party
PPS	Partido Popular Salvadoreño, Salvadorean Popular Party
UCA	Universidad Centroamericana, Central American University (a Jesuit institution)
UCS	Unión Comunal Salvadoreña, Salvadorean Communal Union
UDN	Unión Democrática Nacionalista, National Democratic Union (a front for the PCES)
UGB	Unión Guerrera Blanca, White Warrior Union (a terrorist group)
UNO	Unión Nacional Opositora, National Opposition Union
UTC	Unión de Trabajadores del Campo, Farm Workers Union

HONDURAS

AGAS	Asociación de Ganaderos y Agricultores del Valle de Sula, Sula Valley Association of Herders and Growers
ALIPO	Alianza Popular, Popular Alliance, (a faction of PL)
ANACH	Asociación Nacional de Campesinos de Honduras, National Association of Honduran Peasants
CGT	Confederación General de Trabajadores, General Confederation of Workers

COHEP	Consejo Hondureño de la Empresa Privada, Honduran Council of Private Enterprise
CONSUFA	Consejo Superior de las Fuerzas Armadas, Superior Council of the Armed Forces
CTH	Confederación de Trabajadores de Honduras, Confederation of Honduran Workers
DIN	Departimiento de Investigaciones Nacionales, Department of National Investigation (the secret police)
FECORAH	Federación de Cooperativos Agraria de Honduras, Agricultural Cooperatives Federation of Honduras
FENAGH	Federación Nacional de Agricultores y Ganaderos de Honduras, National Federation of Growers and Herders of Honduras
FESITRAN	Federación Sindical de Trabajadores del Norte, Federation of Workers of the North
FMLH	Frente Morazanista para la Liberación de Honduras, Morazanist Front for Honduran Liberation
FNP	Frente Nacional Patriótica, National Patriotic Front
FUNANCAMPH	Frente de Unidad Nacional Campesina de Honduras, Honduran Front of National Peasant Unity
INA	Instituto Nacional Agraria, National Agrarian Institute
OSOS	Organización Secreta de Oficiales Subalternos, Secret Organization of Junior Officers
PCH	Partido Comunista de Honduras, Honduran Communist Party
PDCH	Partido Demócrata Cristiano Hondureño, Honduran Christian Democratic Party
PL	Partido Liberal, Liberal Party
PN	Partido Nacional, National Party
PR	Partido Revolucionario, Revolutionary Party
PS	Partido Socialista, Socialist Party
SITRASFCO	Sindicato de Trabajadores de Standard Fruit Company, Union of Workers of Standard Fruit Company
SITRATERCO	Sindicato de Trabajadores de Tela Railroad Company, Union of Workers of the Tela Railroad Company
SITRAUNAH	Sindical de Trabajadores de UNAH, Union of Workers of UNAH
UNAH	Universidad Nacional Autónoma de Honduras, National Autonomous University of Honduras
UNC	Unión Nacional de Campesinos, National Peasants Union

NICARAGUA

AMNLAE	Asociación de Mujeres Nicaragüenses, Luisa Amanda Espinosa, Association of Nicaraguan Women, Luisa Amanda Espinosa
ANDEN	Asociación Nacional de Educatores Nicaragüenses, Nicaraguan National Association of Educators
ANS	Asociación de Niños Sandinistas, Association of Sandinista Children
ATC	Asociación de Trabajadores del Campo, Association of Farm Workers
CAUS	Central de Acción Unidad Sindical, Center for United Union Action
CDS	Comités de Defensa Sandinista, Sandinista Defense Committees
CGTI	Confederación General de Trabajo Independiente, Independent General Labor Confederation
COSEP	Consejo Superior de la Empresa Privada, Superior Council of Private Industry
CST	Central Sandinista de Trabajadores, Sandinista Workers Center
CTN	Central de Trabajadores de Nicaragua, Workers Center of Nicaragua
CUS	Confederación Unida de Sindicatos, United Confederation of Unions
FAD	Fuerzas Armadas Democráticas, Armed Democratic Forces (anti-Sandinista group)
FAO	Frente Amplio de Oposición, Broad Opposition Front
FPN	Frente Patriótico Nacional, National Patriotic Front
FSLN	Frente Sandinista de Liberación Nacional, Sandinista National Liberation Front
GPP	Guerra Prolongada Popular, Prolonged Popular War (an FSLN tendency)
INRA	Instituto Nacional de Reforma Agraria, National Agrarian Reform Institute
JS-19	Juventud Sandinista, 19 de Julio, Sandinista Youth, 19 July
MDN	Movimiento Demócrata Nicaraguense, Nicaraguan Democratic Movement (Robelo's party)
MPS	Militia Popular Sandinista, Sandinista Popular Militia
MPU	Movimiento Pueblo Unido, United People's Movement

PCD	Partido Conservador Demócrata, Conservative Democratic Party
PCS	Partido Cristiano Social, Social Christian Party
PLI	Partido Liberal Independiente, Independent Liberal Party
PPCS	Partido Popular Cristiano Social, Popular Christian Social Party
PSD	Partido Social Demócrata, Social Democratic Party
UCA	Universidad Centroamericana, Central American University (a Jesuit institution)
UDEL	Unión Democrática de Liberación, Democratic Union for Liberation
UDN	Unión Democrática Nicaragüense, Nicaraguan Democratic Union (anti-Sandinista group)
UNO	Unión Nacional Opositora, National Opposition Union
UPN	Unión de Periodistas Nicaragüenses, Union of Nicaraguan Journalists

Bibliographical Essay

GENERAL STUDIES OF THE AREA

There has been disappointingly little, of a scholarly nature, written in English on Central America, and what there is has tended to focus either upon the problem of unification or the specter of communism. The most recent full-length study of Central America, although one which concentrates chiefly on the historical background, is by Ralph Lee Woodward, Jr.: *Central America: A Nation Divided.* New York: Oxford University Press, 1976. A brief, but more recent survey of government and human rights is the work of Robert Drinan, John McAward, Thomas P. Anderson, and Bruce Cameron: *Central America, 1980: Nicaragua, El Salvador, Guatemala.* Boston: Unitarian Universalist Service Committee, 1980. Among older studies of the region, the following are still useful: Richard Adams: *Cultural Surveys of Panama, Nicaragua, Guatemala, El Salvador and Honduras.* Washington, D.C.: Pan American Sanitary Bureau, 1957; Thomas L. Karnes: *The Failure of Union: Central America, 1824-1960.* Chapel Hill: University of North Carolina Press, 1961; John D. Martz: *Central America: The Crisis and the Challenge.* Chapel Hill: University of North Carolina Press, 1959; Franklin D. Parker: *The Central American Republics.* London: Royal Institute of International Affairs, 1964; and Mario Rodríguez: *Central America.* Englewood Cliffs, N.J.: Prentice-Hall, 1965.

On the question of regional economics, William R. Cline and Enrique Delgado have done useful work in editing *Economic Integration in Central America.* Washington, D.C.: Brookings Institution, 1978. Jeffrey B. Nugent's book: *Economic Integration in Central America: Empirical Investigations.* Baltimore: Johns Hopkins Press, 1974, has a mass of data intelligible chiefly to the specialist. See also, Gary W. Wynia's *Politics and Planners: Economic Development Politics in Central America.* Madison: University of Wisconsin Press, 1972.

For fuller discussions of certain problems related to this study, the reader is referred to two articles by the present writer: "The Ambiguities of Political Terrorism in Central America." *Terrorism: An International Journal* 4 (1980): 267-76; and "The Social and Cultural Roots of Political Violence in Central America." *Aggressive Behavior* 2 (1976):245-55. A number of books dealing with Latin America contain sections on Central American problems. These include: Robert J. Alexander: *Communism in Latin America.* New Brunswick, N.J.: Rutgers University Press, 1957; Edwin Lieuwen: *Generals versus Presidents.* New York: Praeger, 1964; and Rollie E. Poppino: *International Communism in Latin America: A History of the Movement.* To keep current with the changing political situation, one should read *Latin America Weekly Report* and *Latin America Regional Report,* both from the Latin America Bureau, London. Two weeklies from Guatemala, *This Week Central America and Panama,* and *Central America Reports* are also useful. Unfortunately, all are expensive for the subscriber.

GUATEMALA

Much of the writing on Guatemala is extremely partisan, depending on how the writer feels about the period of the revolution, 1945-54, and the subsequent events. For a lurid journalistic account of the Arbenz years, see Daniel James: *Red Design for the Americas: Guatemalan Prelude.* New York: Day, 1954. A more scholarly account from much the same point of view is Roland M. Schneider's book: *Communism in Guatemala,* New York: Praeger, 1958. Mario Rosenthal found the postrevolutionary period to be just fine, especially the years of his hero, Ydígoras Fuentes, in *Guatemala: The Story of an Emergent Latin-American Democracy.* New York: Twayne, 1962. Subsequent books have tended to take the other side. The classic work on politics and society is still Richard N. Adams: *Crucifixion by Power: Essays on Guatemalan National Social Structure, 1944-1966.* Austin: University of Texas Press, 1970. Eduardo H. Galeano's volume: *Guatemala: Occupied Country.* New York: Monthly Review Press, 1969; is useful but marred by the author's prejudices. Much better are two books by the ex-missionaries Thomas and Marjorie Melville: *Guatemala: Another Vietnam?* New York: Pelican Books, 1971; and *Guatemala: The Politics of Land Ownership.* New York: Free Press, 1971. They share Galeano's pessimism about the state of affairs, as does Roger Plant in *Guatemala: An Unnatural Disaster.* London: Latin American Bureau, 1978. His book has much useful information. A second edition will be forthcoming. For other views on the subject, see the volume edited by Susanne Jonas and David Tobias: *Guatemala.* Berkeley, Calif.: North American Congress on Latin America, 1974. The various articles of Stephen Kinzer are an excellent guide to the country, especially: "Guatemala: the Hard Line." *The Atlantic Monthly* 245 (1980): 4-14.

Human rights remains a burning issue in Guatemala. An authoritative study by a distinguished jurist is that of Donald T. Fox: *Human Rights in Guatemala.* Geneva: International Commission of Jurists, 1979. Other views, equally depressing, are given in the National Lawyers' Guild publication: *Violations of Human Rights in Guatemala.* n.p.: Unity Books, 1979; and Edelberto Torres Rivas: "Guatemala: Crisis and Political Violence." *NACLA Report on the Americas* 14 (1980):16-20.

EL SALVADOR

The Soccer War, 1969, between El Salvador and Honduras has generated quite a bit of literature. For the immediate causes of the conflict and its direct results see the present writer's: *The War of the Dispossessed: Honduras and El Salvador, 1969.* Lincoln: University of Nebraska Press, 1981. William Durham: *Scarcity and Survival in Central America: Ecological Origins of the Soccer War.* Stanford, Calif.: Stanford University Press, 1979; and J. Mayone Stycos: *Margin of Life: Population and Poverty in the Americas.* New York: Grossman, 1974; both cover the anthropological background of the war. The title of Stycos's book is misleading as it deals exclusively with El Salvador and Honduras. The book also contains excellent photographs by Cornell Capa. Mary Jeanne Reid Martz looks at international aspects of the war in: *Central American Soccer War: Historical Patterns and Internal Dynamics of OAS Settlement Procedures.* Athens: Ohio University Press, 1978; as does Franklin D. Parker: "The Fútbol Conflict and Central American Unity." *Annals of the Southeastern Conference on Latin American Studies* 3 (1972):44-59.

On the general background of El Salvador, the present writer's book: *Matanza: El Salvador's Communist Revolt of 1932.* Lincoln: University of Nebraska Press, 1971; chronicles much more than the uprising itself, but a more complete background can be gained from reading Alastair White: *El Salvador.* New York: Praeger, 1973. The geographic situation is splendidly given, along with a great deal else of useful information in David Browning's poetic and charming, yet scholarly volume: *El Salvador: Landscape and Society.* Oxford: The Clarendon Press, 1971. Useful political studies are Stephen Webre: *José Napoleón Duarte and the Christian Democratic Party in Salvadoran Politics.* Baton Rouge, La.: Louisiana State University Press, 1979; and Charles W. Anderson's article: "El Salvador: The Army as Reformer." In *Political Systems of Latin America,* edited by Martin C. Needler. Princeton, N.J.: Van Nostrand, 1964. Anyone interested in seeing how wrong predictions can be should read David R. Raynold's work: *Rapid Development in Small Economies: The Example of El Salvador.* New York: Praeger, 1967; in which the author declared that El Salvador had reached the "take-off point" and was about to soar economically.

For the abysmal human rights record of El Salvador under the Romero regime, see Robert Drinan, John McAward, and Thomas P. Anderson: *Human Rights in El Salvador: 1978.* Boston: Unitarian Universalist Service

Committee, 1978; and the Inter-American Commission on Human Rights: *Report on the Situation of Human Rights in El Salvador.* Washington, D.C.: Organization of American States, 1978.

HONDURAS

Honduras remains a virgin land still awaiting its scholarly bridegroom. The only comprehensive study of its political institutions is the 30-year-old work by William S. Stokes: *Honduras: A Case Study in Government.* Madison: University of Wisconsin Press, 1950. The economic development of the country has, however, generated more work. Of interest are: James A. Morris and Steve C. Ropp: "Corporatism and Dependent Development: A Honduran Case Study." *Latin American Research Review* 12 (1977):27-68; Axel Ivan Mundigo: *Elites, Economic Development and Population in Honduras.* Ithaca, N.Y.: Cornell University Press, 1972; and Benjamin Villaneuva: "The Role of Institutional Innovations in the Economic Development of Honduras." *Land Tenure Center Newsletter* 34 (1968).

NICARAGUA

The period of Sandino and the coming to power of Somoza are detailed in a splendid book by Neill Macaulay: *The Sandino Affair.* Chicago: Quadrangle Books, 1967; while the years of the Somozas in power, especially the early years under Somoza García, are studied in Richard Millett: *Guardians of the Dynasty: A History of the United States Created Guardia of Nicaragua and the Somoza Family.* Maryknoll, N.Y.: Orbis Books, 1977. The introduction to Millett's book by Miguel D'Escoto is also illuminating. Professor Millett is planning to follow this up with a study on the last days of the Somozas, entitled *The Fall of the Dynasty.* Another study of interest is Thomas W. Walker: *The Christian Democratic Movement in Nicaragua.* Comparative Government Studies, no. 3. Tuscon: University of Arizona Press, 1970.

There is not yet much work out on the post-Somoza era, though Professor Walker is now editing a volume entitled *Nicaragua in Revolution.* Two interesting articles with different points of view are William M. LeoGrande: "Revolution in Nicaragua: Another Cuba?" *Foreign Affairs* 58 (1979):28-50; and James Petras: "Whither the Nicaraguan Revolution?" *Monthly Review* 31 (1979):1-22.

Index

214

About the Author

THOMAS P. ANDERSON is Professor of History at Eastern Connecticut State College. Until 1969 he was Assistant Professor of History at Wheeling College, West Virginia.

Dr. Anderson has published widely in the areas of history and politics. His books include: *Matanza: El Salvador's Communist Revolt of 1932* and *The War of the Dispossessed: Honduras and El Salvador, 1969.*

Dr. Anderson holds a B.A. from Saint Louis University and an M.A. and a Ph.D. from Loyola University, Chicago.

.8
D

27707

Anderson, Thomas P.
Politics in Central
America

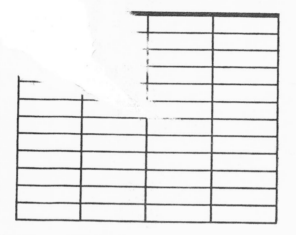